BATTLEGROUND
KOREA

BATTLEGROUND
KOREA
THE BRITISH IN KOREA

CHARLES WHITING

SUTTON PUBLISHING

First published in the United Kingdom in 1999 by
Sutton Publishing Limited · Phoenix Mill
Thrupp · Stroud · Gloucestershire · GL5 2BU

British Library Cataloguing in Publication Data
A catalogue record for this book is available from the British Library

ISBN 0-7509-2085-8

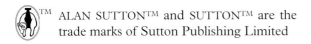

ALAN SUTTON™ and SUTTON™ are the
trade marks of Sutton Publishing Limited

Typeset in 10/12pt Plantin Light.
Typesetting and origination by
Sutton Publishing Limited.
Printed in Great Britain by
Redwood Books, Trowbridge, Wiltshire.

Contents

Acknowledgements

I would like to offer my grateful thanks to the following groups and individuals who have helped me in the writing of this book: Mr Carl Silletoe, Dr Paul Maquet (Belgium), M. Jean Milmeister (Luxembourg), Professor Hobie Morris, (Springfield, New York), Mr Tom Dickinson, Mr Frank Ellison, British Korean Veterans Association, J.J. Thompson, Major-General R. Downward, Mr D. Collen, Mr Alan Lauder, Mr Norman Louis, Mr Denton, Mr Raymond Brown, Mr M. Lamoury, Mr John Herbert, Mr E. Bartlett and Mr Conyers.

Thank you all.

Charles Whiting
1999

Introduction

South Koreans call their country 'the Land of the Morning Calm'. But in the autumn of 1950, when the first 2,000 British soldiers arrived in that country there was little of the 'morning calm' about it. Instead they encountered sorrow, snow and sudden, violent death. The fleeing GIs they met after they landed at the South Korean port of Pusan told them, 'You can have it, buddy . . . *give it back to the Gooks*.' But they didn't. They stayed and fought, just like the vast majority of American soldiers who bore the brunt of the fighting in the three years of bitter conflict that followed.

The British squaddies who fought in those battles on the other side of the world realized from the start that it would become a forgotten war. Most of their compatriots knew little, and cared less, about this remote country. Despite the enormous casualties incurred by soldiers and civilians on both sides – some 1,200,000 in all – this 'UN Police Action' was destined to become a mere footnote in the history of the cold war.

Britain sent 40,000 men to that war, of whom 687 were killed, 2,498 wounded and 1,102 taken prisoner. Yet when the Korean War ended in July 1953 there was no nationwide rejoicing, no mass hysteria in Trafalgar Square with people getting drunk and falling into the fountain. The youthful veterans came home unheralded and unsung, seemingly forgotten by the nation and the British government. They even had to pay for their own war memorial. Nevertheless, although they were unaware of it at the time, those young men helped considerably to shape – *and perhaps even save* – the world for the rest of the twentieth century.

Korea saw the only armed conflict in the whole of the decades-long Cold War, and the soldiers' efforts on the bloody battlefields of Korea helped their political masters in Whitehall to prevent a nuclear holocaust. Britain led the reaction against Washington's proposed use of the atom bomb in 1950, which would surely have resulted in Soviet Russia's retaliation. Poor, broken-down and hopelessly in debt owing to the new Welfare State, London had no real political clout, not even on moral grounds. After all, capitalist, imperialist America had financed that very 'from the cradle-to-the-grave' safety net!

However, Britain was still able to take her place on the world stage, thanks in many ways to those same squaddies loyally supporting the Americans in Korea. The British had been the first to rally to the American cause and send troops, an example soon followed by the rest of the free world. Indeed, the Royal Navy fired the very first salvoes of the 'UN Police Action' at fast torpedo boats of the North Korean Navy. And it was British troops who helped to halt the Chinese advance in April 1951, a crucial turning-point in the war, and which led to the long-protracted peace talks a month or so later.

Although it would take years to finalize a lasting truce between the two opposing forces, the stand of Brigadier Brodie's decimated 29th Brigade, with their American allies, on the Imjin River convinced the Chinese and their North Korean puppets that they would never succeed in pushing the 'round-eyes' back into the sea from whence they had come. As the men said, 'It's only half a victory, but it's better than none at all.'

For South Korea it was a very real victory. Its citizens never did get the kind of democracy America promised them back in the 1940s, but their lifestyle and freedoms are vastly different from those of their cousins on the other side of the 38th Parallel. In North Korea, with its Stalinist cult of leader-worship, it is regarded with suspicion when a citizen owns even his own bicycle! In 1998 the first of the British veterans went back to South Korea at the invitation of the South Korean Legation in London. They were welcomed and fêted as heroes who had helped to make that formerly backward country one of the fast-growing economies in the world.

'Even that terrible pong had vanished. It was roses and sweet violets all the way,' as one soldier quipped after his return. He was referring to that all-pervading stench of *Kimche*, which had appalled the young squaddies back in the 1950s. For the most part the veterans, mere youngsters when they had first sailed to war on the other side of the world, hardly recognized the 'Land of the Morning Calm'. Their 'Forgotten War' had not been in vain after all . . .

Book One

Whither is fled the visionary gleam?
Where is it now, the glory and the dream?
Wordsworth

CHAPTER ONE

The Long Hot Weekend

Saturday evenings in the Tokyo 'Big House' were inevitably the same. It was five years since the 71-year-old General (known behind his back as 'Old Mac') had come to rule a defeated Japan, and by now the routine had been well established. After supper, which was always the same – soup, salad, bread and coffee – the evening entertainment would commence. The general would rise from the dining table promptly after twenty minutes – 'a good meal is a quick meal', he always said – and enter the pantry next to the dining-room. Here, years before, a large hole had been cut in the wall for a movie projector and a movie screen had been installed. Now the old man with the patrician face would plant himself in his red rocking chair, 'circumcise' his large cigar with ritualistic ceremony, and wait for the movie to be set up. This was the man who had conquered Japan for the Allies in the Second World War and had ruled the 'land of the rising sun' ever since. Now he was preparing to enjoy his simple Saturday evening treat. It was all very 'homey' and American. The only thing that was lacking was the popcorn bags.

Already fifty stacking chairs had been set up for his staff and servants, and even for the evening's honour guard. For although his GIs made fun of Old Mac's pretensions – they hadn't forgotten that their predecessors of the shooting war in the Pacific had called him 'Dug-out Doug'[1] – they were still honoured to be the Supreme Commander's guests. They settled down. The General did, too. To one side of him was Jean, his pretty second wife, half his age; on the other his smooth aide and adviser, Sidney Huff. First came the newsreels from the States, flown in specially. Best of all, the General liked those depicting natural catastrophes. In loud asides to Jean or Sidney, he would explain how he would have dealt with them. If there were shots of the stateside Army–Navy football games, he would root loudly for the US Army – naturally. The only newsreels he really disliked were those about his *bête noire*, the Soviet dictator Josef Stalin. *They* had the old man sitting on the edge of his seat with nervous tension.

Finally the newsreels would end and the titles for the main feature would begin. The General wasn't a simple man by any means, but he did like comedies or action films. His favourites were Westerns, especially when he could have his adored and pampered young son Arthur at his side. How he loved that boy! This Saturday night, the movie was considered too adult for 'little Arthur', but it didn't matter. On the morrow, Sunday, he would have all day to devote to the boy.

However, appearances were deceptive. The relaxed old general sitting in his red rocking chair, enjoying a Hollywood B movie, was not quite the homely old bird he appeared to be. His personal world was far removed from that of the average American. His vanity and paranoia were almost certifiable: he was convinced that the rest of the human race, with a few exceptions, was out to do him down.

He was tremendously proud of his Scottish heritage, but he still hated the whole continent of Europe and, in particular, Britain where his family came from. Even so, British egoists such as Churchill, Montgomery and the Chief of the Imperial General Staff Lord Alanbrooke admired him without reservation. Alanbrooke, that canny, cautious Ulsterman, proclaimed that he was 'the greatest general and best strategist the war has produced'. Nevertheless the general still detested these high-placed admirers and their American supporters, such as America's senior soldier General Marshall (who once described him as 'our most brilliant general'), because he felt all of them were conspiring against him.

He idolized his soldier-father, who had also won America's highest honour, the Congressional Medal of Honor. Yet at the same time he was dominated by his mother, nicknamed 'Pinky'. When he went to West Point as a young cadet, his mother followed him and booked herself into a nearby hotel so that she could see whether her son's lamp was burning and check that he was still studying! Later, when she expressed her disapproval of his first wife, the general got divorced. Thereafter, he kept a beautiful Eurasian mistress, lavishing presents on her. He gave her underwear, teagowns and the like but not much in the way of outer clothing. When she complained, he told her there was no need for such stuff. Her first duty was to him in bed. What did she want a coat for?

Later, when she decided to end their relationship, the general was terrified that she might 'go public' and that 'Pinky' would find out. This 54-year-old general, who had won every award for bravery on the battlefield that a grateful USA could bestow on a soldier, was unable to deal with the lady himself. Instead he sent another officer to buy her off. On Christmas Eve 1934, in Washington's Willard Hotel, the officer did so, handing her a sheaf of hundred-dollar bills. For a while MacArthur's love life ceased. But as soon as 'Pinky' died, the 'mummy's boy' revolted against her for the last time. He wooed and won Jean, a woman half his age, and subsequently fathered a son, Arthur, the source of his greatest happiness.

Now eight years after that marriage to his beloved Jean, he was finally enjoying himself. He was famous. He had achieved great things. He had won the Pacific War with fewer casualties than his former aide Eisenhower had lost in the six-week-long Battle of the Bulge in Europe. Now he ruled the beaten Japanese and most of Asia, which now came under the American sphere of influence. He had a lot to be proud of.

Thus General of the Army Douglas MacArthur, the Conqueror of the Pacific, Ruler of Japan and Lord of South-east Asia, enjoyed the evening of

24 June 1950.[2] Once the movie had finished and he had said his goodnights, he would go to his room to sleep, falling into a dreamless slumber immediately his head hit the snowy white pillow. It had always been this way. To those close to him – and all his life he seemed to have been under the scrutiny of some clever, observant individual or other – he appeared to be a man with no conscience, no worries and no concerns for the future. In his overweening *hubris*, he might have asked himself (if he had ever considered posing such a question), why should he?

In Tokyo his former enemies, the Japanese, who now revered him, would doubtless have agreed. The tall patrician general, with his sun-glasses, battered peaked cap and corncob pipe, seemed to them ready to live for ever, just like their own ancients, whom they revered. The Japanese maintained that there were only two things that might disturb MacArthur's steady progress to a great age. One was that he might decide to run for the office of the President of the United States (after all, the General's disdained former aide Eisenhower appeared to be heading in that direction), and the other was the prospect of another war. But although the Russians were continually making threatening noises since they had acquired the atom bomb, nothing ever seemed to come of what really amounted to sabre-rattling. Indeed, on this particular Saturday night, which fell almost exactly in the middle of the war-torn twentieth century, it was as if those in command on both sides of the Cold War had finally grown up and decided there would be no more war. All in all, as the movie at the Big House came to an end, it looked as if the general would live on to achieve that great age.

This was just as well. His Army of Occupation in Japan, generally known as 'the Constabulary', was not capable of fighting a full-scale war. The US Eighth Army, under the command of stubby, pugnacious General Walton 'Bulldog' Walker, one of Patton's former Corps Commanders in Europe, was now a pretty rundown outfit. It consisted of four divisions, all understrength, and only 20 per cent of its effectives were veterans of the Second World War. Worse, the troops were armed with the leftovers from that struggle of five years before. Such weapons were already obsolete, such as bazookas that had been unable to stop German tanks back in 1943 and Sherman tanks – 'Ronson lighters', their crews called them contemptuously – which had been no match for the German Panthers and Tigers or for the Russian T-34s – the type of tank they would be most likely to encounter in any new conflict.

More importantly, the manpower available to MacArthur in case of war was poor. Morale was shaky, and had been ever since the end of the war when the 'Wanna-go-home' riots, sit-downs, even outright mutinies had commenced in Europe and spread to the Pacific. Eisenhower, the Supreme Commander, had been appalled when his veterans, desperate to demobilise, had barracked his headquarters in Frankfurt and, marched like a rabble in uniform through the bombed streets. The result was that the Pentagon ordered a massive demobilization programme without any thought to the future military commitments of the United States Army. As one American general described the situation, the USA 'had fought the war like a football game . . . after which the winner leaves the field and celebrates'.

Over the intervening five years the Pentagon and Congress had weakened the Army, in particular the forces in Japan, by defence cuts[3] and a slackening of entry requirements for volunteers, many of whom apparently joined up because they had been unemployed or wanted to get a free education. Posted to Japan, these reluctant heroes had lived the life of Riley. Military training had been minimal. The dollar had gone a long way, especially on the Japanese black market. The 'babe-sans' had been cheap, easy and willing, and even privates had been able to afford servants to do their chores; most lowly military establishments employed servants to work in the cookhouses and do tedious jobs like refuse-collecting. And corruption at virtually every level was widespread. As one of Walker's divisional commanders later expressed it: 'The soldiers had become a flabby force accustomed to Japanese girlfriends, plenty of beer and servants to shine their boots.'

The general in question, William F. Dean, who had commanded the 44th Division in Europe and now commanded Walker's 24th Infantry Division in Japan, enjoyed a lifestyle that seemed little different from that of his 'flabby GIs', albeit at a more elevated level. Well over 6ft tall and weighing 200lb, Dean had led a very busy life ever since he had volunteered for a Pacific assignment. He was tasked with helping to set up a new Korean government-to-be for when the American occupiers left this formerly Japanese-controlled territory. On 15 August 1948 the US occupation of South Korea had come to an end. Now that his civil role had come to an end, he had taken over command of the US 7th Infantry Division, moving with it to Japan one year later. In October 1949 he had been appointed the divisional commander of the ill-fated US 24th Infantry Division, based at Kokura on Kyushu, Japan's most southerly island.

Dean didn't know it then, but Fate had dealt him a bad hand. His headquarters lay close to the Korea Strait, which separated Japan from Korea. Invaders had sailed across it for centuries, but always it had proved unlucky for the aggressor; indeed this was the strait in which a divine wind – the *Kamikaze*[4] – had forced back a Korean fleet trying to invade Japan in ancient times. The nearest point on the Korean mainland was the port of Pusan,[5] soon to become the focus of world attention.

On that Saturday night, General Dean was happily unaware of how that geographic situation would affect the rest of his life. Instead, like most of Walker's Eighth Army in Japan, he 'partied', as the new phrase of the time had it. He had accepted an invitation to a celebration at the HQ's Officers' Club. Dean deliberately set out to make himself look a little foolish. So he chose for his costume the dress of a Korean gentleman which he had acquired while serving in that country. Due to his great height and bulk, 'the black stovepipe hat . . . sat foolishly high on my head and the long robes proper to a *yangban* [a person who does not work] flopped somewhere about my knees'.

Dean thought his costume was 'a considerable success'. He recalled: 'It was obvious that the officers I had been working hard for several months enjoyed seeing their divisional commander looking thoroughly ridiculous!' Whether they did or not was never recorded, and before that year was out most of those who attended that party would be dead, prisoner-of-war or completely disgraced.

As for the commanding general himself, all he remembered of his one and only time as a *yangban* was that 'it was an uneventful party, just one more officers' club dance like thousands of others; and . . . the high hat became highly uncomfortable before the evening ended.' However, Dean consoled himself with the thought that he would never wear the *yangban* gear ever again and that he 'had no real reason to go to Korea once more'.

But he was sadly mistaken, and he could not have known that this June Saturday night in Japan was perhaps the last happy time of his life. In what was soon to come, he would win America's highest award for bravery and for a while he would hit the headlines in a way he had never done before in his long Army career. But he would pay for it. He would lose his division and never be given another command. To be charitable, perhaps he was too sick ever to lead troops again. Three years of his life would disappear behind the barbed wire of the cage. And when his bravery, even his very name, had been long forgotten, he would still be remembered by the West as the highest-ranking prisoner ever to be captured by the Communists in the nearly forty years of the Cold War.

Five years before, 46-year-old General Dean had been on the winning side: one of the US Seventh Army's divisional commanders now busy on the German–Austrian frontier taking the surrender of the *Wehrmacht* on the run from the Red Army in hot pursuit from the East. Then that heady May, when the victors enjoyed the spoils after eleven months of hard campaigning right across Europe, the American Top Brass indulged themselves. They rode in captured trains or looted Mercedes. They posed for the newsreel photographers, as if these one-time majors and colonels – who back in 1941 had been heading for slippered retirement in America's warm south, where the living was cheap and they could afford to play golf on their limited pension – were world-famous Hollywood movie stars. Indeed nothing seemed to give them greater pleasure than being photographed taking the surrender of some scar-faced 'Nazi general', or even better a well-known 'Nazi war criminal'.

General Dahlquist, a fellow general of the Seventh Army, who commanded the US 36th Infantry Division, was actually photographed shaking the hand of no less a person than Hermann Goering before seeing him off in a small aeroplane at the German spa town of Kitzbühel. It had been a fatal mistake. An obscure 'Nazi General' could be overlooked, but not such a high-ranking member of the Nazi *Prominenz* as 'Fat Hermann'.[6] Dahlquist, who had fought his division well through France and Germany, was relieved of his command.

That May, General Dean was more fortunate. (One couldn't say from his subsequent actions that he was a very *wise* man.) Later that week, Seventh Army's Intelligence section arrested another alleged war criminal in the 44th Division area. Dean, however, kept out of the way. This time there was no shaking of hands before the cameras or exchange of pleasantries between the generous captor and humbled captive, although the German in question was the highest-ranking *Wehrmacht* officer taken in that sector of the Seventh Army's front. All the same the German, whom Dean (as far as we know) never met, would have a decisive effect on Dean's future.

He was Field Marshal Ferdinand Schoerner, one of Hitler's favourite commanders. The big robust, sanguine Bavarian had held the front in the East against the Russians when smarter German generals had long before given into despair. Unlike most generals of his rank, German as well as Allied, Schoerner commanded from the front. He roamed the front line with his bodyguard, threatening, praising, cajoling. Behind him he left officers and men strung up from trees and telegraph poles with the grim legend painted on placards dangling from their necks, 'Defeatist', 'Coward' or simply 'Traitor'.

He was a general after the Führer's heart in those last few weeks of the war. Everywhere he changed commanders, turfed out the 'rear-echelon swine', as the footsloggers called the desk-bound officers to the rear, armed them with rifles and set them to the firing line. Naturally to the 'stubble-hoppers', as the front-line soldiers called themselves in mock contempt, he was welcome. They had never seen a full field marshal this far forward. Schoerner promised the ragged infantrymen the best food and uniforms and told them he'd shoot anybody – 'and I mean *anybody*' – who failed in his duty or deserted the line. Then after delivering that threat, the big Bavarian with the fleshy red face would hand out cakes and sweets to awe-struck simple private soldiers.

Unfortunately for Shoerner, by the time he had turned his troops north to surrender to the Americans, in particular to Patton's XX Corps, commanded by another US general who would take a key part in what was to come in 1950, Gen Walton 'Bulldog' Walker, he had already been classified as a war criminal. Known to Russians as 'the Beast of Silesia', for crimes against Poles allegedly committed in Poland's western province, they demanded that the Americans should surrender Schoerner to them.

For a week, while the Americans of the Seventh Army HQ at Augsburg wondered what to do with the Field Marshal, who had not actually willingly surrendered to them (he had been denounced by his batman while trying to escape in civilian clothes), the Russians persisted in their demands. They quoted the Yalta Agreement. It stated that any German officer who had committed a war crime while serving on the Russian front should be handed to them for trial. In the end General 'Sandy' Patch, commander of the Seventh Army, gave in. He agreed to have the alleged war criminal transferred to America's erstwhile ally.

What transpired next is shrouded with mystery. Officially, Field Marshal Schoerner was sentenced to twenty-five years in the Gulag by a Soviet military court for war crimes. A year after that happened, his former chief-of-staff General Oldwig von Natzmer accused Schoerner of doing that for which he had punished so many of his soldiers during the war, desertion in the face of the enemy. Thereafter, the ex-Field Marshal Schoerner became a symbol of cowardice for many West Germans, more especially when he arrived in the West to testify against one of his former commanders on behalf of the Soviets. It was obvious that former high-ranking members of the *Wehrmacht* knew more about the nefarious activities of Schoerner, supposedly serving time in the Gulag, than the naive Americans, who had handed him over to 'Uncle Joe's boys' so eagerly.[7]

They did indeed.

For soon after Schoerner's sentence had been passed, he had been transferred *not* to the Gulag but to the 'academy' being run by fellow German Field Marshal Paulus, who had surrendered Stalingrad to the Russians during the war, together with what was left of his battered Sixth German Army. Here Paulus and his pro-Russian fellow generals, who had gone over to the Russians, prepared not only propaganda to be used against the West but also military plans for aggressive action against their former comrades and their new American masters. After all, most of 'Paulus's Academy', as it was called in Moscow, had been trained in the same staff colleges in Germany. Who other than they could know just how Russia's possible future opponents in war thought!

As was written long afterward by Hollywood script-writer and novelist Peter Viertel, then a member of the US Intelligence team which had arrested Schoerner back in May 1945. 'That procedure (the delivery of Schoerner to the Russians by the US Seventh Army) turned out to be a grave mistake . . . (it) ultimately led to Schoerner's supervision of the great armored attack.' For on that Saturday night while the aged General of the Army MacArthur slept and his subordinate officers and their troops enjoyed the cheap delights of Occupied Japan, on the other side of the Korea Strait, history was about to be made.

Schoerner would play his part and it would result in the reversal of the roles he and Dean had played five years before. The German would be the victor and captor this time. Dean, for his part, would be the loser and captive. Soon Dean would consider it a great achievement to have discovered the 'best way to kill a fly'. – 'I ought to know. I swatted 40,671 flies in three years and counted every carcass. There were periods when I was batting .850 and deserved to make the big leagues.' Well, it was one way not to go mad, he must have told himself all those years ago.[8]

That last weekend in June 1950, the United States sweltered in hundred-degree temperatures, the first heatwave of the summer. In those pre-air-conditioned days in the States, those who were able abandoned the tiny screens of the latest craze, TV, for the air-conditioned luxury of the movie theatres.

While the kids watched Walt Disney's *Treasure Island* featuring that splendid British actor Robert Newton as Long John Silver, the adults watched an equally talented Brit, Alec Guiness, in Cary's *The Horse's Mouth*.

Ex-Supreme Commander Dwight D. Eisenhower, at that time head of Columbia University and waiting for his call for greater things, was holed up with Zane Grey's last cowboy novel, *The Maverick Queen*. Dean Acheson, Secretary of State for Foreign Affairs, more British than the British, escaped the heat at his Maryland home, and also read himself to sleep.

As for the Washington big-shots who directed the political and military affairs of the superpower to be, they relaxed from the stifling temperatures now that the American President, that perky little ex-haberdasher Harry Truman, had left the capital for the weekend. Undoubtedly he too was trying to escape the killing heat. White House correspondents had been told by the President's spokesman that they would be wasting their time if they stayed in the nation's capital. They'd have to wait till Monday before there would be any new 'presidential activity'.

One or two of the nation's most important men were still attending to their business, but not in Washington. The Chairman of the US Joint Chiefs of Staff Omar Bradley was somewhere over the Pacific, flying home from a 'fact-finding' mission to Tokyo. In a way it was something of a jaunt for the lantern-jawed four-star general, who had never fired a shot in anger prior to the Second World War and had spent most of his time teaching maths at West Point. In 1944/45 he had been Eisenhower's capable though not brilliant commander of US ground forces in Europe. Eisenhower had had his PR men try to work on 'Brad's' image, but it hadn't been very successful. He wasn't very colourful and in a US Army full of generals who were nicknamed 'Wild Bill', 'Iron Mike', 'Lightning Joe' he had to be content with the 'GI's General'.

Understandably Bradley, who wanted a quiet life now, thought that MacArthur, whom he had visited in Tokyo, was 'like Patton and Monty, . . . a megalomaniac'. Everywhere he had visited he had been appeased by the assurances of the local military commanders that there were indeed problems in Asia which concerned America in Asia, but nothing which could remotely be thought to lead to a 'shooting war'.

Intelligence presented Bradley with some evidence that the North Koreans were preparing to invade South Korea. But the two puppet states, one controlled by Russia and the other by the USA, had been at each other's throats for nearly two years now. Both sides routinely invaded the other's territory with 'partisans' sometimes up to a strength of more than a thousand. Indeed the new CIA was running its own guerrilla operation in the North, 'Force 6006'. Bradley, the regular soldier, had always known that Intelligence officers were traditionally 'nervous nellies', so he didn't take too much notice of the rumours, especially as he heard from Brigadier General William Roberts (who had served under him with the famed US 10th Armored Division in Europe, and who had been the chief of the US Korean Military Advisory Group for the last two years) that the South Korean Army would easily deal with any invader from the North. As Bradley recorded, 'Since I knew Roberts to be a professional soldier of good judgment, I took his word for it, *feeling greatly relieved that we had no cause for concern in Korea.*' (author's italics)

Indeed Washington, capital of the emerging American superpower, being forced against its will to take on more and more of the burdens being left behind by the disappearing British Empire and those of France and Holland, would *afterwards* seem to have been too quiet that hot Saturday in the last week of peace. For far away on the other side of the globe in an Asian country of which the average American had never heard, things were happening that would change Americans' lives in one way or another dramatically, and indirectly those of their children, and of *their* children too.

It was noon in New York, the home of the United Nations which had been deadlocked by the Russians for six months now; early afternoon in the Mid-West, where President Truman had just landed at Kansas City Municipal Airport; and 4.00 a.m. on Sunday[9] at something called the '38th Parallel' . . .

Six years before, in what now seemed another age, the US Top Brass in Europe had been enjoying a similarly lazy Saturday, when the bad news reached them. Then, on that Saturday 16 December 1944, it had taken some ten hours for the startling information to arrive at Eisenhower's HQ in Versailles that the supposedly defeated Germans had done the impossible: they had launched a massive surprise counter-attack on the Belgium Ardennes. US troops were reeling back everywhere. America's Gettysburg of the twentieth century – the Battle of the Bulge – had commenced.

This June Saturday in 1950 it took *eight* hours for the news to reach Washington. At 8.00 p.m. Eastern Daylight Saving Time, a certain Bradley Connors, a minor US official in Washington, was called by Donald Gonzales of the United Press and told that the UP correspondent in Korea was sending garbled reports of heavy North Korea attacks all along the 38th Parallel. Did the State Department know about it? Connors said he didn't, but he'd find out.

At first he was out of luck. Everything had apparently closed down till the following Monday. He tried to patch up an emergency connection to the US legation in the South Korean capital of Seoul. But before the harassed minor official could do this, the State Department's own communication centre received a cable stamped 9.26 a.m. from the US ambassador, John J. Muccio himself.

It brought very bad news. It read: 'North Korean forces invaded Republic of Korea at several places this morning . . . It would appear from the nature of the attack and the manner in which it was launched that it constitutes an all-out offensive against the Republic of Korea.'

Again time passed. It had been just the same on that cold overcast Saturday evening at Eisenhower's HQ half a decade before. Eisenhower and Bradley and the Supreme Commander's other military cronies had shot the breeze, played poker and celebrated 'Ike's' fifth star by drinking a precious bottle of 100 Pipers Scotch that one of the lesser generals had brought along as a present. Then as in 1950, there seemed to be little urgency in the actions of these men manning 'Fort Washington'.

In the end Secretary of State Dean Acheson was awoken at ten that night, and he agreed to the suggestion that a special meeting of the UN Security Council should be called for the next day to ask for a ceasefire. The US Deputy Representative to that international body, Ernest Gross, who was in New York, was to take care of the matter while Acheson informed the President of what had just happened.

Finally Acheson got through to President Truman at his home. The family had eaten supper and Harry S. Truman was beginning to yawn; he was plainly ready for his bed. In Independence, Missouri, the President's home town, folks went to sleep early. He soon woke up, however, at Acheson's opening words: 'Mr President, I have very serious news. The North Koreans have invaded South Korea.'

Truman, who despite his faults and all the snide remarks made about 'the little storekeeper' during his lifetime can now be seen as possibly the best American president in the second half of the twentieth century, reacted at once in typical fashion. He told Acheson he would fly back to Washington at once. Gently the moustached dandy dissuaded him. Better get a good night's sleep, he advised the President. All that could be done this Saturday night had been done. He, Acheson, had got the business with the UN started. Now they had to wait for further information. He personally would deal with Frank Pace, Secretary of the Army. Then he hung up, knowing that the next battle wasn't going to be fought in Korea, but at the headquarters of the United Nations at Lake Success, New York . . .

'*My God, Jack*,' exclaimed in dismay Trygve Lie, 54-year-old Norwegian General Secretary of the United Nations, from his home in Forest Hills, on hearing what had just happened in South Korea from John Hickerson of the State Department, 'this is war! . . . *war against the United Nations!*'

It was.

Ever since Korea had been split up into North and South Korea along the line of the 38th Parallel, the north occupied by Russia and the south taken over by the USA at the end of the Second World War, the two new Asian countries had been the wards of the UN.

For the first time in its existence since 1945, UN found itself at war – and as was to be the case in all the UN wars and 'peace-keeping actions' to follow over the next half century, the United Nations didn't possess one single soldier to do its fighting for it. What many had felt was the patent absurdity and futility of that organization, seen by them throughout all its existence to have been there solely to act as a talking shop where politicians could spout hot air and officials could enjoy a gravy-train career (until they were found out once too often), was now to be exposed for all the world to see.

Over the next three terrible years, young men of a dozen different nations, who had probably never even heard of Korea before that fateful June weekend of 1950, would fight and die in their hundreds, thousands and, in the end, in their hundred thousands; and all that the UN could do was to talk. *Fifty years on they are still talking . . .*[10]

CHAPTER TWO

Police Action

Suddenly – startlingly – that pre-dawn morning, the North Korean positions dug in along the 38th Parallel had erupted into violent angry flames and noise, as if the door to a gigantic blast furnace had been flung open: a massive flash of orange light on the horizon to the north; a frightening hush; the whirr of hundreds of shells hurtling towards the dugouts and foxholes of the soldiers of the South Korean Republic[1] . . . Next moment, all dust, noise, panic and sudden death. It had been a typical Russian tactic during the Second World War: one thousand heavy guns firing on a limited front with their fire saturating the enemy until they were either dead or broken, fleeing in disorder for their lives.

That surprise attack on 25 June 1950 had worked. Almost immediately the ROK 12th Regiment had broken and run, leaving the key town of the area, Kaesong, undefended. By 9.30 that terrible Sunday morning, the victorious North Koreans had taken the town with few casualties, capturing half a dozen US advisers attached to the ROK Army in bed, some in piquant circumstances.

The South Koreans, trained by the Americans but without heavy weapons (for reasons known only to the US Government), led by colonels and even generals who had been corporals and captains in the Japanese Army during the Second World War, were seemingly no match for the attackers from the North. One hour after Kaesong fell, the main spearhead of the North Korean Army, the 3rd and 4th Divisions, had routed the ROK 7th Division around the town of Cholwon and North Korean tanks were racing for the South Korean capital of Seoul, which was fated to change hands several times in the long bloody conflict to come.

Now the initial Russian tactic of the massed opening barrage was replaced by a German one, worked out by no less a person than that 'war criminal' ex-*Wehrmacht* Field Marshal Schoerner. It was the same armoured strategy which had caught France and Britain totally off-guard back in 1940. The *Blitzkrieg*!

Hundreds of low-slung T-34 Russian tanks, manned by 22,000 North Koreans who had fought first in the Japanese Army and then as 'volunteers' for either their Russian or Chinese Red Army captors, rattled forward in tight columns through the mountain passes of the Oniin Peninsula. Just as in the great days of Rommel, Guderian, von Manteuffel and all the rest, the T-34s forgot about their flanks. They were left open. The follow-up infantry would deal with any South Korean soldiers who had the temerity to try to hold out in the hills on both sides of the roads. Besides, Schoerner had already made provision for any problems in that quarter. He knew that the ROK Air Force was virtually non-existent, just a handful of obsolete US planes. He, for his part, had planned to have his armoured columns supported by their own 'flying artillery', the Stukas of 1950. These were the Russian-built *Stormovik* dive-bombers. Now these Second World War Russian planes, easily recognizable by their gull-shaped wings, accompanied by the handy barrel-bodied Russian *Yaks*, came falling out of the burning sky. Zooming down the roads and along the hills at tree-top heights, whipping the grass wildly with their prop. wash, they bombed the retreating ROKs. The latter's panic grew rapidly: here and there were seen authentic cases of soldiers tearing off their cheap canvas shoes so that they could run faster.

Demoralization set in rapidly. The pace of the retreat increased: by ten that morning, it had turned into a virtual rout, and officers started to desert their men. The cruelly-treated, ill-paid soldiers, harassed by Schoerner's columns of tanks and self-propelled guns against which they didn't even have a bazooka to defend themselves, began to make their own decisions. Leaderless anyway, they threw away their weapons and military caps and donned looted civilian clothes wherever they could, disappearing into the mass of pathetic white-clad refugees trudging south to some destination known only to themselves. By the end of this terrible Sunday, the ROK frontline divisions had lost twenty per cent or more of their effectives and were a broken force. It seemed that nothing now could stop the triumphant North Korean armoured columns barrelling south to Seoul, the ROK capital.

That morning the mysterious head of the North Korean state, Kim Il Sung, speaking from Pyongyang thundered over the radio to his people,

> Dear Brothers and Sisters! Great danger threatens our motherland and its people. What is needed to liquidate this menace? Under the banner of the Korean People's Democracy, we must complete the unification of the Motherland and create a single independent state! The war which we are forced to wage is just war for the unification and independence of the Motherland and for freedom and democracy!

Even as the dictator spoke to his people about 'freedom' and 'democracy', his soldiers were cruelly binding the hands of captured ROK officers behind their backs with wire and blasting the backs of their skulls away. Democracy in action, one might suppose . . .

'The General' was not fated to enjoy his Sunday with his adored son Arthur and wife Jean. Instead he was awakened by an anxious aide at about the same time as the moon-faced North Korean dictator was making the speech to his country; the aide told MacArthur what had happened across the

Korea Strait and added for the 'General's further information (though it appeared to the young staff officer that his news hadn't really penetrated) that his staff had already been informed.

MacArthur nodded and indicated that he wanted to be left alone. Later he would write of that moment: according to him he felt it was 1941 all over again when the Japanese had invaded the Philippines. He felt 'an uncanny feeling of nightmare . . . it was the same fell note of the war cry that was still ringing in my ears. It couldn't be, I told myself. Not again! I must be asleep and dreaming. Not again!'

The truth was more prosaic. As he would snort later in the day, 'This is probably only a reconnaissance in force. If those asses back in Washington only will not hobble me, I can handle it with one arm behind my back.' If one can really eat words, he would have time and enough in his dotage to wish he had eaten those!

Now in his carpet slippers and frayed grey robe, with his false teeth in place, however, and his thinning (and probably dyed) hair smoothed back, he paced his bedroom. Presently his pretty young wife came in; 'General,' she said, her face worried, 'I heard you pacing up and down. Are you all right?'

He told her the news from Korea and she paled. Why, MacArthur never explained. Like all egomaniacs he was never very much concerned about other people's real feelings, even when the other person was his wife. Perhaps she was thinking of their nerve-wracking flight by torpedo boat from the Philippines to Australia, across a Japanese-dominated ocean back in 1942.

Later his dog Blackie and his son Arthur burst in for a romp, but Jean turned them out and left the 'General' to his brooding. Finally he emerged and some of the toadies who made up his staff felt he had lost ten years at the news from Korea; it had an invigorating effect on the old war horse. Others thought he was still confused, uncertain what to do about the 'gooks' in the north.

Finally it was two other and lesser men who started making the real decisions for him. Both were hard, secretive and decidedly unpleasant men, but both felt they were right and knew what had to be done now.

The first was John Foster Dulles, lawyer, right-winger, pre-war representative of Nazi big business, who knew where the bodies were buried, both in Germany and in the States. With his twisted face and ugly mouth, he certainly would never have won any beauty prize; but he was a born survivor, staying at the top through all the scandals and suspicions right to his death. Now, unconvinced that the ROK Army could look after itself as MacArthur thought, he cabled Acheson in Washington, adding to the Secretary of State's mounting worries this Sunday: 'Believe that if it appears the South Koreans cannot contain or repulse the attack, United States forces should be used even though this risks Russian countermoves. To sit by while Korea is overrun by unprovoked armed attack would start a world war.'

A startling statement indeed! Here is a statesman urging action in a very undiplomatic manner and risking a world war between East and West. For, contrary to Dulles's words, Russia (who Dulles supposed was behind the 'surprise' attack) might well intervene if America sent troops to support South Korea. That would be a much likelier scenario for an all-out war between Russia and the USA than that proposed in this statement.[2]

The second American who acted decisively that Sunday morning was a soldier; to be exact, MacArthur's Chief-of-Staff Gen Almond. He was a newcomer to MacArthur's staff, not one of the old 'Bataan Gang', as MacArthur's wartime staff members who had stayed on with him in Tokyo were called. He was a new boy from that European Theatre of Operations which MacArthur hated with passion; for he believed it had deprived him of the men and resources he had badly needed in the Pacific during the Second World War.

Although Almond was no prima donna like MacArthur, he was cut in the same mould to a certain extent. He never took time off; his job was his hobby. He was a traditionalist who lived to a certain extent in a romantic idealized past as did MacArthur. For Almond it was the Old South of the American Civil War and all that went with it, in particular a distrust of blacks, mainly the blacks in a still almost totally segregated US Army.

Thus, while virtually everyone else on MacArthur's staff that Sunday set off for a garden party in a requisitioned Japanese villa – and that summer all senior US officers and officials possessed such villas, packed with willing servants who could be paid for the week with a pack of Lucky Strike – General Almond went back to work. He realized somehow that this was more than a minor local crisis. So he called his aide, Captain Fred Ladd, who would become one of the key witnesses of what really happened that day in the 'Big House', and whispered to him discreetly: 'Get two or three cars lined up – we're going back to the office.'

'Are we coming back here?' the smart young aide ventured.

The stern-faced veteran of the Italian campaign of 1944/45 shook his head. 'No,' Almond snapped. Half an hour later he was in the Dai Ichi Headquarters building preparing for what he knew had to come. What did the US have in Korea? . . . What were the strengths of Walker's four infantry divisions in Japan? . . . Could reinforcements be found hurriedly in the local area? . . . How did Walker's Eighth Army measure up in terms of armour? . . . There was no doubt about it, General Almond, at least, was preparing for war. UN police action be damned! The USA was going to Korea to fight a major conflict.

In the winter of 1944, Gen Almond commanded the all-black 92nd Infantry Division in Northern Italy as part of the US 5th Army which had been slogging its way up the boot of that country since September of the previous year. The 92nd, with all its senior officers white, including battalion commanders, had not been intended for combat. But political pressure back in the States, plus the fact that Almond was the brother-in-law of Gen Marshall, the US Chief-of-Staff, had worked the trick. The 92nd, completely green, under the command of officers who were 'retreads' or unwelcome in white regiments, had been sent overseas.

Almond, the southerner, felt he knew how to handle 'blacks'. But his belief was that they needed white officers, not their own kind, to make them fight. As he told the newly arrived black 366th Regiment: 'I did not send for you. Your Negro newspapers, Negro politicians and white friends have insisted on your seeing combat and your share of casualties . . . I shall see that you get both.'

Almond certainly did.

His senior officers seem to have led from the rear. Almond himself was seldom seen at the front; and to the rear, when his young black officers came out of the line, they were forbidden to frequent the officers' clubs used by their white comrades-in-arms. After some astute planning in which a photographer took a picture of an American black officer being kicked out of the club at Viareggio, which resulted in the all-white officers' club being closed, things went from bad to worse.

In the end the 92nd Division broke in combat and 'ran away', if one doesn't put too fine a point on it. The Top Brass showed no sympathy. They made no attempt to cover up as they would have done for a white division. Marshall, that 'organizer of victories' but a southerner too, commented that it would have been better if the 92nd had been sent to the far north where it never gets dark. For in the dark, 'nigrahs run away'. Fifth Army Commander Gen Mark Clark maintained that the 92nd Division's record was 'bad' and 'less favourable than any of the white divisions (under his command)'.

Five years later when Almond came into prominence as MacArthur's Chief-of-Staff, *Time* magazine lauded him for what he had done with that particularly tough assignment, the 92nd, back in 1944. The journalist wrote:

World War II . . . tossed him the hottest potato in the USA, command of the 92nd Infantry Division. The 92nd was mostly a Negro outfit and the cynosure of the sensitive Negro press. Its rank and file had the handicap of less-than-average literacy and *more-than-average superstition*. The 92nd did not learn combat discipline easily. Almond handled his difficult assignment with determination and dogged persistence . . .

In fact, Almond had been so desperate to get overseas and prove himself in combat after two decades or more in the US Army without ever hearing a shot fired in anger that he had used his own influence and that of the Negro lobby in Washington to take a black division that he manifestly disliked and distrusted into battle. The result had been that division had fled the field twice and had been finally relegated to the role of stretcher-bearers and odd-job men.

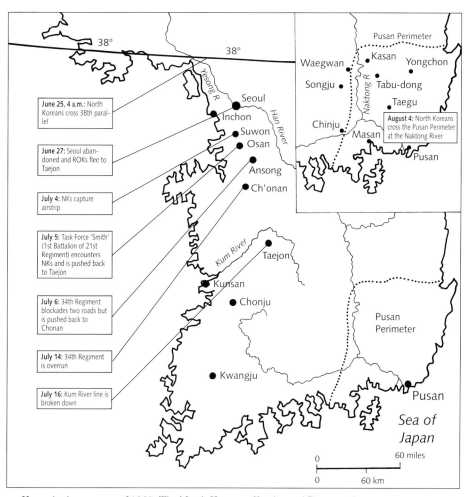

Korea in the summer of 1950. The North Korean offensive and Pusan perimeter.

Now Almond was going to direct a combat operation once more.[3] This time he would be a senior staff officer, however. But the man he would serve directly under was just as hard-nosed, as vain and as opinionated as Almond was. Moreover, MacArthur was a possessor of a titanic ego, an unstable man given to histrionic threats of suicide, a delight in the platonic attentions of whores and an obedient uncritical audience to flatter his personality. The combination was hardly one that was going to win a war.

That Sunday morning, one piece after another, bad news poured into the Washington State Department. Most of it seemed confused and couldn't be verified on the spot. But Ambassador John Muccio's decoded cables appeared to give the truth of what was happening – and they didn't made good reading. Tank columns from the North were sweeping everything before them: what few Second World War tanks the ROK possessed were outgunned and outclassed, and nothing could now stop the 'Gooks' from taking Seoul and Kimpo Airport.

Muccio himself was preparing to flee at any moment – President Rhee wanted to go already, but Muccio had argued he *had* to stay because if he went, the whole of the ROK Army would collapse. According to Muccio, the Korean President had agreed to do so, but by nightfall Rhee was on the run like the rest of his high officials and many of his Army officers as well, for they knew exactly what would happen to them if they fell into North Korean hands: the Koreans were renowned as being particularly cruel throughout Asia, which was notoriously cruel to prisoners. Hadn't the Japanese themselves, who scorned the inferior Koreans, used them to torture their white prisoners during the Second World War? One day later, after ordering that all seven hundred US civilians in Korea should be evacuated immediately (although he didn't seem to know how this could be arranged) Ambassador Muccio would follow the President, heading as fast as he could south in a jeep 'looking for the South Korean government'.

President Truman in the US seemed as indecisive as his State Department officials. The brisk, pushy little Mid-Western businessman, renowned for that sign which adorned his desk in the White House – *The buck stops here!* – did not appear able to react with his customary confident authority. Even as North Korean Yak fighters strafed Rhee's official residence in the South Korean capital, Truman in *his* capital dithered.

Just before he had left for Washington, the President had attempted to cool the situation by telling reporters at the airport: 'Don't make it alarmist. It could be a dangerous situation, but I hope it isn't. I can't answer any questions until I get all the facts.'

But that Sunday evening, facts were hard to come by. By now Acheson knew that 'South Korean arms were clearly outclassed'. Communications were already breaking down between Washington and the representatives of Rhee's government. MacArthur, who was closest to the scene of the surprise attack, was keeping uncharacteristically mum. So far he or his staff had not even made any suggestions how the endangered US civilians in South Korea should be evacuated to Japan. But in a way, Secretary of State Acheson must have been secretly glad that MacArthur was keeping out of things, not wanting that particular prima donna involved at this stage of the business. It would another two days before MacArthur would get around to telling a departing Foster Dulles in Tokyo that 'The only thing we can do is to get our people safely out of the country', i.e. Korea.

Naturally the one-time only 'Field Marshal' in the US Army[4] was now resigned to taking his orders from Washington whenever military matters were concerned. In this instance, they had to come from the US Joint Chiefs of Staff, in particular General Bradley who was head of that group.

But just as in that other major crisis in his military career, the German surprise attack in the Bulge six years before, Bradley was surprised, sick and slow to act.[5] Indeed on arrival in Washington, suffering from an abdominal ailment, that night he told the chiefs-of-staff: 'I am of the opinion that South Korea will not fall in the present attack unless the Russians actively participate in the operation. Therefore, if Korea falls, we may want to recommend even stronger action in the case of Formosa (still held by the pro-American Nationalist Chinese) in order to offset the effect of the fall of South Korea on the rest of East Asia.'

For those few in the know, it wasn't very encouraging. That statement could have been interpreted as a suggestion to give up South Korea and concentrate on the next Russian objective, if indeed Russia was behind the new invasion of South Korea. Fortunately the top brass was made of sterner stuff than the ageing, ailing Bradley.

The first hastily-prepared Presidential briefing was held late on Sunday night at Blair House in Washington. Sitting around the place's large dark mahogany dining table, all the key military and political advisers available were assembled to help Truman make his decisions.

They agreed that for the time being Acheson should concentrate on getting UN in New York to work on the two warring parties as they were 'kind of wards' to that organization. Privately most present that night must have thought in the term used by one of the brass years later, 'it was a crock of shit'. Since Russia had walked out of the UN Council the previous January and left its officials to enjoy their tax-free gravy train existence in peace, nothing much had come out of that international body save a lot of hot air.

Apart from that, after some confused discussion Harry S. Truman made three decisions: General MacArthur would be told to use all available US Army and Navy planes and ships to evacuate US civilians from South Korea (if necessary the planes were to venture across the war-torn 38th Parallel to do so); to provide the hard-pressed ROK forces with ammunition, but *not* weapons; and finally, to have the US Seventh Fleet patrol the Formosa Strait just in case the North Korean attack was actually a feint for an all-out attack on that National Chinese bastion, Taiwan.

It wasn't much and there was nothing particularly dangerous about the measures the President now expected MacArthur to take, save that order for his planes to penetrate North Korean airspace to 'rescue' any Americans stranded there. (Later analysts of the Korean War wondered who those 'civilians' might be apart from consular officials.)

However, the President and his advisers who had that night in Washington placed most of the onus of what had to be done at once on Gen Douglas MacArthur, would have slept less peacefully later if they had known the General's reaction to the new crisis.

Four hours after the Blair House meeting closed, Syngman Rhee personally telephoned MacArthur in Tokyo. An aide told him coldly that the General couldn't be disturbed, and advised the hard-pressed Southern Korean President to call back in the morning. Rhee, always conscious of his position as an 'American puppet' and the possessor – for an Asian – of a notoriously short fuse, flew into a rage and blurted out over the phone: 'Had your country been a little more concerned about us, we would not have come to this! We've warned you many times. *Now you must save Korea . . .'*

Naturally by the night of Sunday/Monday when Rhee made that angry phone call to Tokyo, most Western European governments, media people and others knew what was happening in Korea. They had received the same correspondents' reports and wire service communiqués as the Americans. Any gaps had been filled out by their own diplomatic representatives in the Far East, including those ill-fated British ones in Korea, the most prominent of whom would later become Russia's master spy, George Blake.[6]

Surprisingly enough, although the Dutch, British and French had major interests in the area, the bits and pieces of what was left of their pre-war Empires, they were not in any way concerned by the dire news of events in that area, nor from their own point of view were the West Germans who, naturally, as a recently-defeated enemy nation had no territorial interests on the other side of the globe. However, for potential trouble within the new German Federal Republic itself, already firmly anchored in the American sphere of influence by its wily chancellor Konrad Adenauer, there was very much concern. Indeed its ordinary citizens were shocked by the news of South Korea's invasion much more than the directly affected Americans were even after their sons and menfolk were being sent out to that country to fight – and die. For West Germany felt itself in the front line: it had just survived the 'Berlin Blockade' and they worried that now, if the Russians were preparing for a showdown with America, the resultant 'hot' war would surely engulf them 'at home'.

There was a run on banks, factories laid off workers, production fell and unemployment rose sharply. People began hoarding goods and foodstuffs once more, as they had done in the bad couple of years after the war. Ordinary men and women with no political inclinations refused to disclose to what political party they belonged. They still remembered the men in the ankle-length leather coats of the Gestapo: who knew what might happen to them if the Soviet secret police and their German colleagues of the newly established Communist *Volksrepublik* came westwards, courtesy of the Red Army? In the event, the Korean War soon to come proved a blessing for the emerging West German economy, fuelling the 'economic miracle' and seeing Germany – as well as Japan, another former world enemy – well on its way to becoming one of the world's leading economic powers.

But what of Britain, America's most powerful and most loyal ally of the Second World War, the 'island aircraft carrier' for the invasion of Nazi Europe in 1944? From Churchill onwards right into our own time, British prime ministers have always boasted they enjoyed 'a special relationship' with 'our cousins from over the seas'. What was Britain's reaction to the new danger in the Far East?

Not much, to judge by the papers published in London that Monday morning as, secretly, a special train steamed into besieged Seoul to evacuate Rhee's top officials and their families (in a more modest technical forerunner of what was going to happen in South Vietnam two decades later). Naturally sport was writ large in the British press; it always was in Monday morning editions. It was summer and as customary Britain was having trouble in the Tests. And 'the workers', as they were invariably called in those days, were acting up again.

Despite the fact that new socialist government under Clement Attlee had already worked hard to achieve the new 'welfare state' and a planned economy, *à la* Karl Marx, things were not going well with the workers. The socialist government's nationalization programme – 'power to the people' – had embraced the Bank of England (1946), the coal mines (1947), electricity (1948) followed by gas and railways (both in May, 1948). For the coming year the Attlee government was also committed to the nationalization of the coal and steel industries.

Still, the rank-and-file workers were not satisfied with what had already been achieved at this 'dawn of the New Age'. On this June Monday when the first sketchy reports of the new supposed communist aggression in Korea reached an alarmed Attlee, the ungrateful workers were as 'bolshy' as ever, and were already striking or about to strike in the docks, railways and naturally the mines. This Monday they were even demanding Soviet-style state-owned holiday camps for the workers!

Thus against the background of newspaper headlines gravely proclaiming 'England Fights Back at London Test' and 'Smithfield: Troops Move Meat', Attlee decided to call a full cabinet meeting on the subject of Korea for the next day. In the meantime he would have a look at the waning Empire's resources. In case of an armed conflict involving America, with Britain possibly (though it was not as certain as it might have been in 1945) following, Attlee wondered what the Army and Navy could offer in the way of a quick response. Soon he was going to find out that it wasn't much.

For two years now Field Marshal Slim had been chief of what was quaintly named 'the Imperial General Staff'.[7] He had taken over from the 'Victor of El Alamein', Field Marshal Montgomery, and wasn't too pleased with what he found to be his legacy at the War Office.

Back in 1945, the British Army had demobilized rapidly, as had the American. But the pace had not been so swift, and with a Labour Foreign Secretary still maintaining that Britain was a first-class power, there had been the need for a large army. 'Ernie' Bevin might have been illegitimate, a former rabble-rousing union leader who couldn't pronounce his 'h's', but all the same he was a passionate believer in Britain's 'imperial' commitments overseas – and to defend those commitments and interests Bevin needed soldiers.

But to maintain a large standing army everywhere from Singapore to Salisbury Plain Bevin needed money, and that money was grudgingly forthcoming. According to most of Attlee's cabinet, the lion's share of the country's wealth should go to the new 'Welfare State', in particular their favourite (and naturally vote-winning) National Health Service. A cynic at the time might have commented that we'd lost an empire for the sake of providing granny with her batwing specs and gleaming new plastic choppers.

As far as Slim's command was concerned, this meant that the Army had been systematically starved of real money since he had taken over office in 1948. Britain might well be a nuclear power, but its army was still armed with the weapons of 1945 and radically understrength as far as the supply of regular soldiers was concerned. To meet this deficit the Government had introduced the National Service Act, which had come into operation at the beginning of 1949. It had envisaged the national serviceman serving a year with the colours and six on the Reserve. But unfortunately this meant that due to the fact that after his training the National Serviceman had to be sent overseas to his new duty station by boat transport (air trooping was too expensive and difficult), he served effectively only five months in an operational theatre.

The Royal Navy and the Royal Air Force, which relied more on regular volunteers, were not as substantially affected as the Army which was hit especially by the wastage of regular NCOs and officers needed to train these short-term recruits. Matters were not helped much by the existence of a strong anti-American, anti-military lobby within the ruling Labour Party (this in spite of the fact that Britain's Welfare State was launched with money borrowed from capitalist America).

Field Marshal Slim – 'Uncle Bill' to his troops of the wartime 'Forgotten Army', his 14th Army in Burma – soldiered on. He was used to shortages, political and military bureaucracy and the loneliness of command. With his resignation in his pocket, he went to see Attlee (who had fought together with him in the same division in Gallipoli in World War One) and told him the Army's commitments were too great. He said that he couldn't carry them out with men who in actuality served a mere five months. He needed an extension of active service, i.e. a lengthening of the time the national serviceman did with the Army. The big bluff Field Marshal, who had once been a schoolmaster like Bradley, but who unlike the latter had commanded everything – in action – from a rifle platoon to a whole army, got it: National Service would be extended a further six months.

Now Slim set about encouraging and understanding these callow young 18-year-olds that the Regular Army really didn't want. As he wrote afterwards: 'I spoke to hundreds and hundreds of them . . . They spoke freely even to generals and did not hesitate to air grievances when they thought they had them. But they did not complain that the training was too hard, the hours too long, the conditions too rough . . . The most attractive thing about these National Servicemen was their eagerness to see active service.'

Fortunately those 18- and 19-year-olds *were* eager for active service. For on that confused June Monday, with Britain – still regarded as a world power (strange as that may seem to the reader today) entitled to sit at the same high table as America and Russia as one of the 'Big Three' – had its army spread woefully thin. In the UK the British Army deployed two infantry and one airborne brigades, and had in Germany an infantry division and an armoured one together with seven tank regiments and two infantry battalions; in Austria and the Mediterranean area they had the equivalent of two and a half understrength infantry divisions plus ancillary and support units of armour, artillery, etc. As for forces in the Far East, apart from the handful of Occupation troops still left in Japan there was an infantry brigade and a commando brigade in Malaya and, in the area closest to Korea, Hong Kong, an infantry division and supporting armoured and artillery regiments: all understrength and armed with obsolescent weapons.

If Attlee prayed that day – and he was a deeply religious man – he must have asked God not to involve Britain in a full-scale war in Korea. Let it remain a 'police action', controlled by that UN talking shop in New York. If it did not, God forbid, he would have to use the British Army whose strength currently was made up of under-trained teenage conscripts still wet behind the ears, a terrible prospect for a man who had been through four years in the trenches of the First World War. But the product of Haileybury College's OTC who had volunteered for the Army back in 1914, a man capable when Prime Minister of rebuking one of his ministers with 'Don't talk about your platoon in the bloody mess!', need not have worried: when the shooting war started – and it would – *Major* Clem Attlee would have good reason to be proud of his bolshy teenage National Servicemen. They might well bellow contemptuously at civilians as their troops trains took them through the stations on their way to the ports-of-embarkation, 'We'd rather fuck than fight!' but when the chips were finally down in those remote barren hills on the other side of the world, they'd fight . . .

CHAPTER THREE

The Bulldog Bites Back

Back in the autumn of 1944, the 45-year-old Gen Walton Harris 'Bulldog' Walker had been commanding Patton's XX Corps in north-eastern France. It wasn't the first time that he had fought in the area, which was drenched in the blood of countless generations of soldiers who had battled for its possession. Back in 1918, the young West Pointer had commanded an US Army machine-gun battalion in the attack north-east to Metz from St Mihiel on the Meuse.

Then he had been a slim, dashing aggressive officer with a reputation for womanizing. Now he was no longer slim, but all the other qualities remained despite his considerable bulk. In 1944 he was a martinet strutting around immaculately groomed with his broad bemedalled chest thrust out over his fat belly, always ready for a scrap. To everyone who observed him, including his army commander 'Ole Blood an' Guts', he obviously modelled himself on Patton who led the Third Army, huffing and puffing and cursing all the time just as the latter did. Patton was amused; Walker's soldiers weren't, because they knew that he wouldn't hesitate to sacrifice their lives for an instant if he could win a battle by doing so.

Now in 1944, Walker was faced with the biggest battle of his career. His chief, Patton, had sworn he could go through the vaunted German Siegfried Line 'like shit through a goose.' But Patton knew he had first to capture the great French fortress city of Metz which, unfortunately, was proving a formidable obstacle: after all, it had not been taken by assault from the west since the fifth century.

Such considerations didn't seem to worry Walker, who at Metz would gain his nickname of 'Bulldog' (apart from which, he actually looked like an angry bulldog most of the time). At three o'clock on the morning of 6 September 1944 Walker's XX Corps jumped off with Patton's words ringing in its commander's big ears: 'See you in Metz.'

But that was not to be. For thirteen solid days of mud, rain and sudden death, Walker's hard-pressed infantry tried to break through the dozen or so larger and smaller forts surrounding the Lorraine city, all of them manned by the SS or officer cadets of the local officers' training school. In the end the attack petered out with Walker's casualties streaming back to the US Army hospitals in Nancy, Luneburg and the like in their hundreds and finally in their thousands.

For twenty-four hours 'Bulldog' Walker lost heart and then he prepared to have another crack at Metz, although even Patton was beginning to doubt the damned place could be taken by an all-out infantry assault. With it codenamed 'Operation Thunderbolt', he sold the idea for the operation to both a reluctant Eisenhower and even to Patton: it entailed an all-out life-or-death assault on Metz – as he told one of his infantry divisional commanders just before the great attack, 'Take Driant (one of Metz's major forts), even if it takes every man in XX Corps,' adding ominously, 'I cannot allow an attack by this army to fail.'

But it did fail. 'Thunderbolt' turned out to be a damp squib and Metz would remain in German hands till the following December; by then Walker's attentions were turned elsewhere. All the same, Patton, who couldn't abide failure and who had threatened that winter to sack more than one corps commander, was pleased with 'Bulldog'; that autumn he wrote 'General Walker is always the most willing and most cooperative. He will apparently fight *anytime, anyplace*, with *anything* that the Army Commander desires to give to him.'

Thus in 1950, while the politicians hesitated about what to do in Korea, this was the General to whom Douglas MacArthur was going to give the problem of sorting out the mess in the south of that unfortunate country. For by now MacArthur had paid a flying visit to South Korea to see the situation for himself, and had met the US Ambassador Muccio, a distraught President Rhee and the most senior US Army liaison officer, Brig Gen Churcher, who had fourteen officers under his command, all eager to 'bug out', to use an expression then coming into currency.

But that was not going to happen. After his plane was buzzed by North Korean Yaks (or so MacArthur's PR men maintained later) on landing, MacArthur toured the immediate area for eight hours. For all his show and vanity, the General knew his wars; he had, after all, been in three of them. There was panic everywhere, not only among the fleeing civilians but also among the ROKs. It all looked very bad to him; later he would maintain that on that day he conceived his plan for the great amphibious landing deep behind the enemy's left flank, but that came later. For the time being he told a dismayed Churcher to stay put and 'put some backbone into the Koreans'. Churcher saluted and said he would, though he did not know how. The ROK Army was in full retreat, and its officers, mostly former low-ranking Japanese NCOs and officers, had no idea of how to handle large-scale formations, especially at war; besides which, most of them were abandoning their regiments and divisions and hot-footing it southwards, fearing for their fate at the hands of their countrymen to the north should they be captured.

After that visit, MacArthur flew back to Tokyo and started setting the wheels in motion. Puffing on his celebrated corncob pipe, stuck up at a jaunty angle,[1] he informed Washington that the only way the situation in South Korea could be restored was by the dispatch of US Army ground forces to that country. He urged General 'Lightning Joe' Collins, the Army's Chief-of-Staff in Washington, that 'Unless provision is made for the full utilization of the Army-Navy-Air team in this shattered area, our mission

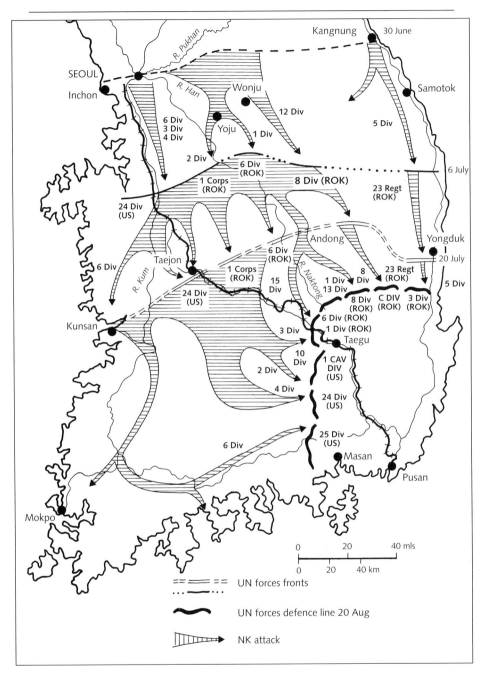

The North Korean advance, July to September 1950.

will at best be needlessly costly in life, money and prestige. At worst it will be doomed to failure.'

MacArthur knew that his forthright cable would put the fiery little Head of the Army in Washington in a dilemma. Collins would have to pass MacArthur's demands over to the President, for MacArthur had insisted that Collins, whom he had awakened in his makeshift cot in the anteroom to the Joint Chiefs' quarters, should take the deciphered cable immediately and directly to the President: then Truman would have to make an overwhelming decision *without prior reference to Congress*.[2] The choice was: should American interfere in South Korea or should the country wait for the UN to act? MacArthur was of the opinion that every hour counted, and indeed, he was for the US to take immediate steps.

While he waited for Truman to be woken and make his decision, MacArthur took a fast look at his military resources in Japan, which in essence were the four divisions of 'Bulldog' Walker's Eighth Army. These divisions – the 24th, 25th and 7th infantry Divisions, plus the 1st Cavalry Division (also an infantry division, despite its name) – were the survivors of those formations which had fought through the Pacific during the Second World War. But only in name. Currently only twenty per cent of Walker's Eighth were combat veterans and even the latter had succumbed to the easy life of Occupation Japan, where a woman could be bought for a pack of cigarettes. Like the rest they were drinking too much, training too little, and spending their weekends in brothels, bars and other dives or 'shacked up' with their women. Of course MacArthur knew all this; his own senior officers were no better. Even though they were bringing over their wives to Japan, they were still keeping their much younger native mistresses on the side; and all of them were drinking and partying far too much.

But even if MacArthur was aware that Walker's Eighth Army was not really ready for combat, he did have confidence in its commander and that he would do his best. At all events, trained and prepared for combat or not, they *were* Americans and they would be fighting against 'Gooks'. So the only problem once the President gave the go-ahead would be throwing them into battle in South Korea as fast as ships and even expensive transport planes became available. Time was running out fast for the United States . . .

On the previous day, Tuesday 27 June 1950, most of the time had been taken up in discussions in Washington, naturally, and in all the other Western capitals which felt themselves involved in the crisis which had emerged so suddenly and startlingly in South Korea. But of all the capitals concerned, it was solely in Washington that there was a sense of urgency, even drama.

As the situation on the other side of the world steadily worsened, an emotional South Korean ambassador to the USA, Dr John Myun Chang, called upon the President and told Truman that his country needed immediate help. Truman is said to have spun the big globe in his office and, slapping his hand down on Korea when it ceased spinning, proclaimed in that flat accent of his: 'This is the Greece[3] of the Far East. If we are tough enough now there won't be any next step.' Dr Chang is said to have broke into tears. Whether from the analogy or from the fact that he didn't hold much faith in the President's intentions to do something, no one ever found out later. He simply stepped into a footnote of the history of the war to come.

At nine that night Truman called yet another meeting at Blair House of his 'war cabinet', as it was now being called by those in the know. Truman knew that he wasn't really going to get far with the UN, whose appeal for a ceasefire had already been turned down by North Korea. The UN as talking shop still dithered and had no clout; after all, the other world superpower was still refusing to take part in its deliberations, almost as if the Russians, if they really *were* behind North Korea, were giving their puppets full rein.

Still, Truman wanted to use the UN. This time he wasn't after a ceasefire: now he wanted to have public support for any action that the US Army might have to take in the next few hours in Korea. In essence, America wanted allies to cover the fact that it was going to have to fight the coming war in protection of its own interests. Now, for the first time in the country's twentieth-century philosophy, the USA was shrugging off its idealistic-isolationist stance and was talking Realpolitik: this last week of June 1950, the sleeping giant was finally waking up to the fact that it was a superpower with vital overseas commitments which had to be defended by every means possible. Though ninety-nine per cent of the American public, still sweltering in the current heatwave, didn't know it, the United States had just entered the new age. From then onwards, after Korea, there'd be just one damned military intervention after another in countries most Americans had never even heard of. America had grown up at last!

That evening France was offered increased support for its Army fighting the communist nationalist forces in Indo-China. (Another burden that the USA would have to take on a decade or so later; Vietnam was born.) All UN countries allied to America by treaty or affiliation were asked to help and to send 'peace-keeping troops'. It may have been one of the first times that that phrase was used, but it had its effect: the fallen National Chinese Supremo Chiang Kai-shek offered 33,000 of his veterans; the Royal Navy placed all its warships in the Pacific under the command of the US Pacific Fleet; and far away in Japan, 'Bulldog' Walker was frantically preparing his reluctant heroes for what was soon to come.

In London, Maj Attlee's socialist cabinet met promptly at eleven o'clock on that Tuesday. Their agenda was much as usual: the regular economic issues which had plagued the workers' representatives ever since Labour had been swept into power back in the summer of 1945. There were important issues – at least to some of the doctrinaire socialists who met at 10 Downing Street that day: the problem of white fish; the integration of the French and German coal industries, very remote then save for the competition they might present to British miners; grants for marginal hill land, etc. But even the left-wingers of the Labour Party had a soft spot in their hearts for that contemporary successor of the old pre-war League of Nations, the UN, and so for once they forgot the economy and the parish pump affairs of 'Great Britain', as it was still called, and concerned themselves with the support of the United Nations in Korea.

Attlee put forward a resolution with which apparently they all agreed, that it was the 'clear duty of the United Kingdom Government to do everything in their power, in concert with other members of the United Nations, to help South Korea to resist this aggression.' More importantly, as far as support for US action was concerned, the British cabinet agreed that the British Far East Fleet should join any offensive action required to deal with North Korea.

Under the command of Rear-Admiral Andrewes, the first British ships (out of the 22 vessels stationed in Far Eastern waters) sailed to join the Americans. With restrained pride Andrewes pointed out that unlike in the last years of the Second World War, the British were as strong numerically as the Americans, and provided the light fleet carrier *Triumph*, the cruisers *Belfast* and *Jamaica*, and the destroyers *Cossack* and *Consort*.

Indeed, a matter of days later, HMS *Jamaica* and the frigate HMS *Black Swan* (known naturally to her crew as 'the Mucky Duck') fought the first naval action of the Korean War. At dawn the two ships were attacked by six North Korean torpedo boats; the action was brief decisive: all the enemy craft save one were sunk. It was 2 July 1950. Britain, purportedly engaged in a UN 'police action', was at war whether she knew it or not . . .[4]

America, however, had still to fire the first shot of *its* war. As far as the Western media were concerned, the various American and UN communiqués were confusing. The journalists, swarming everywhere in Tokyo, Lake Success, New York and Washington trying to get a clear account of what was going on, wanted to know whether the USA was at war, or whether Washington was just a major player in the attempts by the UN to solve the problem of Korea, or whether the US Army was going to participate in an armed Allied attempt under UN control to intervene and *force* North Korea to withdraw its invading army.

Two days after the British Cabinet had made *its* decision, Truman was asked at a presidential press conference to clarify matters:

'Mr President, everyone is asking in this country are we or are we not at war?'

Truman didn't hesitate: 'We are *not* at war,' he snapped back.

The journalist was, however, not prepared to give up that easily. He persisted:

'Mr President, could you elaborate on that statement "we are not at war", and could we use that in quotes?'

Caught off guard for once, the bright perky Mr Truman did 'elaborate'. 'Yes,' he answered, 'I will allow you to use that in quotes. The Republic of Korea was set up with United Nations' help. It was unlawfully attacked by a bunch of bandits who are neighbours in North Korea. The United Nations held a meeting and asked the members to go to the relief of the Korean Republic and the members of the United Nations *are* going to the relief of the Korean Republic to suppress a bandit raid on the Republic of Korea. That is all there is to it.'

It was all very wooden and rather simplistic, as if the President felt he was talking to a none-too-intelligent child. But he had underestimated the correspondent if he thought that was the case, for next moment the latter asked the President, 'Would it be correct then to call it a police action under the United Nations?'

Truman fell for it hook, line and sinker. 'Yes,' he answered promptly, 'that's exactly what it amounts to.'

In other words, if it came to war, it wouldn't be America alone fighting it; the US would be just one of a number of UN nations conducting 'a police action'.

Truman's opponents would never let him forget those fateful words that day. One hundred thousand American young men killed, wounded, taken prisoner, to carry out a 'police action'! It would cost Truman in the end most of the enthusiasm the nation might have had for the long protracted war in Korea – and probably the Presidency too. After all, what red-blooded American wanted to die in a 'police action'?

But, as that first grim week was coming to an end, it was clear to all those in the know that American troops were soon to be engaged in a real all-out shooting war in Korea. On that same day as Truman gave his unfortunate press conference, Tokyo reported that South Korea's 65,000-strong Army was virtually destroyed. It had already lost over 40,000 men killed, wounded, or taken prisoner, and an unknown number had deserted. As MacArthur saw it, the days of pussy-footing around were over. Air and naval support of the South Koreans wasn't going to be enough. Walker would have to send in his woefully unprepared Eighth Army, whose men might not look very good to MacArthur's critical trained eye but who'd frighten the hell out of the 'gooks' to the north . . .

Exactly one week after he had been masquerading as a Korean *yangban* at the officers' fancy dress dance at the 24th Division's Officers' Club, Gen William Dean was stopped in his car on his way to the local airfield at Itazuki. The MPs who stopped the two-star divisional commander told him he had to return immediately to his headquarters at Kokura. Dean didn't need to be a crystal gazer to guess why: something secret must be on its way from HQ. It was, but even though he expected that his career was in for a change, not even in his wildest dreams had he guessed what he was being offered now: he was going to take his division forthwith to Korea; more importantly, he had been given overall command of an American land expeditionary force. A relatively unknown general with no great track record, he was not just going to war again after five years of peace; he was also going to lead a whole US Army, Walker's Eighth, into that war!

But getting his 'sad sacks' of the 24th Infantry Division to Korea to fight proved trickier than the General had anticipated: transport was difficult and air freight was a madhouse, and ultimately he himself would set off from Japan to South Korea to take charge *three times* before finally reaching his new headquarters. In the meantime, however, he sent 'Task Force Smith' (a token force of 406 riflemen under the command of Pacific War veteran Lt Col Charles B. (Brad) Smith) ahead to the area of the key port of Pusan, whence they would journey by train to the front line which was apparently located between Seoul and Suwon. Thereafter he would try to move his division, 'scattered near half a dozen ports with no ships ready'. As Dean wryly concluded, 'It was an interesting assignment.'

Soon that 'interesting assignment' was going to turn into overwhelming bloody disappointment and Gen William Dean would disappear from American ken for the next three years . . .

Three days after Dean finally arrived in Korea, the men of Task Force Smith, apprehensive and nervous, wet and not a little hungry, were occupying a 'blocking position' south of Suwon Airfield near the little town of Osan, a ramshackle place which they could see vaguely but smell even more. As always in Korea, the local towns and villages gave off an awful stench: a mixture of *Kimche*, the national dish; garlic; the 'honeydew' carts used to transport human waste to fertilize the paddies; and unwashed human misery. But in the rising tension of this damp July dawn, even the stink was forgotten. Back at the port-of-embarkation in Japan they had told themselves confidently they'd 'be a week in Korea, settle the gook thing, then back to Japan'. Now that confidence had vanished. This dawn they peered nervously to their fronts, seeing movement where there was none, coughing a lot, rising to take a piss in the nearest ditch, a sure sign of tension in green infantry.

Then it started. Just after seven that morning, an NCO called to his company commander, 'Hey, look over there, Lieutenant,' he said in the casual manner of American soldiers, 'Can you believe it?'

Hastily the officer, Lt Day, asked as he spotted the eight T-34 tanks advancing towards them, 'What are they?'

The sergeant knew the answer. He'd worked at his armour recognition tables back in Japan, 'Those are T-34 tanks, sir . . . and I don't think they're going to be friendly towards us.'

After five years, Field Marshal Schoerner, late of the *Grossdeutsche Wehrmacht*, was going to get his own back on the 'Amis'[5] for the way they had treated him back in that fateful May defeat in the Second World War.

After their initial shock the Americans started to react with what they had, which wasn't much. Capt Dashner cried above the rusty rattle of the T-34s' tracks, 'Let's get some artillery on 'em!'

A few moments later the US guns opened up with a roar. Great spouts of brown earth erupted from the bright green paddy to the defenders' front. Here and there an American veteran opened his mouth to stop his eardrums being punctured. The rest, the greenhorns, continued to stare with horrified fascination at the low-slung tanks with their long overhanging 75mm cannon still coming up on their positions. The American cannon couldn't stop them!

Two brave young American officers took up the challenge with their bazookas, Davids facing up to Goliaths. As the first T-34 raced through the narrow pass between the GIs' positions, one of them opened up. A bang. Scarlet flame stabbing the grey dawn. The hollow boom of metal striking metal. Suddenly a great shining silver star appeared on the Russian tank's steel side. Someone cried, 'He's hit!' A few opened their mouths to cheer. But the cheer died in their throats. The T-34 was still moving, its long cannon twitching from side to side like the ugly snout of some predatory monster. After a few minutes, the Americans then struck lucky, with their 105mm 'Long Tom' cannon living up to its Second World War reputation: its shell struck and stopped a T-34 dead in its tracks. Thick white smoke started to pour from the Russian tank's ruptured engine, and a panic-stricken tanker slid out of the escape hatch. All the same he started firing his burp gun as soon as he landed on his feet. Not for long. He was torn apart by angry American small arms. But before he died, he shot and killed one of Smith's GIs. That unfortunate young man was the first American to die in Mr Truman's 'police action'.

Three hours later what was left of Smith's task force was fighting for its life. Here they were, half a battalion of poorly-trained bewildered young men, outnumbered by 'gook' infantry supported by the best tank in Korea, forced into a position of no hope. Their nation was the world's superpower, possessor of the atom bomb, mighty high sea fleets, great airforces which could bomb Korea off the map, owner of the greatest source of wealth in all history, and the industrial and economic powerhouse of the Western world, yet all it could field to stop these peasant-soldiers in their poor-quality cotton uniforms and their cheap sneakers, was a couple of hundred infantrymen armed with the weapons that had last been used in a war fought five years before!

In the end Task Force Smith faced up to the inevitable. It could either surrender or retreat. The senior officers hesitated; Smith said he'd ordered the Task Force to hang on. But as the casualties began to mount once more, with the medics working full out and running short of supplies, he changed his mind: 'I guess we'll have to (retreat)', he told his officers reluctantly, adding unhappily, 'This is a decision I'll probably regret the rest of my days.'

So they started to pull back. At first it was orderly. Then the men on heights spotted their comrades down below moving out. Fearful of being left behind they abandoned their positions. They started to wade through the stinking paddies, cursing and already beginning to drop their heavier equipment, the usual things that frightened soldiers always abandon first, leaving a trail of olive-drab equipment behind them.

'It was every man for himself,' Lt Day of the Force remembered many years later,

> When we moved out, we began taking more and more casualties . . .
> Guys fell around me. Mortar rounds hit here and there. One of my
> young guys got it in the middle. A sergeant ran over to help him. To no
> avail. All that he could do was to pat him on the head and say
> encouragingly, 'Hang in there!' Another platoon sergeant got it through
> the throat. He began spitting blood . . . For the rest of the day he held
> his throat together with his hands . . .

In the end the survivors got away, fleeing in twos and threes, all military cohesion vanished. Behind them they left the silent dead, sprawled out in the wet paddy in the grotesque positions of those done violently to death. Only 185 men of the original 500-odd of Task Force Smith reached their own lines . . .

By the end of that first dreadful week of July 1950 the USA was at war, though it was a war never officially declared or ever approved by Congress. In fact, the Congress was never even asked for an opinion. Truman was in too much of an 'all-fired hurry', as he expressed it. But things were going badly for the Americans in Korea. The 'gooks' were not the easy meat that some American officers had thought they were. Indeed MacArthur opined that the US Eighth Army was running out of 'real estate'. The troops were becoming demoralized, too, as they suffered defeat after defeat and started to become aware of just how cruel, even sadistic, their enemy was. More than once they recovered bodies of dead GIs who had been murdered in cold blood with their hands wired behind their backs. As a result the same 'bug-out fever' which had attacked South Korean troops at the start of the North Korean invasion had begun to infect Walker's Eighth too.

Walker, pompous strutting little martinet though he was, turned out to be a pillar of strength. Watching the evacuation of Chonan by Gen Dean's battered 24th Division, Walker approached the young officer commanding the first platoon coming over the brow of the hill where the two officers were standing. 'What are you going to do down there?' he demanded.

The lieutenant replied with words that he thought were expected of him, 'I'm going to slug it out.' Watching, Dean thought 'the boy was certain he was on his way to death.' Walker thought differently. He lectured the youngster what he was *really* going to do. 'Now,' he snarled, 'our idea is to stop those people. We don't go up there and charge or slug it out. We take positions where we can have the advantage, where we can fire the first shots and still manage a delaying action.'

The young officer's fate is unknown but, whatever he did, he succeeded only in delaying the North Korean advance for a short while; then they came on and the hard-pressed war-weary GIs were on the run again. As one of them, Cpl Stephen Zeg, told a reporter: 'I'll fight for my country, but I'll be damned if I see why I'm fighting to save this hellhole.' Undoubtedly he spoke for thousands of Walker's troops trying to defend what was becoming known as 'the Pusan front'.

For Pusan had become the most important spot in the whole of South Korea. Through it had come the whole of the US Eighth Army, soon to be followed by British, Belgian, French, Turkish, Australian, Dutch, Philippine troops, even a handful from the little Grand Duchy of Luxembourg. But if it was the Allies' major port-of-entry, it would also be the one through which they would evacuate their troops if necessary; and as that awful month started to draw to a close, that eventually seemed ever more likely.

Something had to be done – and done soon!

CHAPTER FOUR

Where the Hell is the Rest of the US Army?

By 18 July Dean's ill-fated 24th Infantry Division was about at the end of its tether. Its 19th Regiment was no longer an effective fighting force. Dean had been forced to withdraw it to the rear. Its sister regiment, 21st Regiment, was in not much better shape. Both regiments could indeed not muster more than a battalion of infantry still capable of fighting. But Dean wasn't even going to chance that. The morale of the two regiments was too low. As one officer of the shattered Task Force Smith, Maj Martain, commented: 'We knew that we weren't doing well. But we kept saying to ourselves, "Well here we are and we've been here a month and where the hell is the rest of the United States Army?"' As far as Gen Dean was concerned, that 'rest' was what was left of his division still capable of fighting, his 34th Infantry Regiment. It was given the task of defending the all-important road centre, vital for the advance of the victorious North Korean Army, located at the city of Taejon. And it was here that a harassed Gen Dean – who now, in retrospect, seems to have gone a little crazy through overwork, worry and constant defeat that month – decided to make his own personal stand.

Much later, the big hefty soldier rationalized: 'My reasons for staying in the town were simple, although of course there can be much argument about them . . . But these reasons were compounded of poor communications . . . and the old feeling that I could do the job better . . . if I stayed in close contact with what was happening.' It was going to be a fatal decision.

On the morning of 20 July, the General awoke early to the sound of gunfire. He pulled on his boots and helmet and went outside. It didn't take a trained eye to realize that his last remaining regiment, the 34th Infantry, wasn't doing a very good job of defending Taejon. Those GIs, who a month before had been 'happy in Japan' with Japanese girlfriends, plenty of beer and servants to shine their boots', were streaming back in defeat. They came in twos and threes and then in dozens. Their eyes were wild and unseeing. Some had already thrown away their weapons. When Dean tried to stop and question them, they murmured the usual '*They're coming*' (and the General knew who 'they' were) and, tugging themselves free, straggled on out of the doomed city; and all the while 'Spiteful rifles of infiltrators and turncoats spat from windows' at the fugitives.

Suddenly, for no apparent reason, Gen Dean lost his head. He did what no divisional commander should do, but which in the history of modern war many have done on losing control. Some try to guide traffic for hours on end. Others kick out men skulking in cellars and try to form ad hoc fighting forces, which melt away as soon as the general departs. Dean made the worse decision of all. 'We decided to go tank-hunting.'

Together with three companions, one of them his Korean interpreter Jimmy Kim, the General set off through the debris-littered streets, with smoke pouring from burning shanties and the regular bark of cannon close by.

Dean didn't have long to find his first enemy tanks. He found two T-34s from that great armoured forced prepared by Field Marshal Schoerner for the drive south. Both were 'dead in the street', with the one's track rolled out behind it like a severed limb. Opposite them one of the 34th's ammunition carriers was burning furiously. Around it lay dead GIs.

The General pushed on. Someone found an abandoned bazooka. They ducked as a lethal stream of tracer sliced the air just above their heads. They turned a corner and stopped dead. There was the enemy. A single T-34, its engine roaring furiously. Behind it some way off there was another one, trying to find its way out of the confusing mess of blocked streets.

The North Korean turret-gunner spotted the little party in olive drab. He opened fire immediately. Red tracer zipped in their direction like a swarm of angry hornets. They raced for cover. Now hardly daring to breathe, they worked their way through smoking brick rubble behind the T-34. From somewhere close by they could hear the angry snap-and-crackle of a fire fight. They ignored it. Their whole attention was concentrated on that lone T-34 tank.

Now they were within fifteen yards of it. The Korean tank was backing down the street. Dean thought they couldn't miss. He was out of luck. 'This was our day for bad shooting,' he recalled ruefully nearly a decade later. The bazooka man was too nervous. He pulled the trigger of the anti-tank weapon balanced on his right shoulder. A blast of flames. A thick whiff of smoke. For a moment the T-34 vanished from view. The next moment it was scuttling down the street unharmed. Carried away by a mad unreasoning rage, Dean pulled out his .45 and started blazing away purposelessly.

As he confessed candidly afterwards: 'It was plain rage and frustration – just Dean losing his temper.'

Dean went on to fight some more. He didn't think until too late that it was time to move out of a dying Taejon. Instead he did more of the same things that broken general officers at the end of their tether do – perhaps he was seeking death rather than defeat. He organized a 'counter-attack force . . . from kitchen-police, clerks and messengers'. Naturally the 'counter-attack force' faded away before it could do any good.

As afternoon approached, it was clear that the 34th Regiment had lost the battle of Taejon, its battalions and companies falling apart. As they lost more and more officers who sacrificed themselves bravely to try to stop the rot, the 34th was cut up into desperate little pockets of resistance. One of Dean's staff officers showed him a message he was sending to divisional headquarters. To Dean, 'it sounded in his version, too much like asking rescue for me personally.' Dean scribbled out his own message. It read: 'Enemy roadblock eastern exit Taejon. Send armor immediately. Dean.'

But there was no armour, and that was that. Later Dean recalled: 'If I had realized that this was the last formal order I was to issue for three years perhaps I might have phrased it better – one of those ringing things that somebody would remember. But I didn't know then, and now I can't think of anything better to have said.'

Thereafter General William Dean, formerly commanding the US 24th Infantry Division, disappeared. The next three years of his life would be spent in solitary confinement in a North Korean cage. Still, though having failed to write 'one of those ringing things' that July day, he went down in history, after all, as the highest-ranking US officer taken by the communists in the whole of the forty-year-long Cold War. It would be fame of a kind, wouldn't it? . . . .

After Dean's disappearance, a hard-pressed 'Bulldog' Walker – now bearing the whole brunt of holding the North Koreans, trying to stop them with his untrained, under-armed Americans of the Eighth Army – threw in the 24th's sister division, the 25th Infantry to try to stop the 'gooks'. Unfortunately for Walker and his chances of preventing the North Koreans advancing any further, the 25th's regiment placed in the blocking position was the 24th Infantry; and the 24th was a three-battalion, all-black (save for a few senior white officers) outfit. The tragedy of General Almond's 92nd Infantry in Italy was about to repeat itself.

The 24th Infantry was not a happy regiment. Back in Japan, in a strictly segregated US Army, the black GIs had been treated as second-class citizens by their white comrades. They were limited to 'GI bars' catering for the needs of 'coloreds'. They too 'shacked up' with Japanese girls, but the latter turned out usually to be members of the 'horizontal profession', the cheapest of whores at that. Naturally the 'rednecks' among their comrades told the usual tales about 'coloreds': that they were descended from monkeys and were possessed of tails and the like.

In Korea the situation had not improved, even though like the whites they too would soon fight for their very lives there. As one of them, Second World War veteran Roger Walden, recalled bitterly long afterwards: 'From the beginning, South Korean companies were attached to various (white) outfits. Long before blacks were eating, sleeping and fighting alongside their fellow Americans, Koreans were living an integrated life in the American armed forces. To deny that this infuriated the black soldier would be ridiculous.'

As Walden added, 'This was only one of the "jokers in the deck" that I witnessed in Korea.'

Now on 20 July, the same day that Gen Dean disappeared into the jaws of battle at Taejon, the 24th Infantry Regiment went into action for the first time. It had been placed in a blocking position in the Hamchang area. Its task to stop the North Korean 15th Infantry Division, its first engagement with the enemy was indecisive. But it didn't appear to matter very much, for soon after its first contact with the victorious North Koreans, the black soldiers were officially ordered to withdraw down secondary roads.

Then the trouble really started. Moving backwards, constantly being outflanked by the enemy, never really having a chance to fight from well-established positions, the 24th started to exhibit a tendency to panic at the first sight of a North Korean. Prejudiced white soldiers booed the blacks as they moved back, calling them 'a bug-out outfit' and worse, forgetting that in many cases they were 'bugging out' themselves.

The situation grew worse. It was said that officers had to form makeshift stoplines and, with drawn pistols, try to keep their soldiers in their positions by means of threats; but that as soon as these officers (white *and* black) left, their troops slunk away yet again.

The pattern grew even worse. Now as soon as it grew dark or yet another heavy rainstorm set in, the blacks used the cover to desert, often casting their weapons away as they did so.

It seemed to serve no purpose that the Eighth Army's HQ awarded decorations for bravery to certain black soldiers. Indeed one of them, Master Sergeant Curtis D. Pugh, was presented with the Distinguished Service Cross, America's highest honour for courage in combat after the Congressional Medal of Honor, by no less a person than General MacArthur himself.[1] The rot had set in and nothing seemed able to stop it. When questioned, black soldiers complained they 'were fighting the wrong war in the wrong place.' For those who knew the US Army and the general attitude to negroes in those days, their meaning was quite clear. They should have been at home fighting their bigoted white fellow Americans.

On 20 July, the 24th Infantry had first really broken and run from the battlefield at Yechon after a few hours of combat. On the 29th of that month, an almost inexplicable panic overcame the regiment's First Battalion. The battalion had just dug in when they were spotted by North Korean artillery observers. With a stomach-twisting howl, the enemy mortars had opened up. Suddenly great brown steaming holes appeared everywhere to the blacks' front like the work of gigantic moles. For some reason, the battalion's officers were not really able to bring down effective counter-fire as would have been customary in such situations.

Casualties weren't very high, but the bombs falling out of the leaden sky had the effect the North Koreans wanted all the same. Here and there the black GIs began to leave their foxholes and hastily arranged strongpoints. The trickle became a flood. In a matter of an hour or so the whole battalion was fleeing to the rear in panic, abandoning their equipment as they ran. Roadblocks were quickly set up, but officers and MPs armed with Tommy guns and carbines simply couldn't stop the fleeing men.

Later the official US Department of Defense history pulled no punches. It maintained that the 24th was in a habit of abandoning its weapons and its positions, risking the lives of comrades in other outfits. It criticized the regiment's chronic unreliability and lack of leadership (though it did not specify whether this was white or black). The official historian wrote: 'The tendency to panic continued in nearly all the 24th Infantry operations west of Sangju . . .'

Some of the blacks involved took the criticism in a sanguine manner. Eddie T. Robinson, who had already seen Second World War service as a submariner in the USN, had been sunk and had served three years of hell as a Japanese prisoner-of-war, recalled his time as an officer with the 24th, 'as one of those black lieutenants with the 24th Infantry Regiment . . . I was in that mad backward rush from the Yalu River . . . Would I do it again? Hell no, I'm old enough now to know better.' Another, who shall be nameless but who was known to the author, retained a cold hatred in his heart for the whites who had taunted him and his comrades at that time for being cowards. 'One whitey called me a yeller nigger to my face. He didn't live long.' He certainly didn't. The future career warrant officer pulled out his pistol and shot him dead there and then on the spot. Arrested by MPs, the black soldier didn't even express regret at what he had done.[2]

By the end of July, 'Bulldog' Walker realized that the 24th was no good as a front-line outfit. But the new role to which the blacks were assigned was still dangerous, but degrading. They were to be used as a kind of buffer and tripwire. Whenever the Reds would attack, the blacks – predictably (or at least Walker thought so) – would break and flee. But behind them he'd place another regiment that would stop the North Koreans by really serious resistance, once the steam had gone out of the enemy's attack. And that was about the end of the black soldiers' part in the fighting in Korea in 1950. The 24th Infantry Regiment had suffered the same fate as General Almond's 92nd Infantry Division in Italy six years before.

Almond's comment is unknown. But we do know that after Gen Matthew B. Ridgway, a southerner himself, took over the Eighth Army (including Almond, now as the leader of the US X Corps), he ordered on 1 October 1951 that the 24th was to be desegregated. It was the real start of a totally integrated US Army.[3]

On 27 July, after yet another failure for the 24th Infantry (and also troops of the newly arrived 1st Cavalry Division), MacArthur and Almond were to confer with 'Bulldog' Walker. They were both disappointed with the performance of his army, but told Walker there would be 'no Korean Dunkirk'. The Eighth would fight to the bitter end, if necessary. MacArthur would refuse to have the Army evacuated to Japan.

The harsh pep talk was the kind of shot in the arm that Patton had always given Walker and his other Third Army commanders. It fitted in well with Walker's bulldog tenacity. Leaving MacArthur, he first went that afternoon to the headquarters of the 1st Cavalry where he chewed out its commander

Gen Gay, once one of Patton's staff officers. From there Walker journeyed to the HQ of 25th divisional commander Gen William Kean, another wartime staff officer in the 1944/45 campaign. Here naturally he complained about the conduct of the black 24th Infantry; then before the Division's assembled staff officers, he gave out his most famous order, perhaps the most famous of the whole Korean campaign. He told the staff, with the sound of the big guns pounding away in the background and jeeps coming and going with urgent and ever more alarming signals from the crumbling Eighth Army front: 'We are fighting a battle against time. There will be no more retreating, withdrawal or readjustment of the lines or any other term you choose. There is no line behind us to which we can retreat.'

The overweight, pugnacious General paused to let the full impact of his words sink in and there must have been staff officers present that hot damp July afternoon who realized for the first time that even *their* lives were in jeopardy. One day soon they might well be out there too, armed with a pistol or carbine, taking their place in the firing line with the dirty, smelly, frightened GIs who normally had to pay the bloody butcher's bill.

> Every unit must counterattack to keep the enemy in a state of confusion and off balance. There will be no Dunkirk, there will be no Bataan; a retreat to Pusan would be one of the greatest butcheries in history. We must fight to the end! Capture by these people is worse than death itself! We will fight as a team. If some of us must die, we will die together. Any man who gives ground may be personally responsible for the death of thousands of his comrades. I want you to put this out to all men in the division. I want everybody to understand that we are going to hold this line. *We are going to win!*[4]

Red-faced and gasping a little from talking so rapidly and so much, Walker paused, searching each face as if seeing it for the first time, as if trying to etch it on his memory for the present – for ever. It was perhaps Gen Walton 'Bulldog' Walker's finest hour.

Walker's 'stand-or-die' went the rounds rapidly. It was said to have greatly inspired his troops, though Walker had not meant it literally. He was still prepared to retreat, but it had to be a planned, coordinated retreat, not the wild scrambles effected to that point by US soldiers throwing their arms away shamefully, surrendering without a fight and without a qualm to the 'gooks', of whom Walker had once said contemptuously, 'they don't have a pot to piss in.' But his mentor Patton would have been proud of him. It was the kind of fighting talk – 'root hog or die' – that he had always expected of his general officers.

But if Walker's celebrated speech didn't really change the conduct of the war in Korea, luck and planning did. By now the supply lines of the North Korean invaders upon which the enemy depended for the continuation of their drive south were stretched to their limit and coming under accurate bombardment by the US Air Force's massive B-29s, against which the North Koreans had no defence except their Yak fighters – which usually couldn't fly high enough to tackle the gleaming silver-winged four-engined American bombers anyhow.

At the same time, Walker's front had contracted. This coincided with the arrival of sufficient Army and Marine reinforcements to hold the perimeter being formed around Pusan. MacArthur helped too by his clever scheme to integrate elements of broken ROK divisions to those of the Americans, thus instituting the so-called 'buddy system' by which small groups of Americans, even down to single GIs, were supported by their 'Korean buddies', soldiers of the ROK Army. Even if these 'buddies' only acted as porters, bearing huge loads on their A-frames in support of the US outfit to which they were attached, they added an immediate 30,000 new troops almost overnight to Walker's Eighth Army.

But there was another element, for which the US military authorities had not calculated, that helped to stiffen the average GI's resistance and slow down the speed of the North Korean advance: something that Gen Kean, commander of the 25th Division, had encountered before in the 'old war' and had used to bolster the spirit of yet another shaky and demoralized US Army. In that same week of July when ace female war correspondent Marguerite Higgins of New York's *Herald Tribune* was reporting: 'I saw young Americans turn and bolt in battle . . . or throw down their arms cursing their government for what they thought was embroilment in a hopeless cause', something occurred which changed the American soldier's attitude radically: the first North Korean atrocities were discovered.

On the afternoon of Sunday 17 December 1944, the then Maj Gen William Kean had been a worried man. He was chief-of-staff to the US 1st Army in Belgium. The day before, the First had been hit by a massive German counterattack through the Belgian Ardennes. Now, on a gloomy overcast afternoon with a threat of snow to come in the grey sky, he was sifting through reports from the nearby front, each one successively more alarmist, at the 1st Army HQ in the health resort of Spa, when he was handed yet another. It was quarter past three when he received the signal from Col David Pergin, commander of the US 291st Engineer Battalion stationed around Malmédy, the next town to the east. The engineer colonel had something dreadful to report: the Germans had apparently massacred a whole battery of captured US artillerymen in cold blood. The full details were not yet clear, but it was certain that SS tankers had mown them down in a field near the crossroads at the hamlet of Baugnez above Malmédy.

For some reason that cannot be ascertained today, the report went straight to the US Army Group, to which the First Army belonged. (After all, the higher command had far more important problems on their hands that afternoon, when their whole front was falling apart, than the fate of a few score obscure artillerymen.) From there it went to Supreme Headquarters at

Versailles to be read by no less a person than Supreme Commander Gen Dwight D. Eisenhower himself.

It read: 'SS troops vicinity L 8199 captured US soldiers, traffic MP, with about two hundred other US soldiers. American prisoners searched. When finished Germans lined up Americans and shot them with machine pistols. Wounded informant who escaped and more details follow later.'

At six o'clock that night, with his HQ now – ironically enough – preparing to flee from those same 'SS killers', Kean recorded in his diary: 'There is absolutely no question. General Vanderbilt [the US TAC Air Force Commander] had told every one of his pilots about it [the alleged massacre] during their briefing.'

Shortly, thereafter, two US correspondents, Hal Boyle and Jack Belden of *Time* magazine, got hold of the story. It sailed through the usual delays of censorship and was in the stateside papers by Monday. Now the news of the massacre spread rapidly through the troops in the Ardennes. Their commanders didn't waste this opportunity to bolster the sagging morale of their troops. It was no use surrendering, they told their men, the 'Krauts' will shoot you anyway.

The 'Malmédy Massacre', as it became known, came as a godsend to Eisenhower. In that first week of the Ardennes there were wholesale surrenders of US troops all along the 1st Army front. Even as the survivors of the 'Massacre' were still being questioned, a mere fifteen miles away 10,000 GIs of the ill-fated US 106th Infantry Division were considering surrender, the biggest since the American Civil War.[5] Now Eisenhower could point out that it would be wider – and safer – simply to fight on despite the circumstances. As President Roosevelt remarked cynically to Secretary of State for War Stimson when informed of the incident: 'Well now the average GI will hate the Germans just as much as do the Jews.'

Now in 1950 American troops were making first contact with communist Asiatic reality in Korea. In local counterattacks they uncovered the brutally cruel true face of North Korea. The latter's fighters, it was now clear, were proving ruthlessly indifferent to the taking of prisoners-of-war. US prisoners were found shot in ditches, hands tied behind their backs; tossed bound into fast-flowing streams to drown; and in one case burnt probably alive in a barn. Wherever the North Koreans decided their American prisoners would be no use for propaganda purposes – and they would soon become past masters at the art – they disposed of them in the quickest manner they knew – a bullet through the back of the skull!

As six years earlier in the Ardennes, US commanders were not slow to make full use of these enemy atrocities. 'Fight and die – if necessary' became the message from the top. 'Surrender and die anyway!' It was a message not lost on the average GI. Now and again he would still run away – indeed in months to come, there'd be another great bug-out – but not in the same numbers as before. Instead he'd stand and fight, knowing what his fate might well be if he didn't. For he had come to hate and fear the 'gooks', but also to respect them for their fighting qualities. He knew, even if the folks back home didn't, that the gooks didn't triumph because they possessed overwhelming numbers, attacking in 'wave after wave' of troops, as the *New York Times* put it on 26 July. Nor did they outnumber the defenders by 'at least four to one', as the same newspaper put it two days later. In fact, the defenders actually outnumbered the North Korean attackers by 22,000 men (92,000 against 70,000) and the Koreans from the north possessed now no more than forty tanks, fewer than the number of tanks possessed by the newly arrived 89th Tank Battalion alone.

No, so far the North Koreans had succeeded because they had been better trained, better motivated and better indoctrinated in the art of winning than had Walker's Eighth Army. Battle-weary, with hardly enough food to keep going, and having suffered very severe casualties since 25 June, the gooks had managed nonetheless to project the illusion of a very strong, confident and victorious army. Their success was not because they had been able to attack in 'human waves' as the myth of the Korean War has had it right into our time, but because they had felt they had been fighting for a 'cause': the communist one of victory over the ruthless capitalist by the downtrodden masses!

For that one terrible month of July 1950, it seemed that the communists in Asia had almost won their section of the cold war. But they failed just short of throwing the puppet Rhee and his American 'plutocratic masters' back into the Korean Sea. Now it was to be the turn of the 'round-eyed devils'. What *would* the Americans do?

CHAPTER FIVE

Major Attlee Makes a Decision

As always in post-Second World War Britain, the government dithered. The days of Winston Churchill and his bold demands on his ministers and military leaders *Action This Day* had long gone. Now Attlee's socialist government sat on its thumb, agonized and wondered what it should do about Korea.

Of course Attlee, like his next major socialist successor Harold Wilson, disliked communists intensely. (Wilson was almost paranoid on the subject of 'reds under the bed'.) The socialist public schoolboy and ex-major was sure that communist infiltrators into the British trade union movement would attempt to wreck the British economy. Moscow, as always, did not want to see socialist governments succeed. They had done it in pre-war Germany and again in post-war France and Italy. Their weapons now would be traditional trade-union sabotage and the new post-war anti-Americanism.

In the summer of 1950 there was ample evidence in Britain of the former – strikes on the railways, in the mines, in the meat industry, even in bakeries, all calculated to disrupt the lives of ordinary men and women, the people who had voted for a Labour Government in 1945. And Attlee was well aware that his government was not really a popular one. In February 1950, it had sneaked through to its second victory at the polls by only the narrowest of electoral majorities.

Neither did the bald pipe-smoking Premier, who apparently was totally colourless, have far to look for anti-Americanism, which was – and still is – exceedingly popular among the intellectual classes[1] who formed public opinion, or thought they did. The contemptuous tag of a 'coca-cola culture' to describe America and its world-wide influence had not yet arrived, but it was on its way. *Major* Attlee, no intellectual by any stretch of the imagination, did not have to look even as far afield as Bloomsbury or Hampstead to discover a dislike of all things American. Although, as we have seen, the Americans, who had no 'socialized medicine' of their own, had paid for the National Health Service and all the rest of that Labour jewel in the crown, the 'Welfare State', there were many at the top of the Labour Party who detested the 'Yanks' intensely: key figures such as Foot, Callaghan, Barbara Castle, and Jennie Lee, wife of Aneurin Bevan, 'the Minister of Ill-Health', as Churchill called the Minister of Health (who incidentally preferred private doctors when he himself was sick). Beneath them there were as well lesser figures in the Labour Party who openly praised Soviet Russia and visited that country even after the cold war had commenced, and Britain had fought communism in Greece, taken part in the Berlin Blockade, etc.

Naturally, even Attlee thought America was brash, 'too pushy', inclined to act without due consideration. The Major agreed with the USA's first appeal to UN to condemn North Korean aggression, but he didn't like American proposals to attribute that aggression to set Asia alight for the benefit of the 'evil Russian state'.

For the whole month of July while the US Army in Korea fought for its very life under 'Bulldog' Walker, Attlee's government appeared to do nothing. As we have seen the British Far Eastern Fleet was dispatched to help UN, in this case in reality the United States, and it actually fired the first shots of the Korean War. But the Fleet was composed of regulars, and was far away with no newspaper correspondents on board at that time, so that its part in the struggle at the other side of the globe could have no immediate effect on the people at home.

At home, it was the same. In the first week after that hot weekend in June, the newspapers indeed headlined the events in South Korea, but without government encouragement and little of importance (except the usual Foreign Office gobbledegook and Downing Street hot air) coming from the government, newspaper editors seemed to lose interest. News from Korea started to disappear from the headlines to the lower regions of the front page and then finally to the inner pages until there were days in mid-July when the London Press reported nothing on the new 'police action'. What they *did* report, however, alarmed a lot of people. There was talk of increasing National Service so that better-trained teenagers would be eligible for overseas deployment, but for what sort of action? Other reports spoke of recalling the 'Z Reserve', i.e. men, mostly infantry, who had served in the Second World War but who were now settled in 'civvie' jobs, married and bringing up young families. One didn't need to be a mind-reader to realize what effect a recall would have upon them.[2]

The Chiefs-of-Staff in London were not too keen on such a recall. For a start, they wondered how long the Americans under Walker would be able to retain their hold on the narrow enclave around the port of Pusan. They had all served in the Second World War too, and didn't place much reliance on the average American soldier to fight unless he was supported by a mass of technology, air and artillery and tanks. And they did not think too highly of senior American officers either: under a dying Roosevelt in the last year of the Second World War, the US Top Brass had run the war pretty much in any way they wanted. If – God forbid – the Americans were kicked out of Korea and decided to use their atom bomb as they had already done twice before in Japan, five years earlier, where did that leave Britain? The result might well be an all-out world war and what troops and resources Britain possessed would be needed urgently in Europe and the Middle East.

All the same, both Attlee's cabinet and his senior service chiefs could not postpone a decision much longer. Washington was putting increasing pressure on them to join what to some there amounted to an anti-communist crusade. It would be an important publicity coup if Britain, the major Second World War ally, joined in, even with a single battalion (which was the case with Belgium, Greece, France, etc.).

Quietly the decisions were made, without too much public attention. The Great British Public was going on holiday to the seaside, complete with children, bucket and spade in those simple far-off days. Just as quietly those buff-coloured envelopes containing the re-call notices that some ex-squaddies had been dreading ever since the start of the action in Korea began fluttering through the letter-boxes of reservists and those of the 'Z Reserve'. Meanwhile in Hong Kong the regulars were being alerted. Finally Attlee had been forced into sending troops . . .

Whatever the feelings of the reservists, young regular officers were delighted with the news. 'It might only be a small war,' they chortled in their masses, 'but it's the only war we've got!' Young captains such as Anthony Farrar-Hockley of the Gloucester Regiment, who had already fought in the Second World War as an under-age volunteer for some of the time and who would soon suffer grievously as a Chinese POW, couldn't get to Korea fast enough and in spite of everything seems never to have regretted going. All the same, nearly half a century later as a full general he thought that the way the troops were subsequently dispatched in 'penny packets' was wrong: because the British finally went as small brigade-sized formations, and not as a division, they were faced with severe difficulties from the start. As he would write in the Official history: 'A bold decision to form the Commonwealth Division[3] at the outset would not have cost more over the term of the war . . . The presence of a major-general in command of three brigades, fully supporting arms and services would have precluded the intermittent misdirection of the 27th and 29th Brigades.'

What General Sir Anthony Farrar-Hockley was saying obliquely was that due to their small initial numbers the British came naturally under the command of American divisional and corps commanders, in whom they would have little confidence. Nor were these young British officers, eager for some desperate glory, too pleased with their own commanders at brigade level. As Gen Farrar-Hockley would write 45 years on: 'Britain has rarely conducted a major campaign without discovering that a proportion of its senior officers lacked the talents for the unrelenting demands of war.'

A nice backhander so many years after the event. But in that bright sunny August exactly halfway through the twentieth century, these young regular officers, who would fight, suffer and die in Korea for a cause now long forgotten in a war that no one really remembers, were not concerned with such great matters. They were going off to the greatest adventure of all, and that was all which counted. They were going to war!

While Britain procrastinated, Gen MacArthur in faraway Tokyo plotted and planned. He realized that the steam had gone out of both sides in South Korea. For the time being the North Koreans and Walker's men, both ROK and American, were being forced to sit on their butts and wait to regain their strength. For his part Walker had dug in along a 145-mile-long perimeter around the port of Pusan, receiving reinforcements, new outfits and supplies etc. but with (in General MacArthur's opinion) little idea of what to do with them. In essence, it was up to MacArthur.

Above his desk in his office in Tokyo, MacArthur had had a sign hung. The framed message read: 'Youth is not a time of life – it is a state of mind'. It was (and is) a very true statement, one that a lot more old men should heed. It would save them a lot of doctor's bills. Not that MacArthur needed to worry about such things. He had his own surgeon, doctor, dentist, a whole unit of white-coated medical attendants. Now, this summer, he didn't require their services. He was too busy concentrating that very active brain of his on how to change the stalemate in Korea in America's favour – and, naturally, gain the headlines for himself.

He decided that Walker needed new troops, lots of them, especially now as the detested Europeans, primarily the 'Limeys', were being so parsimonious with their soldiers. But where would he find them? It must have been in the last days of July that General MacArthur recalled the generous offer made by the 'Gimo' on the island of Formosa right at the start of the 'police action' to send 33,000 troops straightaway to Korea. Thus it was that in the last week of July, without permission from President Truman or anyone else in Washington for that matter, the old warrior decided he'd fly to visit the 'Gimo' and find out if the offer still held.

The 'Gimo' was tall, handsome in an oriental manner, Generalissimo[4] Chiang Kai-shek, former ruler of China who, after fighting the Japanese, assorted warlords, ambitious underlings and the Chinese communists for nearly a decade had been finally turfed out of his native country and had landed in the island of Formosa, where he plotted with his American-educated, beautiful and very cunning wife to make a triumphant return to China.

As before the 'Gimo' was only too pleased to help. MacArthur was delighted and, before the US State Department could stop him, had empowered the former to issue a statement pledging 'Sino-American cooperation . . . and determined leadershipment in the common fight against totalitarianism in Asia . . . and the menace of communism.'

MacArthur pretended to be surprised when the 'Gimo's' statement hit the headlines in the States. Naturally, as he explained, he hadn't known about the 'Gimo's' intention to issue it. He had gone to Formosa to 'meet my old comrade-in-arms of the last war'. In fact, he was appealing to the US public to force Truman's hand. MacArthur wanted not only to save the day in Korea for the USA, but also to rally the whole of Asia, meaning Nationalist China – perhaps even a re-armed Japan – in an all-out fight against communism. That would mean a war with communist China!

Truman must have hit the roof. What MacArthur was aiming at, he must have thought, was a third world war, involving not only China but also Soviet Russia as well. It was an intention that certainly appealed to the hawks in America who, confident in their country's possession of the nuclear deterrent, wanted, in the words of Gen Le May's famous statement of a decade later, to bomb the 'commies' back to the Stone Age.

For a while Truman 'gave serious thought' to 'relieving General MacArthur as our military commander in the Far East and replacing him with General Bradley'. However, that would come later: Truman relented at the last moment and kept MacArthur on in command. But with the British press (*Manchester Guardian*, *Observer*, *The Times*, etc.) ready to condemn MacArthur's attitude and the tremendous risks involved, the latter had to give way on the issue.

He didn't like it, of course. MacArthur always hated criticism. As some of his critics at the time observed, 'Doug really does believe he can walk across water – and quicker than Jesus, too.' Someone had to be blamed. In MacArthur's fantasy it was those 'fancy pants' in the State Department who had succumbed to 'British pressure'. The 'Limeys' had forced Acheson to dictate that his, MacArthur's, plan to involve National China not only in the fight against North Korea but also against Red China itself, whatever the consequences, was misguided. It was, as one of his advisers told him, 'a clear illustration of the devious workings of the Washington–London team'.[5]

There was worse to come, as MacArthur saw it, from the devious British; but for the time being he was still secure in his office and the direction of the war in Korea. But the damage had been done in London. MacArthur's aggressive behaviour gave birth to what was called 'MacArthuritis', as it was called in the inner circles of the Establishment. The General's ability to make such statements as he had done on Formosa and China without prior consultation with UN and in particular with Attlee's government led the British to fear that MacArthur could lead the Western world into a war against not only China but also the Soviet Union.

President Truman didn't help things either. For three months later he held a press conference in which he alluded to the atomic bomb and 'contingency planning' involving that same terrible weapon. This frightened the striped pants off Major Attlee and in the end he decided to fly to Washington to discuss with Truman in person the bomb, the Korean situation and, above all, General Douglas MacArthur. Thereafter MacArthur's days in command in Asia were numbered . . .

Nine years before, on New Year's Day 1941, General Douglas MacArthur had been agonizing over the decision about just when he should blow up a bridge before the advancing Japanese in the Philippines. His army had been thoroughly thrashed and now he was trying to save the retreating remnants across the Calumpit Bridge, which spanned the fast-flowing Pampanga River. He knew in his heart of hearts that his 24,000-odd American and

Filipino troops were doomed even if they did manage to cross the bridge safely with the Japanese hot on their heels. They would be trapped. Still he had to make the attempt, for he knew too that President Roosevelt wouldn't allow him, one of America's greatest soldiers, to fall into the hands of the Nips.

It had all been very much 'nip-and-tuck'. But he had saved his ragged weary beaten force – for a while. The Japs had been thrown back and the bridge had been blown up. His men had passed on to a kind of gigantic POW camp of their own making where they fed themselves (starved, would have been a better word) until the enemy had come to round them up. For his part General MacArthur had escaped by boat to Australia together with Jean and young Arthur (naturally wearing a kind of cut-down uniform and a garrison cap, to the delight of the photographers) to become for all time 'Dugout Doug' to his abandoned army – those who survived.

On that same day in Asia, another weary band of soldiers had marched down jungle roads infested with Jap infiltrators, heading for the causeway which separated Malaya from Singapore. Once they had crossed it, the next soldiers to appear would be the Japs. In the end 200 survivors, led by their pipers, managed it. Behind them the British sappers blew up the land bridge and Singapore was cut off for good. In due course, that shameful mass surrender which would lose Britain its Indian Empire in a day took place. But those last two hundred survivors of the once nearly 1,000-strong proud Argyll and Sutherland Highlanders had done their duty to the last.

Earlier, further up the coast at Hong Kong, some of the British garrison still fought on, although the Crown Colony had surrendered to the Japs. Four Royal Marine sergeants barricaded themselves in the Garrison Sergeants' Mess and, well-oiled with booze, beat off all comers, even a light Japanese tank, until the inevitable happened. A lone and crazed officer who had lost his fiancée, a nurse, raped and bayoneted to death when the Japs had massacred the British Army personnel at St Stephen's College, armed himself with grenades and a tommy-gun and went out to 'kill Nips'. He was never seen again. And a platoon of the Middlesex Regiment fought to the last man. Not one of them survived the bitter enemy onslaught. Truly they lived up to the regiment's army nickname 'the Diehards'.

Now nearly a decade later the first battalions of those two infantry regiments, one English and from the south, the other Scots and from the north, prepared to fight similarly fanatical Asiatics once again. Again the 1st Battalion of the Middlesex Regiment, commanded by Col Andrew Man, was stationed at Hong Kong. But in the summer of 1950, the 'Diehards' were more concerned with ceremonial drill – 'bull, wallop and Chink bints' – than with last-ditch stands.

It was the same with the 1st Battalion of the Argyll and Sutherland Highlanders, commanded by Colonel Neilson. They had done a little training as part of the British 40th Division, 'the Hong Kong Field Force' as it was called in the terminology of the nineteenth century, but that was it.

Their main task up to mid-August that year was 'flying the flag', ceremonial parades with 'bags of swank' and 'braw lads' marching smartly behind a pipe band, dressed in spotless white tunics.

On Friday 18 August the business of 'blinding 'em with bullshit', 'bags o' swank . . . remember who ye are', and 'Chink bints, who knew how to treat a man like a man' (for a small price) came to an end. For it was on that day that a top-secret signal from Whitehall was flashed to the Crown Colony. The Leicesters (soon to be replaced by the Middlesex) and the Argylls had been alerted for departure; and as the rumour soon started to spread, it was quickly clear to the thickest squaddie that the two infantry battalions were going to Korea.

The officer who was soon to take them there was Brigadier Coad, a burly highly experienced infantry officer, who had commanded the 5th Battalion, the Dorsetshire Regiment right through the campaign in Western Europe in 1944/45. That battalion which belonged to the 43rd Wessex Division, led by Gen 'Butcher' Thomas, had fought in Normandy, at Arnhem, the Battle of the Rhineland and right on to the end at the capture of Bremen.[6] It had suffered tremendous casualties just as had the rest of the 43rd Division, over a thousand dead and wounded a month for eleven months, so that by May 1945 the 43rd had had a complete turnover of strength. By the end, Coad had been promoted to Brigadier and after the war he received a subsequent promotion to major-general. But he didn't last long in that rank, reverting to his old wartime one of brigadier by the time he reached Hong Kong.

Coad was brave and tough, and certainly knew how to handle infantry, but he certainly *didn't* know how to handle Americans when he came in contact with them in Korea. It was soon going to be a major handicap for him and his two-battalion brigade. For instead of the usual three-battalion brigade, he had to content himself with two battalions, both understrength and with three-quarters of their personnel national servicemen who had never been under fire before.

Still, Coad – burly, staid and lacking imagination, perhaps a typical regular British infantry officer of his time and experience – applied his customary energy to the problem. Calls went out to the other battalions of the 40th Division for volunteers to bring the Argylls and Middlesex up to strength, and they were soon forthcoming.

Indeed, as it became known back in the UK that the two battalions were going to war, keen young officers eager for action gave up cushy or plum jobs to volunteer for service with them in Korea, although both battalions had their full complements of officers.

Dashing 24-year-old Captain Colin Mitchell of the Argylls was typical. That summer he was ADC to Lt Gen Sir Gordon MacMillan, commander of Scottish Command. After active service in Italy and Palestine, the infantryman, who had already commanded a company at the age of 22, didn't mind the giddy 'social whirl' of a 'boudoir soldier' – he even learned to dance the reels obligatory in Scottish regiments – but not when there was a war on. War meant death and death meant promotion, and the handsome young captain knew it.

MacMillan was reluctant to let his ADC go: he had not done the required two years. Finally the General agreed on the condition that Mitchell found a replacement. 'After frantic telephoning I found him a new ADC,' the future Colonel Mitchell recalled many years later, 'within a matter of hours. He took it all in very good part. So I was free to set out for my third campaign.' (He would survive and twenty-odd years later, known now to the Press as 'Mad Mike' for his deeds, bold and unconventional in Aden, he fought and saved the regiment he loved. But that would be much later.)

So now he was involved in the chaos that the sudden move to the new war entailed for his Battalion and that of the Middlesex Regiment. Inoculations for the many diseases supposed to be rampant in Korea were overlooked or forgotten. Weapons were 'borrowed'; in the case of the 'Jocks', sometimes 'found' before they were 'lost'. Bits and pieces of uniform and equipment were begged from the hard-nosed 'quarterblokes'. Ammo, that most vital part of a man-in-the-line's kit, was even 'bought' from other units. A hundred and one things had to be dealt with in five short days before finally Brig Coad's 2,000 men sailed in the light fleet aircraft carrier *Unicorn* and the cruiser *Ceylon*, escorted by one lone Australian destroyer. The 'Woolworth's Brigade', as the force was mockingly called, was on its way to battle. The British were coming!

While the 'Woolworth's Brigade' sailed steadily for the 'Land of the Morning Calm' as they learned to call Korea, cynically or otherwise (for some of them would find it a very pretty country despite the overwhelming stink of the place), Gen MacArthur, their new Supreme Commander, had got over his setback over National Chinese intervention in the war.

Already his fertile old mind was planning and plotting yet again. With his great ego, he would not allow himself to keep out of the limelight. At the moment all media attention was being focused on 'Johnnie' (as he called the Eighth Army commander) Walker's defence of the Pusan perimeter. The latter's fight or die declaration at the 25th Division's HQ had caught the public's attention. Temporarily, the 'Hero of Bataan' had been forgotten. That was something MacArthur intended to rectify quickly.

MacArthur, assisted by 'Ned' Almond, reasoned that if Walker stopped the 'commies' at Pusan and then broke out with the aid of the many new American and European formations which were now arriving in the Eighth Army's area, he'd suffer severe casualties. The North Koreans, the cream of their army, would fight like the very devil. It would be better, the two of them thought, if they did what MacArthur had always done very well and very successfully in the latter years of the Second World War, i.e. to stage an amphibious landing to the enemy's rear. As he wrote to the US Joint Chiefs-of-Staff in Washington as early as 23 July 1950: 'Operation planned mid-

September is an amphibious landing of two division corps in rear of enemy lines . . . The alternative is a frontal attack which can only result in a protracted and expensive campaign.'

The Chiefs weren't too excited about the project. In particular Bradley, their chairman, didn't like it and thought it 'bold and very risky'. MacArthur thought Bradley's opposition was a result of sour grapes because he had not wanted Eisenhower's 12th Army Group Commander in the Pacific after the Second World War had concluded. He persisted, going ahead with his planning against all opposition, maintaining that time was of the essence. The Russians were rushing mines by the hundred thousand to the North Koreans to be set in every harbour and sealane along their whole eastern coastline facing Japan. Soon there wouldn't be a harbour available where his soldiers and marines could land.

Then MacArthur gleefully dropped another hot potato in the laps of the Chiefs-of-Staff. He had found a harbour for his planned landing. As the Chiefs under Bradley hastily found the place on their maps of Korea, they must have gasped with shock. Its position, its geographic details and the tides around it made it, they must have reasoned, the worst possible place in the whole world to select for an amphibious landing. Located some 170 miles from Pusan, the harbour could be entered only by a long and exceedingly narrow channel, shallow and easily blocked: the whole dominated by a fortified island named Wolmi-do. If that wasn't bad enough, the huge tides which ran around the harbour were favourable for only a few days each month so that there would be a twelve-hour gap between the first and second wave of aggressors from the sea. To cap it all, the harbour itself was protected by a seawall which would have to be scaled, for it was 12 feet high, exactly twice the height of a tall man. How could even the 'Leathernecks', famed as they were for their toughness, determination and reckless frontal assaults, attack and capture a place like that?

Again the Chiefs-of-Staff attempted to dissuade the old man, with his battered cap and corncob pipe trademarks, in Tokyo. MacArthur remained adamant. On 23 August MacArthur met the whole of the top brass involved, including the Army's Chief-of-Staff 'Lightning Joe' Collins, in the mahogany-panelled conference room in Tokyo's Dai Ichi Building (Number One Building), his headquarters. One by one the generals and admirals put forward their objections – the place, the tides, the lack of time for preparation . . . On and on they went, while MacArthur listened calmly, puffing at his old pipe. (Perhaps this was his only sign of agitation; normally he wouldn't smoke his pipe in public in Japan because he felt it made him look to the 'Nips' like a 'broken-down old farmer'.)

When they were finished, MacArthur let loose with a 45-minute exposé of his assault plan. To coincide with Walker's Eighth Army breakout to the south, his X Corps would lead, over the heads of the Marine generals concerned, the assault on Korea's west coast. In the end the two forces, X Corps and Walker's Eighth, would converge on Seoul and recapture it.

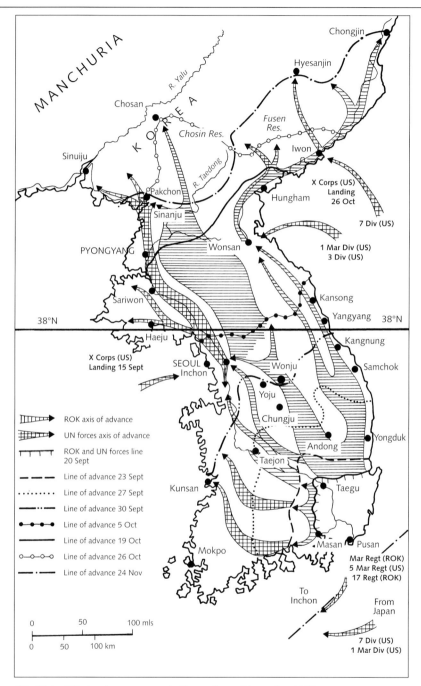

MANCHURIA

K O R E A

R. Yalu

R. Taedong

Chongjin

Hyesanjin

Chosan

Fusen Res.

Chosin Res.

Sinuiju

Iwon

Pakchon

Hungham

Sinanju

X Corps (US)
Landing
26 Oct

7 Div (US)

PYONGYANG

Wonsan

1 Mar Div (US)
3 Div (US)

Sariwon

Kansong

38°N   38°N

Yangyang

Haeju

Kangnung

X Corps (US)
Landing 15 Sept

SEOUL
Inchon

Wonju

Samchok

Yoju

Chungju

Yongduk

Andong

Taejon

Kunsan

Taegu

Mokpo

Masan Pusan

Mar Regt (ROK)
5 Mar Regt (US)
17 Regt (ROK)

To
Inchon

From
Japan

7 Div (US)
1 Mar Div (US)

ROK axis of advance

UN forces axis of advance

ROK and UN forces line
20 Sept

Line of advance 23 Sept

Line of advance 27 Sept

Line of advance 30 Sept

Line of advance 5 Oct

Line of advance 19 Oct

Line of advance 26 Oct

Line of advance 24 Nov

0   50   100 mls

0   50   100 km

The United Nations' counter-attack, September to November 1950.

MacArthur had other things in mind for his troops as well, bold ambitious plans, but for the time being he concentrated on seaborne attack. He stressed his firm belief in the psychological advantage of the landing. At Pusan, the North Koreans were still attacking, believing they had 'Johnnie' Walker on the run. Suddenly, out of the sea at the most unlikely spot imaginable far to the north of Walker's hard-pressed perimeter, would appear a mighty allied naval force composed of ships from seven navies. After they had pounded the surprised defenders to pulp, some 25,000 US Marines and specialized army troops (including 230 British commandos in a special raiding party) would come riding in over the waves to sweep all before them. It would break the back of the North Korean Army and finish them. Korea – he didn't yet say all of Korea – would be liberated from the Reds. In Asia, the cold war would come to an abrupt and victorious end in the favour of the West.

In a dramatic near-whisper, the old General finished, 'We shall land at Inchon and I shall crush them!' The surprise Inchon Landing was on. The turning point of the Korean War had arrived.

CHAPTER SIX

The Woolworth's Brigade

Back in the United Kingdom that early autumn, the business of steadily readying new formations for Korea (and possibly elsewhere if the cold war spread: a terrifying thought always at the back of Attlee's and the planners' minds) went ahead. Most of Britain's best armour and infantry were in Germany, facing the Soviets eye-to-eye along the eastern border of what had been the British zone of occupation up to comparatively recently. In Britain itself there were still good formations, steady unfashionable infantry regiments in which the officers didn't have private means, never being invited to Court nor appearing on the London social scene being photographed for the *Tatler* and the like. But these 'bread-and-butter' regiments were mostly engaged in training national servicemen. Based on a nucleus of battle-experienced NCOs and company officers (all their senior officers having apparently seen action in Europe or Asia and thus wearing the brightly-coloured ribbons of the DSO, MC, etc. which testified to their bravery[1]), their ranks were filled with teenage recruits.

These 18- and 19-year-old lads weren't exactly bolshy. Most of them had been through the blitz as kids; had suffered rationing (in 1950 still in existence); had elder brothers and relatives who had fought in the 'real war'. All the same they were slightly different from their teenage predecessors of that 'real war'. Not only didn't they like the 'bull' just as the earlier generation of recruits hadn't – if it moves, salute it, if it don't, paint it white' – they openly resented it. They still learned how to 'spudbash'; polish the inside of their square mess-tins (leaving a very unpleasant aftertaste); square their blankets and arrange their 'biscuits';[2] 'march to attention' and warble 'mucky' songs – 'Where was the engine-driver when the boiler bust – they found his bollocks and the same to you . .'

But when they first appeared in their 'winkle-pickers', drainpipe 'slacks', and oiled 'styled' hair and a red-faced 'lance-jack' screamed at them, 'What the frig d'ye think ye are, frigging Tony Curtis? GET THAT FRIGGING HAIR CUT!' they resented it, for that was the way they *wanted* to look. Youth, even working-class youth, wanted to appear fashionable and 'with it'.

At first a lot of them resented their loss of freedom: Mum making their tea; watching the new-fangled 'telly'; 'a crafty shandy' at the pub when they were barely of age to drink. They didn't think much of red-faced sergeants bellowing at them in the 'middle of the night' to get 'yer hands off yer cocks and on with yer socks – move it, you idle men'; officers who looked them up and down on parade with disdain, lisping over their shoulder to the platoon sergeant, 'take that man's name, sergeant, idle on parade'; MOs who raised their penis with a pencil as if that organ was indescribably filthy and muttering something about 'clean that John Thomas properly man – get that foreskin right back and scrape out the muck!' What was a 'John Thomas'?

Yet in time they forgot 'civvy street' and its supposed freedoms and delights. For the first and only time in their lives, these 'virgin soldiers' would exist in an ordered environment, where their daily affairs were regulated from reveille to lights out. They'd discover pride in their unit, themselves and their pals. At night after the 'wet canteen', drunk on a 'sniff of the barmaid's apron', they might well chant 'Kiss me goodnight, Sar'nt Major . . . tuck me in me little wooden bed . . .' But, literally sometimes, that was what their NCOs did for them. They looked after them and again reinforced that feeling, for the short period most of them spent in the British Army, that they belonged.

Therefore, it wasn't with the national servicemen that the authorities, preparing possible candidates for posting to the fighting in Korea, had their problems. Indeed many of these first members of the post-war teenage culture, which has stayed with us ever since, volunteered actually to extend their length of service so that they could risk their young lives in that far-off 'Land of the Morning Calm'. A Private Denton, at that time an 18-year-old, was training with the West Yorks just outside his native city of York. An officer trying to fill out the ranks of the Leicesters, still in Hong Kong waiting to go to Korea, asked the platoon for volunteers for a posting to the Midlands regiment. 'All of us were still under eighteen,' Denton explained nearly half a century later, 'and the Government had said nobody under 19 would be sent to Korea. But when the officer asked, the whole platoon, all just eighteen, snapped to attention, stepped one pace forward, as you were supposed to do, and volunteered!' Soon after, like many more of his age group, Denton was on his way to his new regiment and Korea.

The problems the Army faced, therefore, were really with the 'old sweats' of the Army Reserve and the younger ones in their mid-twenties, who had been enrolled at demobilization into the 'Z Reserve' whether they liked it or not. No one had asked them to join the 'Reserve' – many of them had long forgotten they had belonged to it. Unlike the Regular Army reservists they weren't given reserve pay. Now the buff forms fluttered through the doors announcing 'In accordance with of your reserve liability it has become necessary to recall you to active military duty. You are accordingly required to report for duty on ——'[3]

The summons didn't go down too well with hundreds of 'old sweats', especially as it seemed that only 'other ranks' were being recalled. (In fact, the British Army had enough officers; hence the need for ordinary squaddies.) Many had just started their first jobs in 'civvie street'. Others had very young children and pregnant wives who depended upon their single bread-winner for support. Hundreds were ex-POWs of the Japanese and Germans. Indeed, in the end, some reservists found themselves going 'into the bag' for yet a second time.

Extraordinary scenes took place at regimental depots, and sometimes at police stations to which reluctant heroes were taken by force, frog-marched there by the red-faced local gendarmerie. Labour exchanges were crowded with worried young men trying to sort out their affairs, pleading with middle-aged clerks to be deferred because of a hundred-and-one varied family commitments.

The cheaper newspapers such as the *Daily Mirror* featured scores of 'hardship cases'. But the *Mirror* (of the wartime cartoon character 'Jane', whose habit of losing her clothes at every possible occasion was to the delight of its soldier readers) which had turned itself into the 'voice of the squaddie' in the Second World War, found it cut little ice with the socialist government it had helped to elect in 1945. Attlee and his generals could be just as hard-nosed as their conservative blimpish predecessors of the 'old war'. The Army needed 'bodies'. It was going to get them.

The Fifth of Foot, the Royal Northumberland Fusiliers, which would later have a distinguished record in Korea, reported a minor mutiny. As so often in such cases, it started in the cookhouse where the mass of the 'other ranks' would usually be faced by two voices of authority only, those of the orderly officer and the orderly sergeant. These two with their armbands would be seen, in addition, merely for a short time when they came in to taste the meal and ask for 'complaints' to be relayed to them by the senior soldier at each trestle table of twelve squaddies.

The drill was probably as old as was the duty of orderly officer. The young officer in question would watch the cooks – always 'thieving cooks' to the squaddies – dish out the food from their great steaming burnished dixies and trays. Occasionally they would taste the food: cheap beef and potatoes mostly in a brown gravy made of flour and gravy powder. But usually they avoided that not particularly pleasant chore if they could. Then would commence the long trawl around the tables. At each one the officer, followed by the sergeant in his sash and armband with his notebook at the ready, would stop, smile a little hesitantly as the soldiers sat to attention, and ask the senior soldier, 'Any complaints, Private . . .?' In most cases the senior soldier would go along with the time-honoured ritual. After all, he knew the 'thieving cooks' would get him if he *did* complain. If he said there wasn't enough, the next time around they would pile up his plate with so much 'grub' that he couldn't get it down. Then they'd 'crime' him for wasting government property. He'd end up on 'jankers' or even worse, if the sergeant-cook was well in with the RSM. So he kept his mouth shut, even if the food was awful, which it was often enough in those days before the Catering Corps went to 'college' and charm school.

It was thus that 'the mutiny' in the '5th Royal Northumberland Fusiliers' – so labelled by Max Hastings in his excellent book on the Korean War[4] – commenced. After a hard day's training exercise the Fusiliers returned to a meal based on bully beef, that old Army standby. The men declared the meat was 'off', though corned beef dated '1918' had often been used and consumed by the soldiers in the early years of the Second World War. The orderly officer, a Lt William Cooper, was summoned to judge on the men's complaint. He agreed. Then according to Max Hastings, 'The men in the mess-hall then staged a sit-in. The adjutant arrived to rebuke Cooper for condemning the corned beef without first consulting the medical officer.' The situation escalated. Senior officers apparently pleaded with the men. 'But even after repeated appeals and orders from senior officers, a dozen recalcitrant mutineers remained, who defied all orders to move. They were finally removed for courtmartial.' Thereafter the atmosphere in the battalion remained poor.[5]

One force being hurriedly prepared for the battle of Korea to come had no problems with either its volunteer recruits or its morale. It was the old and very battle-experienced 41 Independent Commando, Royal Marines. The 41 Commando had experienced its first real action in the invasion of Sicily in July 1943. Later that year it had experienced its second invasion at Salerno, where it was nearly wiped out and eventually sent back to the UK for a rest and reconstitution. D-Day followed in 1944 and in the winter of that year, they made yet another – little-known – attack on the Dutch island of Walcheren, in which one in three of the 'Green Berets' was killed or wounded.

Now – why, the British didn't yet know – the Americans appealed to Whitehall for the immediate dispatch of specialized commandos, able to carry out raids on enemy coasts and other duties not yet specified. The Royal Marines, whose commandos had virtually disappeared from their peacetime establishment, jumped at the chance. Tall, lanky, hook-nosed Maj Douglas Drysdale, who had led one of the Marine Commandos in the Far East in the latter stages of the Second World War, was hurriedly restored to his old rank and ordered to reform the Forty-First for almost immediate departure for Japan and active service.

Lt Col Drysdale jumped at the chance. Volunteers weren't lacking: there were scores of Marines who were sick of the 'bull' associated with peacetime service afloat or ashore where Marines were often relegated to a role they hated – the 'ship's Gestapo', i.e. armed naval police. Within three short weeks, the new Colonel had assembled over two hundred men, including swimming beach-reconnaissance parties,[6] demolition experts and heavy weapons specialists, plus the usual run of tough, young, all-round fighters who had made up the wartime commandos.

Due to the confused security pertaining at the time, Drysdale and his new command were forced to wear civilian clothes and fly some of the way – the top brass frowned at the cost of using this new-fangled means of civilian transport – to the Far East. Here they 'kidnapped' as reinforcements a further 150 Marine Commandos heading for Malaya. Although their security was laughable, they reached their last stop, Japan, before ops commenced, almost without a hitch: one of Forty-One's number found himself in trouble with his wife when she read in her morning newspaper that her sergeant husband was 'an eager volunteer'. Soon these 'eager volunteers' would become heroes not only in their own country, but also in that of their ally, America.[7] But the 'butcher's bill' would be costly. Before 1950 was over they would have achieved a lasting glory, but would have lost half their number in doing so. Indeed in the end the surviving number of Col Drysdale's 41 Commando was only strong enough to provide a 'garrison reserve' for the American Marines at whose side they fought.[8]

Finally the new troops sailed. They had been formed into a new brigade under the command of Brigadier T. Brodie, another veteran of the Second World War, called the 29th. Its patch was a white circle on a base of a black square. Later when the squaddies of the 29th Independent Brigade first met the freezing cold of Korea in autumn and winter (minus forty degrees), they would maintain that it represented a 'frozen rectum', gained by sitting with a bare rear on a thunderbox in those killer Korean winds. But all that was later.

Now the men of the 'Frozen Rectum' Brigade sailed. They were the infantry of the 1st Battalion Royal Northumberland Fusiliers, the 1st Battalion Gloucestershire Regiment and that of the Royal Ulster Rifles, plus the 45th Field Artillery, 170 Independent Mortar Battery R.A. (a bright idea on somebody's part, for the mortarmen's 4.2-inch mortars were going to come in very useful in the hillfighting to come) and the 11 (Sphinx) AA Battery, armed with quick-firing Bofors anti-aircraft guns. The force's armour was provided by the 8th Irish Hussars of Balaclava fame and C Squadron, 7th Royal Tank Regiment, armed with an antiquated but one of the most-feared weapons in the Allied armoury, Churchill flame-throwing tanks known as 'Crocodiles'. (In the 1944/45 campaign the enemy had usually run when the Crocodiles appeared on the battlefield, as part of 'Churchill's Funnies'.[9]) To support this strong brigade, there was the 55th Field Squadron Royal Engineers.

The officers and men who now started their leisurely cruise along the (now century-old) Imperial route to the 'far-flung' stations of what remained of the Empire to the Far East did not belong to the glamorous smarter regiments of the British Army. They weren't the 'Brigade', the 'Cherrypickers', the 'Skins' or any of those fashionable regiments to which rich men sent their sons.[10] They were the ordinary provincial men, for the most part, who had joined the Army for adventure or lack of money, just as their fathers and grandfathers and their fathers before them had done ever since the time of Col Cardwell. In the late 1870s, the good Colonel had devised a system for ruling the British Empire, one third of the world, with only seventy-five regiments, each having two battalions of which one stayed at home at the depot while the other got its 'knees brown' at some outpost of that Empire. Since that August afternoon in Japan five months before, that system had changed. There were no longer 'second battalions'.

So the British government – wittingly – sent out its soldiers, old sweats and teenage national servicemen to fight an old-fashioned war, more comparable to the static trench warfare of the 'Great War' than to that of the Second World War. They were poorly armed and poorly clothed for the winter to come, and lacked the reinforcements that a second battalion would have provided in case there were casualties.

These men, who sailed that long 'Imperial' route, singing at intervals that popular song of the time, 'I'm gonna get you on a slow boat to China', still believed perhaps that they were the guardians of a powerful empire. Weren't they sailing from one British port or staging station to another right across the world? Hadn't the War Office announced in a press release before they left that the 29th Brigade was 'the best equipped military force ever to leave Britain'?

In truth they would be suffering worse privations than those fighting in the Crimean War of a hundred years before. In essence, as far as weapons, food, equipment, supplies, etc. were concerned, they would become wards of the American Army. Even when they disagreed with the orders the 'Yanks' gave them and were, in some cases, openly contemptuous of their allies, their American commanders called the tune – and they, perforce, danced to it. They had no alternative.

The British Empire lay a-dying, though they did not know it. Britain's role in world affairs was diminishing rapidly. Even their culture was changing virtually overnight. (One of the transports the Army used was the *Empire Windrush*, which two years before had carried the first batch of emigrants from the West Indies to Britain.) By the time these young soldiers grew old they wouldn't recognize the 'Great' Britain they had sailed to defend that autumn. In the end, when they did arrive at the headquarters of the US corps under whose command they came, they found that they were regarded as objects of curiosity, as if they were creatures from another world. They were stage-managed by officers of a kind as yet unknown to the British Army: glad-handing PR men who thought them quaint and took every opportunity available to have the 'Limeys' photographed for propaganda purposes and 'the folks back home'; though *their* folks would never see those US Army Signal Corps pictures . . .

It had been no different when earlier in the last week of August, the Woolworth's Brigade had arrived from Korea. Then, Brig Coad had been welcomed by an enthusiastic American glad-hander with a cheery 'Glad you British have arrived – *you're the real experts on retreating!*' 'Bulldog' Walker's fiery words about there being 'no Dunkirk' for his Eighth Army had apparently not reached that particular cheerful young officer.

Brig Coad's reaction is not recorded. Perhaps it was good for Anglo-American relations that it wasn't. But now they were here, British squaddies: the rank-and-file were a bit younger than their predecessors of the Second World War. They were, however, the descendants of those bawdy, cheerful characters who had fought Britain's battles for the past couple of centuries or so. Soon they would show they lacked neither the bravery, the skill nor the humour of their forefathers. Quite a few of them would die or bear the scars of what was to come for the rest of their lives. They hadn't wanted to come here, to the 'Land of the Morning Calm'. But they had accepted it as they had hitherto accepted their dreary routine existence of 'work, wallop and wenches' (with more of the first and precious little of the latter two). It had just been their fate.

But in retrospect, in their old age, a lot of them grudgingly admitted that it had perhaps been the high point of their lives, even the happiest time, an unforgotten change from the unrelenting boring routine of the rest of their years. Col Barker, one of the historians of the Korean War,[11] recorded the 'gloomy buoyancy' of a Yorkshire squaddie as he marched to war: 'Just my luck my name begins with "L" . . . It'll be down at t'bottom of t'war memorial – with all the dogs cocking their legs on it.' In the weeks, months, even years to come in Korea, they would all be truly pissed on cruelly more than once. But they'd never really let it get them down. They were British soldiers, weren't they?

CHAPTER SEVEN

Surprise Attack!

13 September 1950

Out at sea MacArthur was in his element. There had been a storm during the night. But that had not worried the old warrior much; he had been through this kind of thing often enough during the Second World War, as had his new commander of the US X Corps, Nat Almond. The general who had failed back in Italy 1945 (probably he would have snorted that *he* hadn't failed; his *blacks* had) was completely confident. On first meeting Gen O. Smith, commander of his main assault element, the 1st Marine Division, Almond had rubbed the veteran of the Pacific War up the wrong way immediately by dismissing the difficulties of amphibious ops with, 'This amphibious stuff is just a mechanical option.' It didn't help either that Almond kept calling the veteran Marine 'son'. As Smith commented later, 'It kinda annoyed me.'

And it certainly did annoy him, more so when Smith started to realize the difficulties of the Inchon landing, with a thirty-two tidal range that was one of the greatest in the world and the fact that the Marines would have first to capture the fortified island of Wolmi-Do, which would give the North Koreans an eleven-hour advance warning of what the 'round-eyed devils' intended. Thereafter, because of the terrible tides, the Marines and their Army comrades would have a mere two hours to dig in on the beach and take the suburbs of a city of some quarter of a million souls before darkness fell. Thereafter, they would lose the advantage of the big guns of the seven-fleet naval task force. A tall order indeed; and Almond, in that arrogant supercilious manner of his, thought it was just a matter of mechanics. Some mechanics!

But that was all in the past. The Marines and the Army were committed. That morning the mixed cruiser-destroyer force, including the British light cruiser HMS *Kenya* and her cohort HMS *Jamaica*, moved into position off the channel leading to Inchon. There they waited. Tension lay in the very air. On the ships the crews, clad in their helmets and anti-flash hoods so that they looked like medieval men-at-arms, waited for the first screech of an enemy shell. They knew the Force was being used as bait. The US admirals wanted the enemy 75mms on the shore to open up at such a tempting target and give away their positions. Nothing happened! The North Korean gunners remained stubbornly silent and the Marines already lined up in their assault serials, with their numbers chalked on their helmets, knew that now they might have to contend with North Korean medium guns as well.

Not that it worried them particularly. Marines had been trained to be gung-ho, but also fatalists to a certain extent, too. If your number was on it, well . . . Besides, most of their officers were battle-experienced, having landed time and time again on the killing beaches of nameless Pacific atolls. One Marine regiment had just come back from Walker's command at Pusan and had been engaged in heavy fighting only a few days before. Even the greenhorns, just out of boot camp, were imbued with the Marine Corps spirit, which involved – in battle – frontal assaults with no regard to the casualties suffered as long as they took their objective.

The first alarm. One of the lookouts, straining his eyes against the grey seascape, suddenly yelled 'MINES!' The low water had revealed the lethal spiked black hulls of Russian-made mines, each packed with a ton of high explosive. The admiral in charge must have muttered a hasty prayer of gratitude to the Almighty. One of his gravest problems had been solved immediately. The trained gun crews, many of them British H.O.s[1] who had stayed on in the service after the war, knew what to do. The 4.5-inch turret cannons thundered. 'Chicago pianos'[2] chattered madly. Marksmen emptied their magazines in energetic rapid fire. Abruptly all was noise, smoke, anger. Scarlet flame stabbed the greyness. Smoke rose, billowing into clouds. Water erupted in whirling white spirals. Everywhere the mines leapt out of the water and exploded in roar of thunder that echoed and re-echoed around the surrounding hills, as if it would go on for ever.

Meanwhile another small group of destroyers dared the communists to open fire just off the fortified island of Wolmi-Do. In the lead was the *Gurke*, only eight hundred yards off shore: nothing more than a sitting duck, taunting the North Korean gunners to open fire and destroy her. Now every man of the crews on the deck searched the sinister humps, which they knew concealed the enemy gun emplacements. For fifteen minutes they waited, though to the tense expectant sailors it seemed like an eternity. Nothing. No movement whatsoever. At last, at one that afternoon, squadron commander Cap Halle C. Allan flashed a signal to his ships, 'Execute assigned mission!'

The naval gunners needed no urging, and as one the massive bombardment of the key island commenced. Salvo after massive salvo swept the island. At three minutes past one the firing ceased. Still the enemy had not returned the barrage. Allan thought he could read the North Korean gun commander's mind: five US destroyers there for the taking, served up to him on a silver platter. But if he ordered his 75mms to open fire, he had served his own death warrant.

But the unknown North Korean was a brave man. He took that chance. Just when Allan thought that Wolmi-Do was going to be taken without a fight, the North Koreans opened fire. At that range they could hardly miss. The *Collett* reeled violently, her masts seeming to touch the water as she was struck four times. Next to her, the *Gurke* was hit twice. The *Swenson* took a near-miss, a shell falling just short of her, sending great jagged shards of red-hot steel hissing lethally through the air. In those few moments before the North Korean gunners died violently, five sailors were wounded and one officer was killed.

They were avenged almost immediately. This was what the destroyers had been waiting for. Their spotters had noted the puffs of smoke and short-lived flashes of cherry-red which indicated every North Korean gun. Minutes later they swamped the island with their fire. A few more solitary rounds and then the North Koreans fell silent. The guns had been destroyed. Now it was the turn of the 'flyboys'. Swiftly the flotilla turned and started to sail the way they had come, clearing a few more mines as they did so.

Now the Channel was clear, the artillery defences destroyed. It was the turn of the 'gyrenes' as they had begun calling themselves. The Navy had done its part with its usual cool professional efficiency. They'd see what the 'gung-ho' guys could do.

Gen MacArthur had gone to war three days earlier. Jean had packed a bag for him, containing among other things an extra pipe, a straight razor and strop and his old battered 'lucky bathrobe'. The same night they had boarded the command ship *Mount McKinley*, just in time to be struck by the full force of the expected typhoon Kezia. It didn't worry MacArthur; his doubts had vanished. He was in a high good mood. That night, as the Yellow Sea heaved and swayed, and the *McKinley* ploughed its way steadily westwards towards the battle-to-come, he entertained the officers of the Navy and Marines at his table. He mimicked prominent American civilians, including the President; surprisingly enough defended his one-time aide, Eisenhower, whom he usually mocked; and pontificated in that sonorous old-fashioned orator's voice of his on everything under the sun. The junior officers were pleased with his performance, flattered that the 'great man' had taken so much time with them. Gen Smith of the 1st Marine Division left the table, however, disliking the 'pomposity of his (MacArthur's) statements'. But then Smith was pre-occupied with the battle to come.

The next night, as the typhoon started to abate a little MacArthur retired early, for the next day would be a busy one. But he couldn't sleep. At two a.m. on the morning of 14 September he ordered his Marine sentry to waken one of his aides. He wanted to talk to someone.

Pacing up and down the swaying cabin in his 'lucky' bathrobe, the General unburdened his heart. Clearly this was a really risky operation. Still, it had been decided upon and it would be carried through. 'Johnnie' Walker, besieged at Pusan, had to be relieved. He couldn't do much of his own accord. Besides the Eighth Army staff were a bunch of 'nervous Nellys'. While his aide listened, mostly in silence, the General concluded with, 'The decision was a sound one. The risks and hazards have to be accepted.' He patted the aide on the shoulder, thanked him and dismissed him. As the listener went out the ship's clock struck five bells. It was two thirty in the morning. MacArthur had overcome his low point. Now he reached for his

Bible – at least, that's what his aide said later. But then legends have to be created. History requires them of great men.

Next morning, clad in his usual leather jacket in which he had been photographed a score of times on such occasions in the Old War and wearing his tarnished old peaked cap, he watched the Marines go in at Wolmi-Do. Now his customary coterie of photographers snapped away, with the General as usual tilting his jaw to do away with his double chin, his whole attention concentrated on those young men who would fight and perhaps die for him.

Fortunately this day not many of the 5th Marines did so. Casualties were exceedingly low. Only seventeen of his young men were wounded in the taking of the fortified island. The news pleased MacArthur greatly. He commented happily that 'More people than that get killed in traffic every day'. Thereupon he invited 'all hands' to coffee and drafted a first signal to the Combined Chiefs-of-Staff, who had been so adamant that the op couldn't succeed, stating: 'First landing phase successful with slight losses. All goes well and on schedule.' Naturally MacArthur was gloating, enjoying one of his last few triumphs. There wouldn't be so many to come in the future.

'Suddenly the wall loomed directly ahead and I felt the boat shudder as it crossed a mud bank,' wrote US Marine Herbert Butts, a few years later about the landing at Inchon. 'I swung the ladder up and was on the second or third rung when the ramp at the forward end suddenly dropped. The ladder fell forward against the seawall beyond . . . Directly in front of us was one of the shellholes the coxswain had sought.'

Hastily the 21-year-old Marine went through the hole with the rest and spread out with them 'in the familiar formations which had been part of our training virtually from the day we had left boot camp at Parris Island or San Diego.'

Glancing over his shoulder, the young Marine volunteer who had recently 'blooded' in fighting at Pusan, saw 1st Lt Baldomero Lopez, who Butts thought was probably a 'Tex-Mex'. He seemed to have acted like one all day. He had been nervous 'like a barefoot man treading the edge of a bayonet'. He liked the young officer, but thought his actions typical of his 'spic' ancestry. Then he concentrated on his company's objective, 'Cemetery Hill', envying at the same time other Marines who were slated to take the Jap-built Asahi Brewery. It would probably be their stinking luck to find it full of 'suds' still.

Then he forgot Lopez and the 'Nip suds' and concentrated on storming forward with the rest of his company. Later, after the attack on 'Cemetery Hill' had succeeded, he asked one of his battle-grimed weary fellow Marines: 'How is Mister Lopez?'

'Dead', was the quiet reply. 'Dead when they got him to the aid station.'

A moment later 'a thick Southern voice' asked: 'Who got that there Asahi Brewery?'

'Second Battalion, I think,' someone answered.

'Lucky bastards,' the Southerner groaned, 'All that beer and us out here!'

Butts lay there in the darkness, wondering. He'd been told that the war wouldn't last 'more than five weeks'. How much more was ahead? 'He promised himself that if the war ended early, he'd find' the Lopez family down in Texas and 'tell them how their son had died to save the lives of his men around him.' (Lopez had thrown himself on a live hand grenade just as he had clambered over that last obstacle, the feared 12-foot-high seawall.)

Later Butts found that his journey would not be necessary. While still fighting in Korea, he discovered that Lt Baldomero Lopez had been awarded America's highest honour for bravery, the Congressional Medal of Honor. And 'that was when I wondered about the cost to him. And whether he really had known what he was doing that grey foggy afternoon at Inchon.'

'The cost?'

'The cost of the Medal of Honor to the United States Government?'

'Fifteen dollars and twenty-five cents – including case . . .'

While young Marine Private Butts wondered that Friday evening so long ago, General MacArthur was afflicted by what he called 'the old familiar nausea'. Retching miserably, he excused himself, staggered to one side and 'threw up'.

But MacArthur's fit of nausea, occasioned by nerves and the strain of the past week, didn't last long. He had pulled it off. The dead young men were no concern of his. They had achieved his victory, when no one in Washington had believed he could do it, and that was that. A few minutes later he was his old self: the photographer's dream, all jutting jaw, pipe stuck at an aggressive angle, aged eyes shaded by dark glasses, showing to the folks back home that this wasn't an old 'retread', but one of the new glamorous 'swinging' generation.

Pointing to a dead enemy soldier, sprawled out at a grotesque angle, body in a pool of already congealing dark blood, he said to a nearby medical officer: 'That's a patient you'll never have to work on, Doc.' The doctor's comment is not recorded; but as MacArthur climbed back into his jeep to continue his tour of the newly won battlefield, he remarked: '[that corpse] is a good sight for my old eyes'.

Now as always in the past, he was carried away recklessly by the heady atmosphere of the battlefield; he demanded to see some newly destroyed and still smoking North Korean T-34s. Smith didn't like that one bit, for he could hear the angry snap-and-crack of a small-arms fight close by. What would the Commandant-General of the US Marine Corps say if he, Smith, went and got 'Dug-out Doug' killed.

MacArthur was adamant. A worried Marine lieutenant tried to stop him. He barred the progress of the top brass's jeeps, crying in alarm, 'General, you can't come up here!'

'Why?' MacArthur demanded.

The agitated young officer told the General, 'Sir, we've just knocked out six Red tanks over the top of that hill.'

MacArthur said, rather obviously, 'That's the proper thing to do.' Still, he climbed out and had a quick look at the North Korean riflemen still firing at the Marines in their camouflaged helmets advancing steadily forward; the photographers were clicking away busily. Then he was satisfied. He returned to his jeep and told the assembled brass that his hunch had been right; the enemy holding Inchon had been second-rate troops, recent conscripts and the like. North Korea's first line troops – what was left of them – were further south, attacking Walker's perimeter at Pusan.

Later MacArthur, with no sense of shame or professional decorum, would proclaim that his landing in North Korea had been a 'classic' battle. At the time it strengthened his resolution not only to recapture Seoul but also to advance *further* than the River Yalu to the north, something he had agreed already with the US Chiefs-of-Staff (though he was not telling them that just yet). All the same, Gen MacArthur seems to have had vague doubts about his future strategy. For at the same time as he declared the Inchon Landings 'a classic', he did add a codicil. It was that the Inchon Landing would not be 'one of the short list of decisive battles of the world' *if* the 'Chinese Communists' entered the war in Korea!

Back in the middle of the war when he had taken over one of three regiments of the 82nd 'All American' Airborne Division, his tough paras had nicknamed their handsome young colonel 'Slim Jim' or more aptly 'Gentleman Jim'. For the 38-year-old airborne colonel was unlike the usual para regiment colonel, stereotypically unshaven, foul-mouthed, cultivating the tough cigar-smoking image that supposedly went with the job of falling out of the sky at 'the end of a pair of ladies' silk panties' to do battle. Quite the contrary, the future General Gavin was always faultlessly dressed, as befitted a graduate of West Point, who supposedly had rescued Marlene Dietrich during the Battle of the Bulge from a 'fate worse than death'. (She could have been his mother!) But he was a fighting soldier, who had jumped into Sicily, where he was 'wounded', as he called his cut laughingly, by an Italian peasant whose trousers he was attempting to cut off to prevent him from running away. There had followed for him Normandy, Nijmegen and much fighting as a ground commander right to the very end on the River Elbe in North Germany.

But paradrops had fallen out of fashion in the post-war Army (though a US parachute regiment had been scheduled to drop to support the Inchon Landing, but didn't) and on this day Gen 'Gentleman Jim' Gavin, as slim and as handsome as ever, found himself representing the Pentagon's Weapons Systems Evaluation Group at the newly captured North Korean airfield at Kimpo. There, he and his experts made an odd discovery. The Yak they found was of no interest. Nor were the spare parts for the Russian MIG jets, though the US team wondered how they had got to this remote place. But the strange discoveries the team made that day, with the guns still thundering in the background, were not in the hastily abandoned North Korean airfield hangars; they were on the field itself.

As Gavin recalled long afterwards,

I was amazed to find an elaborate arrangement of hard stands and revetments all around the airfield. They were as good [as] or better than any I had seen in the airfields of Europe in World War II.

He concluded:

Obviously some sophisticated thinking had gone into the planning and much labor and effort had been expended in anticipation of using the airfield by a modern air force. Either the North Koreans were wasting their time which seemed unlikely or a first class air power was about to intervene in the war.

The question was, which one?

CHAPTER EIGHT

Scotland the Brave

Now it was the turn of the British.

At 4.30 that September morning, the officers and sergeants started to rouse their companies. But in many cases it was not necessary: both the old sweats and the national servicemen knew that today they were going into action; many had not slept well. Instead their minds went round and round with thoughts of what that action might bring.

So they were awake in the pre-dawn gloom. In the distance the guns of the heavy barrage rumbled. Somewhere a machine-gun was ticking like an irate woodpecker. Every now and again flares hissed into the sky and hung there, illuminating everything below in their sickly unnatural red and green light before dropping to earth like fallen angels. What they signified no one knew or cared. It was all part and parcel of the orchestration for what was to come.

So they prepared, while the cook orderlies brought up canteens of 'sar'nt-major's char': a thick rich-brown brew, made richer by pouring in tins of creamy Carnation milk. It would help the soldiers to wash down their Yank C-7 rations, straight out of the olive-drab cans. They had been forbidden to light their Yank 'sternos' to heat them up.

For the most part the old sweats, the minority in the Argylls and Middlesex, did nothing. They knew from experience that if a bullet or shell 'had yer number on it', that was that. A few, who still believed that you could defy fate, put on clean vests so that if they were hit 'germ-free' cloth would be forced into the wound and they wouldn't contact gas gangrene from dirty clothing. Some put their steel shaving mirrors in their left battle-dress blouse pocket. They'd heard of the bloke who had been saved from death by a bullet striking the steel glass. In another mob, natch! It was always in another mob.

The national servicemen were too bewildered by it all to take precautions or do anything else specific for that matter. They were on a military conveyor belt, perhaps to death itself, but there was nothing they could do about it. For the most part they simply accepted what was happening to them, the only real sign of their nervousness and anxiety being the frequency with which they 'went for a slash'. The NCOs knew the signs. They chivvied the teenage soldiers, whose faces looking even more boyish under the 'tin hats', but they weren't so rough on them as they usually were.

Now it was dawn. Time to move out. Laden with their packs, rifles, grenades, bits-and-pieces, mortars, mortar shells and the usual gear that the 'poor bloody infantry' (the 'PBI', as they called themselves without self-pity) carried into battle, they started across the paddies and hills in long head-bent columns, walking into battle.

Their officers were confident, or seemed to be. They had told their soldiers the night before that there had been a great landing at some place called Inchon to the north. Now the Eighth Army commander 'Bulldog' Walker expected the 'gooks' to their front to be in full retreat soon. If they weren't, then they'd be cut off in the great pincer movement from Pusan and Inchon, scheduled to meet at the South Korean capital, which General MacArthur in Tokyo had planned for the Allies in this remote smelly country.

The brigadier and the two regimental colonels were not so sanguine. As three battle-experienced officers, with a very real sense of their own importance and the traditions of the British Army, they didn't particularly like their present task. They had no independent role: the Americans were definitely in charge. The US commander of the I Corps – 'Eye Corps' – to which they were attached, was businesslike and pleasant, but Brig Coad in particular was not impressed with Gen Churcher of the US 24th Infantry Division under whose control they were going to fight their first battle in Korea.

Churcher, who right at the beginning back in June had been ordered by no less a person than MacArthur himself to stay behind in Korea to see what he could do with the mess, had now taken over the 24th Infantry Division. Dean's old division, routed and defeated right at the start of the 'police action', had been reformed and sent back into the line under Churcher. Once the US 1st Cavalry had hacked a way free out of the Pusan perimeter, Churcher's 24th would move through the gap and head north.

But as Brig Coad saw it, Churcher had 'failed to get a grip' on his new command. The men seemed to spend endless hours talking on the phone to their girlfriends back in Japan, regardless of security. (As it turned out, the North Koreans knew the Allies were going to try to break out of the Pusan perimeter.) As well, the men discussed orders and were distinctly casual about carrying them out. Perhaps, Coad thought, it was their democratic way of running an army, but he was definitely put out when he saw American colonels lining up with their men for 'chow'. As one of his battalion commanders put it: 'Why waste the time of a highly paid officer by making him standing in a queue for his grub?'

Most of all Coad didn't like the lack of information available to him. Twice already he had had his plans changed at very short notice, and having completed his military education under 'Butcher' Thomas of the 43rd British Infantry Division, a former First World War artillery officer in the trenches, Coad always liked things worked out to the last. An attack had to be planned to be foolproof, as far as the Brigadier was concerned. Now, instead of being in reserve until the great break-out from the Pusan perimeter had been achieved, he had been ordered to send his First Middlesex under Col Andrew Man into action this September morning. The 24th Division's armoured Reconnaissance Company had gone and got itself cut off . . .

Three miles west of the River Naktong, which I Corps had to assault and cross before they really started the attack north, the Yank armoured recce troops, complete with tanks, had stalled. West of the river, which had not yet been crossed by friendly troops, the Americans had been trapped on the road near a tumbledown Korean hamlet and were being subjected to heavy enemy mortar fire. The 'Limeys' had to go and rescue them, though Churcher didn't say 'rescue'; he wouldn't!

Hastily Coad and Col Man of the Middlesex worked out a rescue plan. The Middlesex would do the donkey work, with a company of the Argylls to take a hill that night covering them. To give 'muscle' to their operation, a battery of American 105mm guns from the 24th Division was to give the 'Diehards' fire support.

Everything went wrong from the start. Moving along to the head of his long line of PBI slogging forward doggedly like heavily-laden mules, Col Man headed for the spot where he was supposed to meet the US forward observer officer for the 105mm near a footbridge over the river. No officer. Later Man discovered that supposedly these Yank 'FOs' were not to move when it was getting dark. The weary troops had another and more cynical explanation for the Yank's conduct; and it also included the initials 'FO'.

Man and his company commanders crossed the rickety bridge, wondering how long it would take the enemy in the hills to their front to spot them. But nothing happened. Surprisingly enough the North Koreans remained silent' though as they encountered the first Sherman and Pershing tanks of the stalled recce company, boarded them and moved off, there was evidence enough of recent fighting. As Col Man recalled afterwards: '[There were] bodies and burnt-out houses. Throughout the short journey, one felt exposed and unprotected: a feeling which solitary United States tanks, stationed infrequently in the valley, along the road, with crews looking anything but happy, did little to dispel.'

The eerie feeling of apprehension was not relieved by the first meeting of the Middlesex soldiers and their American allies in the battered hamlet in which they later felt they were trapped. Man was too good and loyal a soldier to write openly of what his feelings were at that moment. But if one reads between the lines of what he wrote later, they are clear enough:

The United States Reconnaissance Company Commander [Man wrote] was closely surrounded with his armoured personnel carriers and his tanks, his infantry . . . being entrenched on a small hill . . . some hundred yards from it . . . The Middlesex Officers were struck by the very concentrated dispositions . . . They could hardly have been sited more closely together, or have presented a more worthwhile target.

Man met the American CO, and queried his dispositions. The American was sitting in his jeep with the engine running. He told Man that he expected his vehicles to be attacked by 'gooks' throwing hand grenades. This was 'Indian country' and apparently anything could happen. Man decided not to mention that, as his vehicles were packed tightly together on the road, they presented a heaven-sent target to the unseen North Korean mortarmen in the hills beyond. Instead he asked for tank support – he finally got three tanks only – to aid his 'Diehards' in attacking the hill features beyond, soon nicknamed 'Plum Pudding' (due to its shape) and 'Middlesex Hill'.

Early next morning, with a bitter icy wind sweeping across the valley straight from Siberia, the Middlesex went into their first attack. There was again surprisingly little enemy reaction. All the same, the US tanks refused to go any further than 300 yards from the hamlet held by the Recce Company. No amount of pleading, orders, threats could move them. Without infantry protection against the supposed North Korean grenade-throwers they simply weren't moving. The Diehards' officers gave up on them and left them to fire their 75mm cannon in 'support' of the advancing infantry. Some no doubt prayed that the Yanks would limit their bombardment to the enemy. For by now the British were beginning to expect everything, including the worst, from the 24th US Infantry Division.

Still, Col Man was pleased with his battalion and in particular his young national servicemen. Despite the fact they had not slept well in the sub-zero temperatures under their one thin blanket and had not eaten breakfast, those who needed to shave had done so; and all had gone into battle washed and shaved, as good soldiers should.

Now they proved they could fight as well. For, puffing and panting up 'Middlesex Hill' under enemy automatic fire, they took it the first time, destroying North Korean machine-gun posts and killing twelve of the enemy, at a cost to the lead platoon of three dead and three wounded.

By now as the assault commenced on the second hill which barred the further progress of the 24th Infantry, American artillery had commenced firing support as agreed upon right at the start. Unfortunately it still continued after the British infantry reached its summit. The company commander of the newly victorious troops thought the 'shoot' had been arranged especially for him by Col Man. Now he radioed his thanks and asked if the barrage could be lifted.

Man cursed. He hadn't ordered the barrage; nor did he know who had. Swiftly he radioed Brigade HQ. They knew nothing either. Nor did they know how to find out; they hadn't wireless contact with higher head-quarters, i.e. that of Churcher's 24th Infantry Division.

Now as the shelling started to become a real nuisance for the victors, crouching and cursing in the shelter of the rocks on the summit, hardly daring to move as great red-hot shards of gleaming silver metal scythed through the air, the Middlesex's B Company radioed that the shells were coming from the missing battery of US 105mm cannon. B Company had asked the Americans to stop firing; they were endangering British troops. They replied 'that so important a mission could, on no account, be stopped as a United States Reconnaissance Company was held up by enemy located thereupon.' No thought, it seemed, for the Poor Bloody Infantry of the 'Diehards' trying to clear the way for the Americans huddled in the relative safety of their hamlet on the road below.

That did it! Colonel Man writing of himself in the third person, told the 'Yanks' 'with considerable restraint' that the 'hill in question was, at that moment, being attacked by his soldiers who were assisting the Reconnaissance Company . . . and added that any further fire on this hill, unless with his permission, would directly affect the lives of British soldiers.'

There followed a 'long and painful silence' before finally a subdued "Roger" was received, followed by a cessation of fire.'

An hour or so later, sweating in the hot sun, the Middlesex took their objective at a cost of two dead and three wounded. One of the killed in action was 2/Lt G. White, a platoon commander. Ironically enough, he was posthumously awarded the US Silver Star for 'his gallantry in action'.

So ended the Middlesex's first action in Korea. It had been a success, especially for the teenage national servicemen. The cost hadn't been too high – a handful of young men killed and wounded – and the US Reconnaissance Company was moving again. All in all, Man was proud of his battalion, though during the course of the action Anglo-American teamwork had been a bit of a farce. Now that farce was going to turn into tragedy.

On Friday 22 September 1950, the Argyll and Sutherland Highlanders moved off into their first real action of the war. They were to support the left flank of Walker's break-out attempt. In particular they were to assault and capture Hill 282.

The Jocks, veterans and new boys, were in good heart. On the whole they had been received better by the Yanks than had the 'Diehards'. Their pipes and kilts had been the usual sources of complaint and curiosity. 'Say buddy, how do you get that racket outa that sheepguts? . . . Hey, what do you guys wear under them skirts?' A bare bottom was explanation enough, but it broke the ice and 'Scottish guys' were judged to be OK. But then the 'Jocks' of the Argyll and Sutherland Highlanders didn't need the 'Yanks' to tell them that. It was something that they'd always known. 'Scotland the Brave' and 'Hieland Laddie' and all that stuff, ye ken?[1]

But now they were faced with the grim reality. The games were behind them. Now they were going to kill and be killed. By nightfall on that Friday they were at the base of Hill 282. The infantry dug in. American artillery were promised for the next day's attack and while the Argylls attempted to sleep curled up under their one blanket each, Brig Coad brought up more ammo and food. Somehow he must have realized instinctively that his men would need it.

At four the attack company was wakened. With their mouths tasting foul, some having headaches and 'dying for a tab', releasing the hot steaming yellow gush of the first urination, hitching up their small packs, slapping the breeches of their Mark IV rifles, tugging at the pouches filled with Bren magazines, they were finally ready to move out. Nothing much in the way of orders. None of the US Marines' gung-ho 'Saddle up' or the Hollywood movies' inevitable, 'Okay, guys, let's go!', the Jocks started to scramble up the hill tracks.

Each man was wrapped in his individual cocoon of private fears and apprehensions. The officers were concerned probably with the problems of command – what to do if they took fire from the right flank . . . Was that movement at three o'clock next to that stunted tree? . . . What were they going to do if their platoon refused to follow them in a crisis (everyone who had ever commanded Jocks in action knew that they could be very temperamental if you didn't keep a tight grip on them) – a hundred and one problems. As for the old sweats, if they were lucky, they concentrated on the things that old sweats always concentrated on: booze and bints!

They were getting closer to the summit now and it was getting lighter by the minute. Already the enemy automatics were beginning to chatter and there was the hollow obscene plonk of a mortar being fired. It wouldn't be long now before they started ranging in.

Over at battalion headquarters at Point 148, Maj Kenneth Muir, the Argylls' second-in-command, heard the firing and probably raged inwardly. He had been kept out of the attack officially. It would be his task, if Col Neilson was knocked out, to take over; and it was something that fiery-tempered officer disliked. He didn't want to step into dead men's shoes. He wanted to be in the action *now*!

But as the first wounded were reported and the carrier party sent forward to bring them back lost its way, he suggested a humble yet active task for himself. He volunteered to take charge of a second body of men who were being readied to replace the casualties. The CO agreed and Muir set off with his thirty men to carry out a task from which he would not return. It was one of those actions carried out in battle when men are swept away by the hot unreasoning craziness of conflict, not caring for the morrow or the consequences. Such men die young – and perhaps not forgotten: in the hearts and minds of the men of his regiment, the one of which he proved he was so proud this last week of September 1950, Maj Kenneth Muir would never be . . .

Now it was nearly nine on the morning of 23 September. By now the Argylls had achieved their objective. For a little while they had some respite as they settled down in the abandoned enemy gunpits. Some managed to find water to wash in and a few cans of food. But not for long. Enemy guns and mortars were beginning to range in on their former positions. Shells slammed into the side of the hill, shaking the very earth. Evil black mortar bombs came tumbling out of the sky to explode in a fountain of flying pebbles and earth.

But it turned out that the American forward observers were too far away from the summit to discover where the enemy guns were and so could not direct the fire of their own cannon. One of them suggested whistling up a British Mosquito reconnaissance aircraft, unarmed but made of wood and very fast, to spot the North Koreans for them. The suggestion was accepted, for down on the summit the Argylls' casualties were mounting rapidly and Maj Muir, coming up with his party having already lost nearly half of it, found there were too many of them for his remaining bearers to take away.

Things got worse. The headquarters of the 24th Infantry Division informed the Jocks that they were withdrawing their guns, which were needed urgently elsewhere. Maj Douglas Reith, the 'Woolworth's Brigade's' brigade major, protested. The Yanks hastily reassured him. The guns would still cover the Scots until relief batteries could be found. It was a plain untruth: the American 105mms were already moving out. The tragedy had commenced.

As their ammunition started to run out and desperate NCOs scuttled from position to position encouraging the Jocks, saying the usual things about conserving ammunition and making 'every round count', the Argylls' officers did their best to hold their position. But it was very difficult. Covered by an intense mortar-and-artillery barrage in the Russian fashion, the North Koreans kept rushing the Jocks' dug-out and foxholes with fanatical courage, being beaten back at the very last moment, leaving a khaki-clad carpet of their own dead and dying behind them every time. The Jocks knew they wouldn't be able to hold much longer for virtually all their small arms ammo was gone: here and there they were robbing the dead and the wounded of their clips, frantically tugging off the 50- and 100-round khaki-coloured bandoliers from the corpses of their fallen comrades.

Once again they requested ammunition and artillery support. Neither was forthcoming. But by now the Jocks had identified the main North Korean centres from which they were being attacked. An air strike was proposed and agreed upon. Hastily the hard-pressed Argylls began to put out their air-recognition panels. Those of their officers and NCOs who had fought in Europe half a decade before had great faith in air support. The RAF and their flying comrades of the US Army Air Corps TAC had rarely let them down. But they'd feared the US bombers – 'The 'US Luftwaffe', as they had named it – which had often bombed Allied frontline positions, including one terrible episode in Normandy when nearly 700 GIs, including a US major general, had been killed and wounded by their own bombers. Now the Argylls waited tensely for the Yanks to come and save them.

Opposite them, however, the North Korean attackers were by now wise to the round-eyes's tactics. They knew only too well that the enemy dominated the air. So they put out some recognition panels of their own . . . or at least that's what was reported afterwards at the Court of Enquiry.

By now the US light spotter plane had arrived. Lazily, ignoring the tracer sailing up to hit it, it circled the embattled heights as it reported back to the

US airfield, where the P-51 Mustangs, pilots in their cockpits and engines running, waited eagerly for the order to take off.

Finally the pilot of the unarmed spotter, who was after all risking his own life to fly so low in order that his identification was correct, reported back to American Fighter Calculation Control team that he had spotted the correct panels and they appeared to be being used by Allied troops holding a ridge feature. Later it would appear the ground controllers took his word for it without further verification; for they had been stopped from getting close to the British battalion on account of 'a small river'. (Naturally that went down very well with the unhappy Jock survivors.) The ground team radioed their command back to the waiting Mustangs. Minutes later the tough wartime planes, which had accompanied many US daytime raids into the heart of the Third Reich only a few years earlier, were racing and bumping down the runway heading for the 'shooting war'.

They were soon there. The first flight circled the smoke-shrouded height. They spotted the panels outlining the positions of the trapped Argylls, or later said they did. Moments later they were falling out of the sky, cannon chattering, sending streams of white tracer 20mm shells at the 'enemy'. The Jocks ducked hastily as the shells exploded all around them, cursing the 'frigging Yanks', yelping in agony here and there as they were hit by rock splinters or red-hot pieces.

Now as the flight-leader levelled out of his death-defying dive, his fat-bellied plane seemed to stagger momentarily, as he released his clutch of deadly eggs. These were the lethal weapons, which had only been used twice against white opponents in Europe. In the Second World War they had been reserved for 'slopeheads' and other 'gooks'. This time they were employed by the Americans against their own allies – and *they* were white, to boot.

The jellied petrol fire-bombs, not too long after to be known to the world during the Vietnam War as napalm, hit the ground below. The hill-top erupted in angry scarlet flame, tinged with black oily smoke. Ammo started exploding. There was a great roar as the bombs seared across the summit like the flame of a gigantic blowtorch. Screaming, panic-stricken, their uniforms already beginning to stink of burning, the Jocks ducked for whatever cover they might find . . . Here and there men crouched in agony, sudden blackened charred pygmy creatures shrinking visibly, shrieking in utter anguish as they died. And then the next Mustang bearing its frightening deadly cargo was directly above them and those who were not already dead and dying were flinging themselves in panic down the slope fifty feet to another position – anything to get out of the way of those all-consuming flames.

In the end as the Mustangs winged their way back to their fields, another sortie carried out successfully, the survivors attempted to bring down the dead, dying and wounded. All them were blackened. Here and there their flesh had burst under the intense heat to reveal pink open wounds set against their charred cracked skins. Teeth gleamed in skull-like black faces like polished ivory. But the task was too much for the survivors. Besides now the North Koreans, realizing what had happened, were attacking all out. Up top one lone Jock who had somehow survived the maelstrom of flames, Pte Watts, was taking aimed single shots, keeping the attackers at their distance. Further back, Maj Gillies had collected a handful of shocked soldiers and was trying to aid Watts. But it was Kenneth Muir, who would die gloriously this day, who really took the initiative. He decided on the spot that the hilltop had to be retaken at once before the enemy gained a foothold. He gathered together another thirty Argylls. Although he had the CO's permission to stand or withdraw at his discretion, Muir decided to go ahead. With a cheer he led his shocked little band back to the summit, littered with their own charred dead.

But already the North Koreans were closed in, attacking from three different points. With the fourteen men now left to him after the attack, he set about collecting what ammo they could find while Maj Gordon-Ingram and six other Argylls gave them covering fire, with the Major firing the company's sole remaining 2-inch mortar himself.

Now the situation was desperate once more. The Jocks were heavily outnumbered. The North Koreans came rushing on, clambering over their own dead, eager to get to grips with the Scots, knowing that the 'round-eyes' were virtually wiped out. The mortar was hit. Maj Muir reeled to one side, gravely wounded.

But the Argylls' stubborn defence was paying dividends. Why these underpaid soldiers,[2] defending this God-forsaken hilltop whose name they never learnt – those who survived – fought on is beyond understanding. Perhaps it was sheer aggression – their blood was up – they'd show the slant-eyed yeller buggers! Perhaps it was for the honour of the regiment. Who knows? But fight they did and actually drove the enemy back.

Then, sadly, Maj Muir was hit by two bursts of automatic fire and mortally wounded. There was no hope for him. As a couple of his men knelt beside him, ignoring the North Korean bullets, he gasped his last words: 'The Gooks will never drive the Argylls off this hill!'

CHAPTER NINE

The War is Won?

Those dying words of an obscure 38-year-old major were not very elegant. That use of the term 'gook' might well have been sneered at by the so-called 'progressives', the 'parlour pinks', who never would be asked to put their lives on the line for whatever principles they held; they would undoubtedly die peacefully in bed. They probably thought them racist and hopelessly old-fashioned. He had not died with some populist cry on his lips such as 'citizen soldiers of the social democracies of the West';[1] but with solely the name of the regiment to which he had belonged for most of his life, as had had his father before him.

In due course Maj 'Kenny' Muir was awarded the Victoria Cross, his country's highest honour (and the US Silver Star as well), and after a while was naturally forgotten. In spite of the fact that he had been prepared to lay down his life for his country, his regiment and, in a way, for a cause, too (though his regiment probably played a greater role than any cause could), he was soon relegated to a footnote in the history of the Korean War, which itself would be equally soon forgotten. The second half of the twentieth century in his Homeland had no place or time for 'heroes' such as Muir. He had inherited another age which had been linked with an austere, even awesome sense of duty, even if it meant paying that final due, the laying down of one's life for it. Rights, but not responsibilities were the order of the day now.

Muir was the official hero, but on that day in September, the Argyll and Sutherland Highlanders had suffered other grievous casualties: seventeen killed or missing and seventy-six wounded. One of its companies had disappeared, leaving it only two rifle companies to help in the breakout from the Pusan Perimeter; and those casualties had not been caused solely by the enemy. It became a matter of heated discussion among the senior officers of the 'Woolworth's Brigade', which regarded itself something of a waif in a far land with no means of communicating with the mother country.

It seems that the American Top Brass tried to hush up the use of napalm on their allies. But the photographers had already taken photographs of the Jocks' dreadful casualties; they reached not only the USA but also the UK, so the American authorities couldn't hush the matter up. It was out in the open. Brig Coad, loyal as he was to the command structure, kept his mouth shut, though he was a very angry man. Walker expressed his personal regrets to him, and the senior British officer in the Far East, Air Vice-Marshal Bouchier, did his bit too for the sake of Allied solidarity. As he reported to his masters, 'I tried to suppress the original press release, knowing it would be probably exaggerated and sensational in the home press'. The good Air Marshal maintained that Argylls had accepted the attack 'without turning a hair'.

In the end, however, there was an enquiry, results of which were not published at the time. As Bouchier reported, there had been understandable but not intentional mistakes, and the American officer in charge was 'immediately replaced and I assume appropriate action will be taken after completion of American investigation'.

It wasn't. The matter was swept carefully under the carpet and the drive north continued, with drafts coming in from all the Highland regiments to make up the Argylls' losses, many of them volunteers. Coad, however, never forgave Churcher and his 24th Infantry Division. He dreaded being placed under his command again. Walker sensed it and allowed the British to revert to the command of US Gen Milburn of I Corps. Almost immediately and on his own complete initiative, Coad informed Milburn (who was another one of Patton's corps commanders, like Walton in the Second World War), that he had changed the name of his command. We don't know what the dark balding American, who always looked as if he needed a shave, thought; but he must have been surprised at that moment, for even in the more democratic US Army, regimental commanders (a British brigade was the equivalent of an American regiment) didn't tell their corps commanders that they were giving a new name to their outfit. He waited. Coad, knowing he was about to have the crack all-volunteer Australian 3rd Infantry Battalion joining his Middlesex and Argylls, didn't hesitate. An angry man, he snapped that with 'immediate effect' the former 'Woolworth's Brigade' would be called the '27th Commonwealth Infantry Brigade'.

But he did more. After Milburn approved his surprise request, Brig Coad demanded his own radio links to superior British headquarters. He was no longer going to use the American wireless network, which had failed the Argylls so lamentably. He wanted to be able to communicate independently with the British Army. Just as surprisingly, the British authorities in Tokyo, and in due course London as well, granted him such a facility. Perhaps under the current circumstances, with Anglo-American military relationships in Korea hanging in the balance, the authorities thought it was wise to humour the irate Brigadier. However, they explained this new link, which would operate independently of Walker's Eighth Army, as a means of 'reporting British battle casualties more swiftly' so that the people back home would not have to wait for the Americans in Tokyo to release the figures.

With that, 'the bitter small change of war' on that remote hilltop, as Korean War Historian Max Hastings has called it, was forgotten. But unknown to those involved that September, the fact that the British now possessed an independent radio link (over which not only British casualties but also operational details of the Allied forces would be reported) was going to have a decisive influence on the campaign in the next few months. For from then onwards, not only would London know what was taking place in the war in Korea, but so also would Soviet Russia and, whenever the Soviet dictator Stalin wanted them to know, the Red Chinese as well . . .

Now it was the turn of the Allies. That September, it seemed that the weeks and even months of successive defeats and the heartbreak and misery of being constantly on the run or being attacked by 'waves' (it was always 'waves') of North Koreans were over. Now it was the Americans and their Western Allies – the British, the Australians, the Canadians and the rest – who were doing the attacking; and, although in places the North Koreans were fighting back almost fanatically, the Western forces were winning – as they ought, for they outnumbered the North Koreans two to one in manpower and five to one in armour. To the Americans at least, armour was very important, for *they* were still roadbound, using their armour and trucks to carry their troops forward, not realizing in the hilly terrain of the Korean interior that it was, as 'Mad Mitch' of the Argylls pointed out truthfully, 'an infantryman's war'. He who slogged up the hills and took them would win the battle, for hills dominated roads.

For the time being the advantage was on the side of the West. MacArthur's bold landing at Inchon and 'Bulldog' Walker's breakout of their position on the Pusan Perimeter had virtually trapped the North Korean Army in a classic pincer movement. Furthermore, the Allied advance from north and south was becoming something of a race, not solely against the North Koreans, but in fact between Almond's X Corps and Walker's Eighth Army as well. By September there was little love lost between the two US generals. Almond, ambitious, pushy, determined to wipe out the stigma of his failed command in Italy, was now regarded as the coming man. At MacArthur's HQ, envious staff officers whispered behind Almond's ramrod-straight back that he was now 'the old man's blue-eyed boy'.

Walker, Patton's former corps commander, with a highly successful record in Europe in the Second World War, had failed in MacArthur's eyes. More than once MacArthur had feared he would have to pull the US Eighth Army out of South Korea altogether. He had not realized what wonders 'Johnny' Walker had done with the forces available. He had shored up the beaten demoralized ROK troops, whose divisional commanders even stole the funds intended to pay for their soldiers' rations and mercilessly beat and even shot soldiers they thought had failed them. During the siege of the Perimeter he had switched the best of his troops from one sector to the other to meet the enemy attacks and had managed by the skin of his teeth to keep his defences intact. He had lived up to his bold statement that there would be 'no Dunkirk' for his army in Korea.

Now Walker wanted the kudos of victory. Schooled in the tradition of his former boss, 'Old Blood an' Guts' Patton, who had always maintained there was only one army fighting in Europe, his Third (with the rest of the US Army Group just, in his opinion, supporting him), Walker had determined that the world should see that his maligned Eighth had won the war.

MacArthur, however, seems to have had other ideas. After the breakout from Inchon, his first priority was to ensure that Almond's mixed corps of Marines and GIs recaptured the South Korean capital of Seoul. The capital itself was a smoking ruin and MacArthur knew it. But Seoul had a threefold significance for him: political, psychological and personal. Over half a decade earlier, he had kept his 1942 promise to return to the Philippines and, in Manila's Malacanan Palace, had formally restored native Philippine rule over the recaptured islands. Now he informed the Joint Chiefs-of-Staff in Washington that he intended to do the same in Seoul's vaulted National Assembly chamber. Despite some State Department objections that this would mean restoring South Korea's corrupt pre-war ruling clique, MacArthur continued on his course. For the act of restoration would give him personal pleasure and at the same time, send out a political-psychological message to the rest of Asia and 'the commies'. American would not tolerate communist-inspired revolution or aggression and would if necessary use force to restore the status quo. In essence, it was the commencement of what Warsaw Pact countries would maintain throughout the cold war was 'American Imperialism'.

Now it was up to the 'PBI' to carry out that plan and accordingly pay the bloody 'Butcher's Bill'. But while they started to move from north and south, Gentleman Jim Gavin, formerly of the 82nd 'All American' Airborne Division, had come to some conclusions about the installations he had discovered.

Back in Tokyo now, he requested an interview with MacArthur's long-time chief-of-intelligence, the bastard son of a German rope-maker, who at some time had changed his name to the more American Charles Willoughby and had become known, due to his lordly and supercilious manner, as 'Sir Charles'. Gavin, as elegant as ever, pointed out to the older man that he thought his discoveries at Kimpo Airfield indicated that a 'first-class air power' was about to interfere in the Korean War. He added that 'intelligence of that sort was taken very seriously in the European War'. Then the paratroop commander made his point. He suggested that 'an intervention by the Chinese seemed most likely.'

Willoughby looked down his long nose at Gavin. He implied that Gavin knew little about real intelligence. He was merely an infantryman using a newfangled means of getting to war – out of an airplane. He rejected the suggestion outright. Coldly he told Gavin, 'If the Chinese were going to intervene, they would have done so when we made the Inchon landing.'

He didn't convince the airborne man. Gavin said the Chinese were probably too stunned by MacArthur's surprising landing at such an unlikely place; they hadn't had time to react and come to the aid of the North Koreans. 'But if they do plan an intervention,' he persisted, 'the preparation at Kimpo is a sure indication that this is what they are going to do, and when they are ready, they will come in.'

Gavin's statement didn't impress 'Uncle Willoughby' as he was also called by the staff. In his 'personal opinion', the Chinese would never cross the Yalu River, which basically marked the border between Korea and China. He gave 'Gentleman Jim' his fake knowing smile and assured Gavin that *he* had his own sources. He *knew*.[2]

Now it was to be the US Marines who were going to pay the 'Butcher's Bill' in MacArthur's drive for Seoul. At the time of the Inchon landing his first question each morning had been, 'Have the Chinese come in?' Now the 'Chinks' had been forgotten – Willoughby, naturally, had seen to that; and MacArthur had trusted 'Sir Charles' for nearly a decade now. Instead, now his first question was 'How far are Smith's Marines away from Seoul?'

Pre-war, the Regular Army had jested that the Marines were 'nursery rhyme soldiers' because just like the children's ditty, their tactics were 'hey, diddle diddle, right up the middle'. The Marines had never had time for 'fancy' plans. Flanking attacks, feints, use of dead ground and all the tactics used by ordinary GI infantry seemed to be beyond their ken. The Marines believed in old-fashioned frontal attacks, regardless of loss. That had been their tactic throughout the war in the Pacific – death and glory all the way – and it would be the same one they'd use in the first year of the war in Korea.

Now flanked by a regiment of the Army's Seventh Infantry Division and the 187 US Airborne, Gen Smith's 1st Marine Division bulled their way towards the South Korean capital. Some said they moved slowly, and criticized Smith's sluggish tactics. But no one criticized the Marines' bravery, for unlike the Army, the Marines absorbed heavy casualties and still kept on doggedly pushing ever closer to Seoul.

It wasn't easy. The North Koreans, trapped as they were, fought savagely to hang on to their gains in the south, turning savagely on the local civilians if they thought the latter were betraying them; shooting prisoners and suspected South Korean partisans; burning all behind them, imitating the scorched earth policy of the Red Army in the great retreats of 1941/42.

Time and time again the brave young Marines came across scenes of senseless destruction and, even worse, North Korean massacres: prisoners thrown into mass graves and slaughtered out of hand!

One day the Marines would find a dozen or so South Korean soldiers or civilians massacred by their own folk from across the 38th Parallel; on another, they'd discover up to four hundred, hands tied behind them and massacred by a couple of machine-guns. It was the gung-ho soldiers' first taste of the cruelty and unthinking brutality of war. 'The old heads' who had been through the Pacific fighting took it in their stride – it was simply a fact of war. The younger ones were at first repelled and then they too became equally savage, as if attempting to cover their own repugnance and horror by outdoing the enemy in their mindless brutality.

After all, the callow young soldiers reasoned, they were fighting against 'gooks', and 'gooks' didn't count. Whenever they encountered resistance, they'd call down artillery and air. The guns would thunder and the Mustangs and Corsairs would come falling out of the sky to machine-gun indiscriminately, dropping the dreaded napalm wherever it suited them, whether their targets were strictly military or not. If innocent 'gooks', South Korean or otherwise, got caught in the bombardment, it was 'tough shit' – 'go and see the chaplain, buddy'.

Still, there was no plan to the actions of these young American soldiers; they were carried out on the spur of the moment by individual soldiers with no attempt at premeditated murder. It was otherwise with the North Koreans, whose savage cruel massacres had been executed on orders from above: the thirty GIs of the unfortunate 24th Division thrust into a ditch and shot from behind; the two survivors of eight others who had been shot and then covered with a thin layer of earth through which the survivors had clawed a hole in order to breathe until rescue came.

The British, on the other hand, had neither the means nor the time for the savage merciless behaviour exhibited by some of the Americans. They had no tanks of their own or aircraft. The British war correspondent R.W. Thompson of the *Daily Telegraph*, who had covered the activities of the elder brothers and perhaps even fathers of these same men in the Second World War, was repelled by the American attitude that the devastating use of machines of war saved lives. As he wrote at the time: 'The slightest resistance (by the North Koreans) brought down a deluge of destruction blotting out the area.' He couldn't have written the same about the 'Woolworth's Brigade', now advancing north the best they could with their limited transport. They simply didn't have the resources.

Not that they couldn't have used them. They were short of everything, in particular of battle-experienced troops. National service 2/Lt Alan Lauder of the Argylls, aged 20 at the time, recalls being flown in from Japan 'the day after Hill 282 (the napalming of the regiment) to Taegu, and being in action within forty minutes!' Young Lauder's previous military experience had been 'when I'd served in the school cadets during WWII'; later he'd be wounded and return for a second dose of Korea.

Lauder's experience seems to have been typical. Veteran Maj John Willoughby of the 'Diehards' thought that many of the Middlesex's young conscripts were in a 'state of shock for many weeks after we arrived'. They accepted orders willingly enough, but they had no idea of front-line combat discipline. One fell asleep on sentry duty (a punishable offence that could result in the death sentence), but Willoughby accepted that the young soldier was probably exhausted, so instead of 'charging' the man in question, he 'simply said, "Wake up you bugger. All your mates could get killed." . . . You could only deal with these things on a fatherly basis.'

Still Walker pushed on his Eighth Army; the weakly disciplined US divisions; the underarmed and undermanned British; the shaky 'reformed'

ROK divisions (callow youths picked off the Korean streets and given US weapons by press gangs) – they were all urged to reach the 38th Parallel and thence to reach the North Korean capital, Pyongyang, before the hated Almond did. On the eve of what appeared to be victory for the Allies in Korea, the war was already entering that dangerous phase which would ensure it would continue for another three long terrible years . . .

But in the third week of September 1950, MacArthur's mind was seemingly closed to the dangers inherent in his plans and in the playing off of one commander against another, that old army game which ensured that progress was made regardless of the cost. He wanted Seoul by 23/24 September: three months exactly after the 'police action' had begun.

The assault on the South Korean capital began on 22 September. Smith's 5th Marine Regiment staged a frontal assault on the western gates of the ruined city. Here the Northern Koreans had set up their strongest defences in hills where their fanatical last-ditch troops had dug in well, with interlocking machine gun fields of fire so that any attacker would not only be facing frontal fire, but also that from both flanks. It was the kind of attack that Marine vets were used to. They had done it over and over again in the Pacific war. But even the veterans would be shaken when they were finally presented with the 'Butcher's Bill' for the capture of what was in essence, a prestige objective for MacArthur: a means of flattering his overwhelming vanity and putting a full stop (or so MacArthur thought) to the end of the Korean War.

As always the Marines went up the hill bravely. All of them wore their camouflaged helmets of which they were so proud. It identified them as 'gyrenes', not GIs. But that fact didn't impress the waiting North Koreans. Their old-fashioned Russian Maxims started to chatter at once, like irate woodpeckers, as they swept the slopes with tracer. Marines went down everywhere. Still they continued their blind frontal assault. Now the ascent behind them was littered with their bodies. Here and there little groups attempted to go to ground. To no avail. Angry, red-faced veteran noncoms urged them on. When curses didn't suffice, kicks and blows did. They advanced again into that crazy lethal maelstrom. But the steam had started to run out of their attack. As brave as they were, trained right from the start in those feared boot camps of theirs, the Marines simply couldn't progress any further against that wall of steel. One by one they went to ground, hurriedly scraping holes in the hard unyielding earth, dying as they did so.

Another company tried again to take the hill line, coming in from a different direction. The enemy machine-gunners were waiting for them. The North Korean fire swept the hillside from left to right. The gunners couldn't miss. The advancing Marines, outlined quite clearly against the bare, rocky slope, were being presented to them on a silver platter. That attack failed, too. The attackers – what was left of them – had to be content with engaging the enemy at long distance, their Brownings duelling with the enemy's Maxims in First World War style.

Meanwhile the First Marines were coming in, attacking in two main drives. Just like their comrades they were meeting heavy resistance, but with the reckless (some army officers said 'crazy') courage of their Corps, they kept on going. One group, Company A, made up of 200 men under the command of six foot four Captain Robert Barrow, decided it was not going to be merely cannonfodder for the 'Gook' gunners.

Barrow had fought with Chinese guerrillas behind the Japanese lines . . . in the Second World War. Now he led his Marines through head-high paddy fields, wading through, as one of them phrased it without any attempt at delicacy, 'goo and shit'.[3] Surprisingly enough they weren't spotted. They emerged back on firm ground, close to the Inchon–Seoul Road, smelling somewhat 'ripe' without a shot being fired.

Now their luck still held. A platoon commanded by a Lt John Swords bumped into a North Korean force and 'cut it to ribbons'. On the Marines went. To the right they could hear the sounds of battle where their unluckier comrades 'slugged it out' with the obstinate defenders. A five-storey Korean building was destroyed. Captured enemy plasma was used to succour their own dozen wounded. Their radio went, so now they were unable to reach battalion HQ. Still they pushed on, firing and moving, mopping up and continuing again.

At dusk that day, five T-34s with their heavy overhanging guns swinging from side to side like the snouts of predatory monsters looking for something to eat rumbled up, the first tanks the Marines had ever fought; but as the Russian-built tanks opened fire at a range of thirty yards, 'they stood cool and tall and let them have it', as Barrow remembered long afterwards. The Marine bazooka teams opened up at once. Scarlet flames stabbed the growing gloom. Despite the fact that their bazookas had been obsolete back in 1945, they still did a lot of damage to the enemy tanks at such close range. A Marine corporal challenged one of the monsters like a modern-day David facing up to Goliath. He struck lucky. His first projectile slammed against the T-34's metal hide with a great hollow boom. The tank rumbled to a stop and a mushroom of grey smoke rose from its open turret like a huge smoke ring. Nobody got out. In the end the Marines damaged two more T-34s and the last one rolled away into the darkness in panic.

But now a new danger threatened the lone company. They were attacked by North Korean infantry who came screaming down the debris-littered street as if they were drugged or drunk, or perhaps both. Hand-to-hand fighting ensued, but in the end the hard-pressed Marines threw them back. But the fanatical defenders were still not finished: half an hour later they attacked again – and again . . . By midnight the North Koreans had assaulted the stubborn Marines five times, until finally a Corporal Billy Webb ventured onto the street, covered with crumpled bodies everywhere, and fired a single shot. And that was that. Webb had just killed the enemy commander. After that there was relative peace. At dawn the weary, hollow-eyed Marines counted the enemy dead. They found three hundred and ten corpses. . . .

Still the battle for Seoul continued. The Marine casualties were mounting rapidly. In the end they'd lose about a sixth of the 1st Marine Division, some two thousand men. Time and time again, individual Marine companies were cut off or were ambushed in the smoking ruins. Still they pressed on, living up to the nearly two hundred years old Marine tradition.

General Almond, by now one of the best hated men by the 1st Marine Division, was not satisfied. The corps commander told Marine General Smith that he was 'dissatisfied with the marines'. Angry and impatient he told Smith, who was something of a plodder (for a Marine) that he wanted Seoul captured now by 25 September; General MacArthur wanted to make his triumphal entry. But as the Marine history states: 'It was neat public relations, but the enemy would not cooperate.' On went the bitter battle for this ruined, militarily speaking, totally useless prestige objective.

Almond gave Smith another twenty-four hours. If the Marine General couldn't capture the South Korean capital by then, Almond would order in an Army regiment to the attack. Desperately he tried to meet the deadline. The honour of the US Marine Corps was at stake. But he simply couldn't make it. In one Marine company 176 men out of the unit's total of 206 fell that day. A Marine won his country's highest honour – and died doing so. Almond wasn't impressed. He sent in the Army, GIs of the Seventh Division's 32nd Regiment. The Koreans started evacuating their troops. Still the fighting continued in the smoke-filled ruins, men dodging in and out of doorways, dying alone and in agony in the brick rubble on the debris-littered streets to be flattened like cardboard figures by the tanks rushing blindly back and forth.

MacArthur, it appeared, couldn't wait any longer. He proclaimed Seoul captured. He was premature, but it wasn't the first time. He had done the same thing back in 1945 when his soldiers had attempted to capture the Old City of Manilla in the Philippines and failed to meet his deadline.

The end came finally on the afternoon of 27 September when Company G of the 5th Marines seized Seouls' Government House; exhausted as they were, they managed to haul down the North Korean flag and replace it by 'Old Glory'. But not for long as we shall see. The cost had been prohibitive. The 1st Marine Division had lost 414 dead and 2,430 other casualties, most of them sustained in the fight for the Korean capital.

But the cost didn't concern the Top Brass. Hurriedly a celebration programme was launched. Immense labour, American and Korean, was diverted from the battlefield to build a bridge across the Han River. It was to be used by MacArthur, who would land at Kimpo airfield from Tokyo and then drive ceremonially across it to the capital building. Here, like some medieval king-maker, he would hand over the building to the aged former ruler of South Korea, Dr Syngman Rhee, the politician who had done as much to start the ruinous war in Korea as had any of his opposite numbers north of the 38th Parallel.

At the beginning MacArthur, who had brought his wife Jean along for the great ceremony, was in a jovial mood. Together with the 75-year-old South Korean President, they crossed the new pontoon bridge, waving at the cheering kids, all – naturally – waving paper ROK flags. MacArthur cracked, as if he was now coming to the end of a long difficult road, 'This is where I came in.' But his face hardened and he grew more sombre when he saw the damage on all sides and heard the rumble of the heavy guns in the far distance. All around him his aides were carrying side-arms, too, as if expecting trouble, and one of them commented cynically while the two great men prepared to enter the smoking government building arm-in-arm, 'There hasn't been so many gats in this place since the last time the legislature sat.' MacArthur silenced the officer with an icy look.

Now someone remembered this was supposed to be a 'UN police action' and not an American war. Hurriedly the Stars and Stripes banner was hauled down and replaced by the non-descript flag of the UN.

It was twelve noon. The two old men, who between them had wrought so much destruction, strode into the building that still stank of burning paper and wood. MacArthur ordered that they would all say a prayer – the Lord's Prayer – for Korea's deliverance. Bareheaded they did so, but not for long, as great plates of glass dislodged from the damaged roof came tumbling down at that very moment. Hurriedly the attendant officers grabbed for their steel helmets.

MacArthur didn't seem to notice. Tears streaming down his aged cheeks, the General told Rhee:

> By the grace of a merciful Providence our forces fighting under the standard of that greatest hope and inspiration of mankind, the United Nations, have liberated this ancient capital city of Korea . . . Now on behalf of the United Nations Command, I am happy to restore to you, Mr President, the seat of your government.

Rhee grasped MacArthur's hand, his prepared text forgotten in the emotion of that moment, with the guns still thundering outside. 'We admire you,' the old hypocrite intoned. 'We love you as the saviour of our race. How can I explain to you my own undying gratitude and that of the Korean people?'

It was all over, it seemed. The 'police action' was over. The good guys had won.

Or had they?

Book Two

Bless 'em all, the long and the short and the tall
For we're saying good-bye to 'em all . . .
You'll get no promotion this side of the ocean,
So cheer up my lads . . . FUCK 'EM ALL!
                    'Soldiers' Song', British Army.

CHAPTER TEN

'Attack North'

Standing on the doorstep of his London home the British minister warned his protégé who was soon to depart for Washington:

'There are three basic don'ts, Guy, to bear in mind when you're dealing with Americans.'

The half-drunk younger man listened to the earnest tone of the Scottish minister, as he pontificated, 'The first is Communism . . . the second is homosexuality . . . and the third is the colour bar.' He looked hard at the tousle-haired handsome new recruit to the British Embassy in Washington and added, 'Do please memorize them, won't you?'

The listener gave him his winning seraphic smile, and quipped in that flippant manner of his which had always annoyed his elders ever since he was an unruly schoolboy at Eton, 'I've got it, Hector.[1] So there, don't worry. What you're trying to say in your nice long-winded manner is "Guy, for God's sake, don't make a pass at Paul Robeson!"'

The remark was typical of Guy Burgess and the rest of his clique, who would one day go down in history as the infamous 'Cambridge spies'. It was as if they had been born to act the gadfly and to cock a snook at the Establishment, although in essence they were members of that same maligned Establishment themselves.

In the years immediately after the Great War when they had been public schoolboys, the three most notorious of them – Philby, Burgess and Maclean – had felt themselves misfits. Philby's father, the noted Arabist and right-winger, had always been away travelling and had never been there for his son; Burgess's father was dead, and he was being brought up by a self-indulgent mother; while Maclean's father Sir Donald had been a stern and dour cabinet minister and MP who had little time for his children.

In the 1930s when they had gone up to Cambridge, the young misfits had deliberately become wastrels, wilful decadents, drinking their days away, proclaiming with all the vast authority of their tender years that the British Empire was rotten and ready to fall apart at any moment. All of them became typical 'parlour pinks' of the time, as did a Rothschild, for example, who could have bought and sold the lot of them without batting an eyelid! Naturally they were ideal targets for communist spy recruiters: they were homosexuals and drunkards; by nature and choice outsiders. But at the same time they were also members of that same Establishment which they were now committed to bringing down.

The war gave them positions and power they didn't deserve. They entered the British Foreign Office and drifted into Intelligence, grew wiser and more cunning – save Burgess – and by the time the Second World War had ended, all of them, each in his own small way, had 'arrived': they had become the bureaucrats and officials who directed the way the Establishment was run.

Of them all, Donald Maclean had advanced the furthest. He had repressed his latent homosexuality, had married for the first time (though he was still a heavy drinker, inclined to go off on weekend group binges, perhaps due to the strain he was under), and was, by the time the cold war had really started, First Secretary of the British Embassy in Washington. From there he had warned his Russian control that the Anglo-Americans were serious about continuing to supply Soviet-blockaded West Berlin by air. And it was the measure of just how serious the Russian spymasters in Moscow took Maclean's information that it was passed on to the Russian dictator Stalin. Now that same former First Secretary, back in London and on the verge of a nervous breakdown,[2] was in the forefront of informing Russia of American intentions in Korea.

We do not know exactly what Maclean and his fellow spies in Washington – Philby and Burgess – passed on to the Russians on this subject, save that one of the last snippets of information found in his house after he had fled to the 'Workers' and Peasants' paradise were details of the Attlee–Truman meeting of December 1950 concerning MacArthur's future.[3] But we *do* know that Stalin had implicit faith in Maclean's information, in light of his report in the previous year that Truman was prepared to use the H-bomb on Russia if the problem of the Berlin Blockade wasn't resolved soon. That episode had been the key factor in Stalin's decision to call off the blockade. So now, as suspicious as he normally was (not even, for example, heeding Churchill's warning in 1941 that Nazi Germany was going to invade Russia, calling it a 'provocation'), Stalin didn't hesitate at this time to accept the English spy's information.

As Maclean and the others saw it, tapping their London and Washington sources (information based on Brig Coad's radio link), MacArthur was not going to stop after his capture of Seoul. He would free the rest of South Korea before crossing in force into the north of that unhappy country, using both Almond's X Corps and Walker's Eighth Army, intending to make a two-pronged drive from the 38th Parallel and close on the Yalu River, bringing hostilities to an end before action could be hindered by the deep snows of winter. In the course of this operation, MacArthur intended to capture the North Korean capital, after completely destroying that country's army. It was clear that after that capital (Pyongyang) was in Allied hands, MacArthur would attempt to unify the whole of Korea. That would be something that Stalin, whose Red Army had created North Korea at the end of the Second World War, did not like one bit. But he was not prepared to risk an all-out, perhaps nuclear, confrontation with the USA on account of that obscure Far Eastern country. However, there was one major power in the area which Stalin thought might be prepared to take on the 'Yankee Imperialists'. Did not the rulers of that country constantly complain to him that the Americans were always threatening them and interfering in their internal affairs? Stalin, that supposedly benevolent 'Uncle Joe', as the Americans had once called him, considered what Red China would do if he now informed its communist leaders of what MacArthur was apparently planning for North Korea. The Soviet dictator thought he knew. China would fight! Accordingly Stalin demanded more information from those upper-class, homosexual British traitors in London and Washington. He knew he was treading on risky ground. But it was a risk he was prepared to take.

Thus it was that, while MacArthur savoured his victory in the South and prepared for the drive to the North (as Washington still saw it, a limited one), he was unaware that his downfall was already being brought about by a bunch of 'limey faggots'. Those 'lovely boys', once dedicated to what they called 'a higher sodomy', who at Cambridge all those years before had once chanted drunkenly, 'boys of rough trade and laddies of leisure give me equal pleasure', had done their bit. Now all depended upon America's greatest soldier, as MacArthur thought himself (as did at the time a lot of other people who should have known better). Would he avoid the trap being set for him in the North? By the time Seoul had been captured, the dreaded writing was already on the wall and some in US Intelligence knew roughly what was going on. But MacArthur was no longer listening. Blinded by his successes in September and his overwhelming vanity, the old warrior would walk blindly to his fate . . .

Riding on the tanks of the US 1st Cavalry Division, the infantry of the British 'Woolworth's Brigade' could hardly believe their luck. They were riding, not slogging up and down hills as they had done so far; they were moving through a 'beautiful land of wooded mountains with deep valleys' with 'the weather warm and the nights fresh', as Captain Colin Mitchell of the 1st Argylls remembered the drive north; and so far they had encountered little resistance.

The experience was exhilarating. Whenever they bumped into any opposition from the beaten retreating North Koreans, the fighter bombers were whistled up at once. Within minutes they appeared from nowhere. Engines going full out, they would drop out of the sky. Cannon pumping shells, machine-guns chattering, they'd hit the 'Gooks' with a lethal hail of glowing white tracer. Then it would be up to the infantry and tankers to scatter the handful of survivors with their heavy machine-guns. Afterwards the Shermans and Pershings would race by shattered smoking strongpoints, the dead 'Gooks' sprawled around in dark crimson pools of their blood and gore. It was all too easy, and as the future 'Mad Mike' remembered many years later, it 'gave a very false picture of the future'.

Not that the squaddies of the three battalions involved – the 'Diehards', the 'Jocks' and the 'Aussies' – worried about such things. Their concern was to live for the day. For most of them their intellectual level was limited to 'wallop' and 'women'. Japanese beer had already begun to arrive and so far they had not fancied tackling the local women. They were shapeless, unintelligible and very dirty. Not that their disinclination would last long. Soon most battalions of all twelve UN nations serving in Korea would be reporting a VD rate of between 11 and 13 per cent.[4]

These working-class soldiers soon to be betrayed by their 'pansy' upper-class fellow countrymen, were not given to soul-searching or intellectual justification for their presence in this strange land. Most of them felt they were 'here because they were here' and didn't go into the bitter histrionics of the average GI: 'Hell give it back to the Gooks . . . let me out, brother!'

Eric Linklater, novelist and war correspondent,[5] interviewing the 'Diehards' that year, felt they were 'non-committal . . . They thought, perhaps, that service with the Diehards was its own justification.' His fellow countrymen of the Argylls were 'more exuberant, more emotional'. A sergeant-major told Linklater, the 'men knew it was Communism they were fighting in Korea. And that is enough to make them serious.'

Serious or not, luck seemed still to be on the side of the 'Woolworth's Brigade'. By the middle of October, the British were way ahead of the main body of Walker's Eighth Army. It didn't worry the Jocks, who seemed to have been operating independently for ever now. By then they had been given an objective: the grimy north-western industrial town of Sariwon, not far from North Korea's coast. With luck, if they reached it in time they'd cut off all enemy troops withdrawing from the great bulge of the coastline below the town.

Curiously enough, as Mitchell records, the key town appeared empty. So it was that a small officers' group found themselves in the centre of a badly bombed Sariwon, consulting a map (the Jocks were already beginning to run out of them), wondering what to do next.

In the event, the decision was made for them. One of the Argylls' officers suddenly pointed to the skyline and exclaimed 'Gooks . . . enemy Gooks!' They didn't wait to find out whether the excited young officer was right enough. 'Mad Mike' contented himself with firing a long burst from a machine-gun at the vehicles on the height and then the little convoy moved off, but not for long. A few minutes later the Jocks spotted a large truck crammed with soldiers, heading straight for them. It was the North Koreans they had just seen.

For what seemed an age, the Argylls' CO and his handful of officers stared open-mouthed at the thirty or so enemy officers in the truck. The Jocks reacted first, however. Their first jeep slewed to a stop in a cloud of white dust. In that same instant the truck screeched to a halt. Too late! A wild fire-fight broke out with Maj Alastair Gordon-Ingram standing in the middle of the street snapping off well-aimed shots like some movie western gunslinger. But one of the Argyll privates reacted more effectively than his officers. He pulled out a 36 grenade. Deftly he lobbed it over the high side of the stalled enemy truck. A thick throaty crump. A puff of angry grey smoke. When it cleared, dead enemy officers were seen sprawled on all sides and the rest were fleeing as if the Devil himself were after them . . .

In Sariwon the confused fighting went on like that all night. Once Mitchell bumped into a file of marching infantry. In the poor light he took them for 'Yanks'. Then the 22-year-old Captain realized that the enemy weren't wearing helmets as the Americans always did in combat. They were the 'gooks'. Both sides ripped off volleys – and both sides missed! It was an absolute farce. The range was so close that the worse shot in the world shouldn't have missed, but they had. As it was described by Mitchell two decades later, both sides went on their ways, unharmed: '[As] there was nothing else to do and the situation suddenly seemed so ludicrous [I was] roaring with laughter.'

Little did the cocky young Highland soldier know that laughter would soon turn to bitter tears. 'Within less than three weeks, both John and Alastair (two of his closest friends in the 1st Battalion Argyll and Sutherland Highlanders) were to be out of the fight for good.' And they wouldn't be the only ones.

But with Sariwon taken and passed, the great advance north continued triumphantly. The Gooks were on the run and, as Mitchell records, 'the cry was On . . . On . . .!'

Attached now to the hated 24th Infantry Division, which Brig Coad didn't trust one inch, the 27th Brigade headed for the River Yalu. Those at the top knew that Washington had ordered that no UN unit should cross the Yalu River to their immediate front, a move that the US State Department and the US Joint Chiefs-of-Staff considered might well provoke Red China into reacting. Any movement further north on the other side of the Yalu would be left to ROK troops; after all Korea – the whole of it – was *their* country. It was a strategy, with which MacArthur supposedly agreed. But already he had other – and more dangerous – objectives in mind. For as 'Sir Charles', MacArthur's supercilious German-American Chief-of-Intelligence, informed his adored master: 'Organized resistance on any larger scale has ceased to be an enemy capability. Indications are that the North Korean military and political headquarters may have fled to Manchuria,' i.e. Red Chinese territory. As Maj Gen Charles Willoughby in faraway Tokyo saw it, the Korean War was virtually over.

The men of the 27th Brigade were beginning to think differently. Opposition was hardening all along, although they were still beating the Gooks when the chips were down. In one case the men of the 3rd Australian Infantry Battalion launched a First World War-style bayonet charge at the enemy, the first of the Korean War. Meanwhile the Battalion HQ Lt Col Charles Green had been attacked by a large number of North Korean infantry. Green's Aussies saw them off smartly, killing thirty-four of the enemy in close combat. It seemed that the 'diggers' couldn't get enough of the bloody business. One US war correspondent observed a 'big red-haired Australian' jump into an enemy trench roaring his head off like a madman. He came out 'bleeding like a stuck hog', but still on his feet. Behind him he left eight dead North Koreans, bayoneted to death.' In the end the 3rd Australian Infantry accounted for 500 North Koreans dead or taken prisoner.

The Australians, however, much admired by their British comrades since all were volunteers and veterans of the fighting in the Middle East and the Pacific, were starting to have to pay the bloody butcher's bill as well now. On 29 October, they took over the point position. Their objective was the town of Chongju. The going was tough, through rugged mountain country, and the 'gooks' seemed to be fighting hard once again. Against growing opposition, the Aussies gained a pass and the ridgelines on both sides and settled down in their shallow foxholes. For the most part they ignored their US rations; and if they possessed any 'grog' that night, none of their chroniclers mentions it. Instead they settled down for an exhausted sleep, though it was not to last for long. The first angry red flares sailed into the night sky almost immediately. Those on sentry duty heard the first rusty squeak of tank tracks. A little later dark shadows began to detach themselves from the darker ones cast by the terrain to the Australians' front. 'Stand to!' the urgent summons was whispered from hole to hole. Cursing and bitching, the weary Australians roused themselves. They flipped back their big bush hats, which they insisted on wearing even in the line; they identified them as Australians and that was something, despite all their cursing, that they were proud of.

Then blowing their bugles, shrilling blasts on their whistles, the Gooks came out of the night, following the tanks and self-propelled guns. Other troops might have sprung from their holes and run, for the Australians hadn't much in the way of anti-tank weapons to beat off the lumbering metal monsters, just a handful of bazookas. They didn't run, though, staying in their positions and fighting it out. This time they were going to have to pay the price. The North Koreans pushed home their attack with their old determination, as if this were June and not October, and were causing all to fly in front of them . . . '*Stretcher-bearer . . . over here, cobber . . . where's those fucking stretcher-bearers!*' The angry hurt cries went up on all sides, as the darkness was split by the violent purple flashes of grenades exploding and the lethal Morse of tracer. For a while it looked as if one of the Australian companies would be overrun: there seemed to be no stopping the fanatical North Korean attack. But in the end the Australians triumphed. Their losses were high and Australia, their mother country, didn't have an inexhaustible supply of replacements. They lost thirty-nine killed and wounded, including their much admired CO, Col Green, an inspiration to this battalion which didn't take to officers gladly, in that fine old bolshy tradition of the 'Aussies'. He died of his wounds the following morning and the heart seemed to go out of the 3rd Australian Infantry Battalion.

Hastily the Argylls were pushing through the grieving 'Aussies'. They entered Chongju without too much resistance. The Australians had broken the 'Gooks'' will to resist. Thus it was on that last morning in October that Captain Mitchell of the Argylls, having just heard that the 27th Brigade had done enough – the Yanks would take over the point now – stood on a hilltop and stared through the receding mists to the north and the unknown. Later he wrote: 'I remember feeling that this was a moment in history.' For the 22-year-old officer, not a particularly imaginative young man, experienced that morning a sense of foreboding: that he and his regiment 'were on the eve of a new battle', but with whom that battle would be fought he did not yet know.

Soon he would find out. Soon the successors to the old 93rd Highlanders, who had formed the 'thin red line' at Balaclava a century before and had gained a battle honour doing so, would win another in this remote country. Not that that would matter to anyone but the Argyll successors to those kilted bearded warriors in the Crimea. For as Mitchell, who would one day save the regiment from being relegated to the military history of a sorely-tried British Army, would remark bitterly: 'But then, few can ever have heard of Pakchon.' How true! For the three-year struggle about to begin in Korea would be a forgotten war. Then, back in the homeland of these soldiers who were suffering and dying for an ungrateful country, the average man in the street was more concerned with whether the new National Health Scheme – 'the envy of the whole world', as Attlee had proclaimed it proudly – could pay for granny's false teeth or not, or ensure that grandad got his 'specs' gratis . . .

By now Gen Milburn, commanding the US I Corps which was responsible for the British 27th Brigade, decided that the 'Limeys' had had enough. All three regiments that made up the 'Woolworth's Brigade' had suffered considerable losses in both men and equipment. There was another consideration, too, which played a part in his decision to withdraw the British from the van of the attack.

Ever since the US Army had become the senior partner in Anglo-American military coalitions, US generals had been aware that their superiors and the 'Great American Public' naturally wanted Americans to win the victories. The scuttlebutt at I Corps HQ was that the war in Korea was about over. Now, it wouldn't look good back home if the Limeys appeared to be gaining the kudos of final victory. Milburn, the veteran of the Second World War in Europe where it had seemed to some that in the last months of that war the British had forgotten they were fighting the Germans in their eagerness to beat their American allies to the final triumph, was not going to have that. Accordingly, he replaced the Middlesex and the Argylls with the US 24th Division's 21st Infantry Regiment.

The regiment which, as we have seen, had suffered greatly in the initial retreat of the summer, started their advance at two in the morning on that same day, 31 October. Two miles west of the North Korean town of

Kwaksan, the enemy tried to ambush the Americans. As usual the US infantry had not learned to get off the roads; they were still highway-bound. But this time the men of the 21st Infantry were waiting for the attack. As 500 enemy infantry supported by seven T-34s descended from the hills on both sides of the road, confident that they had surprised the 'round-eyes', they were met by a hail of fire. The minor battle raged most of the day. But the Americans, who outnumbered the Gooks by six to one and were confident of their new weapons and renewed fighting power, beat the attackers off time and time again.

In the end as darkness began to fall on that cold October day, the surviving North Koreans abandoned their dead and dying and fled back into the safety of the surrounding hills, never to reappear. The Americans of that same division, whose commander now languished in a North Korean POW cage, so emaciated that his men wouldn't have recognized him,⁶ had won.

Now Milburn, perhaps on orders from 'Bulldog' Walker who wanted some of the headlines too, for his Eighth Army,⁷ commanded that the 21st Infantry's First Battalion should take the point.

Eagerly Lt Col Charles B. Smith, CO of the First Battalion, accepted the challenge. Relentlessly, almost brutally, he urged his men, mostly replacements by now, forward. By noon of 1 November they had reached Chonggo-dong, eighteen miles from Sinuiju and the key Yalu River. Later American students of the battle for Korea would say it was just a matter of sheer coincidence, but this battalion, once known as 'Task Force Smith', achieved the furthest penetration of all of Walker's Eighth Army.

What was the coincidence? Just that Smith's force had been the first US unit to engage the North Koreans near Osan on 5 July 1950. Then, it had been ignominiously routed. Now, Walker and Milburn must have thought the wheel had turned full circle: that bitter defeat had been reversed and the American Army was back where it had started. But like one of those gaily-painted Russian dolls that contain yet another one inside it, this latest victory reversing the old defeat contained yet another new defeat to come. For up in the hills, watching the Americans as they dug in that afternoon, there were new enemies whose drab shapeless uniforms bore no badges of identification save the enamel red star of Communist China.

CHAPTER ELEVEN

Chinks!

It had been a long voyage for the 'Geordies', six weeks to be exact. As in the old days of the new fast-declining British Empire, the northerners of the Royal Northumberland Fusiliers stopped at 'Alex', Port Said, Colombo and all the rest of those 'exotic' ports which for generations of soldiers had dotted the British Army troop-ships' route to the East. In the Suez Canal they had heard the old cries from soldiers already there to 'get yer knees brown, mate' – this to men who had got their 'knees brown' when the young conscripts below had still been in short pants. At Port Said, the 'wogs' in their bathrobes had lifted them to show the gawping soldiers lining the rails high above their 'bumboats' the desirable sexual effect that came from the perusal of the 'dirty, naughty postcards' they were peddling.

For the Geordies, the men of the 8th Royal Irish Hussars, and the lads of the Royal Artillery and Engineers who made up the contingent of 2,000 men on board the *Empire Halladale*, these occasions had made welcome breaks in the boring shipboard routine of morning drills and afternoon 'housey-housey' gambling sessions. But after they had left Singapore behind in the last stage of their journey to battle, Nature soon roused them from their boredom. As the big trooper entered the China Sea, now six thousand miles from 'Blighty' she was hit by a tremendous cyclone. As Fusilier Thompson, known to his mates as 'Thommo', recalls: 'All aboard were tossed around like paper dolls . . . The ship was near to sinking with massive waves lashing her constantly amidships.' In the end 'the Captain had no option but alter course and steer towards the Chinese mainland . . . in order to ride out the massive waves'. Little did the *Empire Halladale*'s skipper know that he had placed himself in yet another danger by doing so, as he would learn later.

Finally the frightening storm ended and the 2,000 men of the Fusiliers, Hussars, Artillery and Sappers sailed on to the port of disembarkation, Pusan. Here they and the rest of Brig Brodie's 29th Independent Brigade Group – the Gloucestershires, the Royal Ulster Rifles, the Royal Tank Regiment equipped with an antiquated but still fearsome weapon, the Crocodile (a flame-throwing Churchill tank) – started to form up for what lay in front of them. One thing they knew – as 'Thommo' of the Fusiliers put it: 'Soon we'll be fighting, we knew that. So let's get it over quick . . . But as events were to prove, it wasn't going to be as easy as that . . .' Fusilier Thompson, the 22-year-old regular and future writer,[1] was right. For while the lead elements of the new British Brigade under Brodie had ridden out the storm in the China Sea, the war in Korea had taken a decisive turn for the worse for the Western Allies.

By then General MacArthur, without consultation with Washington, had decided he would exceed his brief and not stop short of the Yalu, leaving the ROK forces alone to move further north, even to the Chinese Manchurian frontier if necessary. Instead, as October gave way to a cold harsh November, he removed all restrictions on the use of UN forces to press forward, in what was to prove a fatal move.

On 25 October, the day that MacArthur opened up the front to non-ROK forces, the dawn was very cold, with icy flurries of snow in the mountains. Still, the ROKs were used to the weather and the terrain – and they were winning. So finding the way ahead completely open, as if their cousins the North Koreans had given up altogether, the victorious ROK 7th Regiment mounted their American troop-carriers, the old Second World War deuces-and-a-half, with their objective this cold day a bold one: they were going to drive north for Chosan, fifty air miles away on the Yalu River. So off they went – mile after mile they passed through that abandoned lunar landscape, the only signs that there had once been an enemy here being the trucks abandoned after running out of fuel or a tank burnt out after being set on fire by its own crew. Everywhere along the dusty roadsides, the villages were abandoned. Even the skinny dogs had vanished. Not a shot was fired. It seemed that the North Korean Army had vanished from the very face of the earth.

Meanwhile as the 7th ROK Regiment drove eighteen unopposed miles by early afternoon, the ROK 15th Regiment, riding on the Shermans and Pershings of the US 6th Medium Tank Battalion, also headed north. They too felt a sense of elation. After all the misery, the cruelty, the sudden violent death, things were going well at last. Perhaps the young Korean conscripts (some as young as fourteen, snatched off the streets and given an unfamiliar rifle, then sent straight to the front!) told themselves they would be going home soon, after all.

The American tankers were a little more wary. By now they had learned just how vulnerable their tanks were, exposed on the roads with the heights on both sides possibly in the hands of enemy infantry armed with anti-tank weapons. Later some of them reported that they had felt a sense of being watched, a kind of unseen scrutiny, which sent shivers 'down the spine like those horror movies back home'. But as the hours passed without any sign of the retreating enemy, the tension started to ease off and the tankers concentrated on getting their clumsy metal monsters round the tightly winding curvy roads of the area. Then it happened. They had just passed through the small dirty, tumbledown town of Unsan and were advancing to a bridge a mile to the front, when the still of the afternoon was ripped apart. There was no mistaking the obscene sound of mortars being fired at them. Next instant the first bombs sailed out of the grey sky and plumped into the paddy to their right with a series of black earth spurts, tinged with angry cherry-red flame. 'Gooks!' the leading company commander yelled, 'Gooks up ahead!'

Crazily the drivers braked to a stop. The gunners swung their turrets round, poised behind their weapons ready to open fire at a moment's notice. ROK officers yelled orders. Korean NCOs shrilled their whistles urgently. Suddenly all was controlled confusion, as the ROKs dropped to the road and started forward in a rough-and-ready skirmish line.

Now the American officers and their undersized ROK liaison officers, who spoke some English, waited impatiently for news. To their front, the ROK troops fanned out to both sides of the bridge, from which the mortar fire seemed to be coming. There was the abrupt snap-and-crackle of small-arms fire. Then a sinister echoing silence. Minutes later some angry-faced, sweating ROK soldiers came hurrying back down the road they had attacked along, bringing with them the first prisoner for interrogation.

Prodding him cruelly when he seemed to lag, they finally halted in front of the waiting officers. The senior ROK liaison officer stepped forward, while the Americans waited eagerly. He snapped something to the man in Korean. The man didn't react. The ROK officer looked angry and puzzled. He was losing face in front of the Americans. He sized up the prisoner. He looked like all the other North Korean POWs they had captured: a small man in sneakers, wearing cotton clothing. He tried again and this time the prisoner did respond. But he spoke in a tongue that the harassed ROK officer could barely recognize. It was Chinese.

On that same snowy 25 October, General Paek Sun Yup, commander of the Second ROK Corps, faced up to some strange prisoners. They had been captured by the forward elements of his corps which had walked into the same sort of trap that had been sprung on the ROK 15th Regiment. The Corps Commander, Japanese-trained, intelligent, a veteran of the Japanese Army's long campaign in China, spoke fluent Mandarin Chinese. Now he eyed his prisoners. A couple were dressed in North Korean uniforms, but all of them wore the reversible smocks of the Chinese Army, which he recognized from Second World War days. General Paek Sun Yup went to work on them in Chinese. He asked: 'Are there many of you here?'

They nodded and muttered 'Many . . . many.'

The ROK General absorbed the startling information, knowing his POWs couldn't be lying. They were indeed mainland Chinese, speaking with the accent of the south. Then he made his mind up. He reported his bad news to Gen 'Shrimp' Milburn, commanding the US I Corps.

Milburn was not convinced. He didn't pay much attention to the Korean General's report. Still his chief-of-intelligence Col Percy Thomas, who *was* concerned, forwarded the information to the Eighth Army commander. Walker, who had now less than two months to live, did accept that the ROKs had captured Chinese soldiers. But he rationalized that the fact played no great role. He stated in his usual bluff no-nonsense manner: 'After all, a lot of Mexicans live in Texas', assuming presumably that the captured

Chinese had been residents of North Korea and had been conscripted into the enemy infantry. In other words, Walker did not believe that China had entered the war, but that only a handful of Chinese had been forced to 'volunteer' to fight against the 'round-eyes'.

MacArthur and 'Sir Charles' 700 miles away in Tokyo took the same attitude. It was something similar to that of Montgomery before the great bold drop at Arnhem during the Second World War, at which time a junior intelligence officer had warned the 'Master' that there were confirmed reports of two SS Panzer divisions in the area: Montgomery had pooh-poohed the information, which didn't fit into his plans. It was the same with MacArthur. He had ended the war in Korea, hadn't he? The Chinese couldn't now change that fact; he simply wouldn't allow it! By the end of October with communist resistance stiffening by the instant, the UN forces had captured twenty-five POWs of Chinese origin. All were vocal. They told their interrogators what they wanted to hear. Still MacArthur refused to admit a Chinese Army presence in Korea.

On 'Bonfire Night' 1950, the weary Argylls had settled down in the area of Pakchon. They were hungry and unshaven and cold and, as British soldiers were wont to do, their first concern was a 'brew of char', a 'fag' and, if the Quartermaster were in a good mood, a half mugfull of issue rum.[2] But their rest was soon due to be rudely disturbed.

Colin Mitchell, the future 'Mad Mike', had just shaved and was sharing a joke with fellow company commander Alastair Gordon-Ingram when there was the sharp dry crack of a sniper's rifle. Alastair yelped with sudden pain and next moment crumpled to the ground with blood jetting from his arm. They were under enemy attack!

In a flash, caught by surprise, soldiers dropped their square mess tins and ran for their posts, with those in position to do so concentrating their return fire on a hill to their left – clearly the unknown enemy's observation post and obviously the place to blind the attackers. Hastily the Jocks whistled up the support of an American field artillery battery which cracked into action almost instantly, and not a minute too soon: already the Argylls' MO was receiving a steady flow of casualties at his makeshift dressing station.

Like hushed winged eagles the US shells sailed over the defenders' heads. They slammed into the hill which shook as if it were a live thing. Thick brown smoke started to rise, but the North Koreans, if that's what they were, continued their attack with a new vigour for a beaten army.

The Argylls' CO organized a 'pepperpot': a trained fire-and-move operation. It required some men to dash forward while others gave them covering fire from the rear; then the first group, having reached its objective, would give cover for the rear group to rush forward in turn. To add muscle to the daring operation, the Argylls asked the American tankers with them to use their turret machine-guns in support. The Yanks who were themselves under machine-gunfire refused point-blank, so the infantry were left to go it alone.

Mitchell took over a platoon himself for the daring attack. They rushed forward, ignoring the slugs whining off the rocks all around. Going all out, crouched low, hearts thumping furiously as if they might well burst the rib cage at any moment, they headed for their objective: a group of low, rough wooden huts. The Jocks' Celtic blood was up. They ignored the enemy fire, snapping off slugs from the hip as they ran. Enemy soldiers slumped to the ground on all sides, or threw up their arms in a melodramatic gesture before falling and dying. Then Mitchell and his men were in the dead ground, wide eyes wild and staring, seeming unable to take in the enemy dead lying everywhere. Mitchell pulled himself together as he slammed to a halt against the wooden wall of a hut. He counted twenty dead bodies in his immediate vicinity, 'but they were unlike any enemy I had seen before. They wore thick padded clothing which made them look like little "Michelin" men'. But there was nothing funny about these dead soldiers in their strange jackets, for Mitchell 'turned one over with his foot and saw that he wore a peaked cap with a red star badge. These soldiers were Chinese!'

Hardly had the young infantry officer recovered from his surprise when he took a second look at the 'dead' Chinese. Suddenly the Chinese opened one eye and 'looked up at me'. He wasn't dead after all! Mitchell, veteran of Second World War fighting in Italy, reacted more quickly than the enemy and pressed the trigger of his looted Luger. The man shrieked with absolute agony as the bullet slammed into him at such close range. His spine arched like the string of a taut bow. In the same instant that he fell back dead, Mitchell shrieked: 'They're alive!' Instantly a 'terrific gun battle' erupted among the barren rocks. For the Chinese, who had been lying 'dead' in the hope that the British would pass them, were springing to their feet everywhere, firing wildly as they did so. But they didn't live long enough to surrender. This time when they went down, they really were dead.

Hurriedly the Argylls, supported by US tanks, pushed on a further mile. But they were now encountering firing on both flanks and it was growing dark rapidly. Yet in the growing darkness of the early winter afternoon, the hard-pressed Jocks could see that something strange was taking place to their front. The whole scrub-lined hillside seemed to be moving!

Then they got it. Camouflaged Chinese were moving forward steadily, waiting for darkness when the Allies wouldn't be able to launch one of their feared air strikes, for as yet the UN forces had complete mastery of the air over Korea. It was time to get out. Under fire the Argylls started to pull back through those ever-willing 'Aussies' that they so admired.

The British didn't know it, but the withdrawal that dark November day in the face of the overwhelming superiority of the 'Chinese volunteers' (as communist propaganda called the Red Chinese Army's intervention in the Korean War) was the start of the 'big bug-out'. The 'Death March', as Mitchell's Jocks chose to call it, was on.

It was Monday 26 November 1950 when the shit hit the fan at the top. For nearly three weeks, MacArthur and Willoughby, Almond and Walker, and various politicians and top brass in Washington had had their heads stuck into the sand – ever since the first Chinese had been taken prisoner. They had simply refused to acknowledge the fact that the 'Chinese volunteer's were in fact a 300,000 strong Red Chinese Army, a lot of it well behind the UN front line already. Even as late as the previous Sunday Tokyo had announced that the UN offensive was continuing 'to roll closer' to the Chinese Manchurian border.

Abruptly on that Monday there was a sudden jarring note. Instead of MacArthur's deep resonant voice stating (as it had done 72 hours before) over Armed Forces Radio that 'This (the new offensive) should for all practical purposes end the war', an 'official spokesman' announced that 'strong enemy counterattacks . . . stalled yesterday the United Nations general offensive'.

Now battlefield reality took over at last. Although correspondents in Tokyo were warned against 'undue pessimism', the newspapermen knew from the long faces everywhere in MacArthur's HQ that things were going badly at the front. Hurriedly Walker and Almond were summoned to the Japanese capital for an 'emergency conference'.

MacArthur asked them for an honest opinion. It was a foolish request really: senior officers committed to one course of action and intent on the personal glory to be gained from it are not inclined to change their opinion at the drop of a hat. But all the facts were against them. Both ROK and UN units all along the front in Korea were being hit hard and were crumbling, some of the ROK outfits disastrously so. The two senior officers were forced to admit that the 'Chicoms', as the Chinese communists were now being called, were in Korea in strength as part of an organized army. The talk of 'Chinese volunteers' was rubbish. More, the Chinese were winning; Almond's X Corps and Walker's Eighth Army were running out of men. Very soon Walker would have to throw in his last reserve, the British Commonwealth Brigade.

Hastily 'Sir Charles' estimated that there were 300,000 Chinese in Korea now. MacArthur radioed Washington and then UN's Lake Success HQ that 'we now face an entirely new war'. The Chinese, he stated, 'sought nothing less than the complete destruction of his army'. Bradley (who must have felt this was a re-run of that horrific weekend of 16–18 December 1944 when he had first realized just how hard the Germans had struck his line in the Belgian Ardennes) phoned Truman: 'A terrible message has come in from General MacArthur.' In his turn the President told his staff: 'MacArthur says he's stymied. He says he has to go over to the defensive. It's no longer a question of a few so-called volunteers. The Chinks have come in with both feet!'

MacArthur's information struck in Washington like a bombshell, shocking both military and civilian authorities into a kind of initial paralysis. They knew that UN – i.e. effectively the USA – couldn't afford to lose this first armed conflict of the new cold war with communism. America's allies, in particular countries such as France, Belgium, Italy and Greece, were potential 'weak sisters' in light of their having strong communist parties. Even American's principal ally Britain had a strong anti-American minority. What would these countries do if America suffered a defeat at the hands of Russian-inspired communist forces?

Naturally the Joint Chiefs-of-Staff, who so far had been virtually ignored by MacArthur, knew that the latter's desperate statement to the President meant he was appealing for more troops. But what few trained reserves were available were needed in Europe. For the Joint Chiefs were inclined to believe that Korea well might be just a feint. Stalin was really concerned with dominating Western Europe. Send the troops to Korea, Washington reasoned, and Stalin might well attack in Europe. What then? The new military coalitions being formed in that continent, which would culminate as NATO, might well fall apart. Stalin would dominate Western Europe, and America – the new superpower and world caretaker – could find itself totally isolated and with no world to be responsible for. For the Joint Chiefs-of-Staff that last day of November 1950, those same generals and admirals who had made America the most powerful force in the world and had won the war in Western Europe and the Pacific, it must have seemed that everything they had achieved had turned to ashes.

There was only one alternative and they hardly dare think about that!

At his press conference on 30 November, the little ex-businessman from the Mid-West brought it all out into the open, albeit inadvertently. As a cautious Bradley (who five years before had found himself in a somewhat similar situation during the Battle of the Bulge) put it: 'Truman . . . put his foot in his mouth, causing universal consternation.'

The panic started when Truman answered a reporter who asked the President what he was going to do now, with what seemed like a second Dunkirk looming in Korea. Truman said: 'We will take whatever steps are necessary to meet the military situation, just as we have always done.'

Before the bespectacled President could really recover from the first of the hard-hitting questions now obviously to be raised, another reporter nipped in, asking, 'Will that include the atomic bomb?'

There is no record of what Truman's advisers thought of that moment, with the camera flashes exploding and correspondents thrusting up their pencils and hoping to ask more questions, but one can guess. They must have clenched their fists in a cold sweat and prayed that Truman didn't say too much. But with all his faults, Truman was a straight-talking fighter. Instead of ducking the obviously leading question, he answered at once, 'that includes every weapon we have!'

Now the Press scented blood. Another chimed in with, 'Does that mean there is active consideration of the use of the atomic bomb?' It was the overwhelming question: the one which the whole world feared being answered. For ever since that dreaded mushroom had exploded over Japan in August 1945, the ordinary man and woman everywhere had lived with the frightening possibility that they and their world would be wiped out as instantaneously as that of the unfortunate Japanese had been.

Truman didn't hesitate. In that downright, plain-speaking (for a politician) manner of his, he snapped: 'There has always been active consideration of its use. It is a matter that the military people will have to decide . . . I am not a military authority that passes on these things . . . The military commander in the field will have charge of the use of weapons, as he always has . . .'

It seemed, then, as if Truman had finally realized just exactly what he was stating before an audience, who would soon spread his comments throughout the civilized world, and was attempting subterfuge at last by passing the buck to the 'military commander in the field', i.e. MacArthur. But it was too late. The fat was in the frying pan and already sizzling away merrily. Now the remaining question was: would he burn that bacon? For everyone present that fateful day in Washington knew that Truman was not only the President of the United States, but also the commander-in-chief of the US Armed Forces. In essence it was he who would make the final decision on the use of the atomic bomb and possibly start a worldwide nuclear conflict, not that vain old soldier in Tokyo.

As soon as he had taken up office in what now seemed another age, Truman had adorned his desk in the White House with a sign that is now old and trite, but which then inspired the American people in their belief that this unknown who now ruled them knew what he was about. There'd be no more 'gobbledegook', no more hesitancy, no more weasel-word politician's talk. This little man with his spectacles, cheery smile and provincial 'sharp' suits was going 'to tell it as it was'. That sign was simple, a little folksy, but unmistakeably clear about the new President's style of government. It read: 'The buck stops here!' Harry S. Truman and the ordinary good decent folk of middle-America had been proud of it. It seemed to signal an end to Roosevelt and his upper-class radicals of the 'New Deal'. Now the question was posed everywhere as November gave way to December 1950, did the President mean it? Did the proverbial 'buck' stop with him? Would he and he alone make that overwhelming decision to use or not to use the ultimate deterrent, the atom bomb?

CHAPTER TWELVE

The Big Bug-out

'*Haul ass!*' this was the order that Brig Basil Coad received at Corps Head-quarters when he drove to the American HQ to find out what the situation was. The front was collapsing everywhere. On the right flank of the Eighth Army where his Commonwealth Brigade was holding the line, the situation was not as grave as elsewhere, since here the Americans and their British allies were still fairly mobile. The Chinese were without motor transport, though they were soon going to capture plenty of it from the retreating Eighth, and couldn't keep up with the men pulling back in their vehicles.

Coad, veteran infantryman of Second World War Europe, might not have understood – or appreciated – the crude command, but he did understand the writing on the wall and, afterwards, was wont to use himself the Americanism that symbolized the whole sorry business that November: 'the 'Big Bug-out'.

Now a harassed Walker, on the verge of being sacked because of the way he had handled his army (already his supposed successor, tough airborne Gen Ridgway, was prowling around the battlefield trying to find 'what the hell's going on') was presented with an impossible task. He was to pull back his eighteen divisions (seven American, ten ROK, one Turkish and two British brigades). This meant trying to withdraw some 300,000 men of various nationalities who were roadbound, separated from each other by the hilly ranges in which radios, especially those of the 'Limeys', didn't function too well. But the tubby little Army Commander, who was losing weight, something he had never done in combat before, did his best. He was not going to allow *his* army to disintegrate as the American divisions at the commencement of the Korean War had done so disastrously.

All the same the Americans were in trouble right from the start. With the Red Chinese holding the hills, the young soldiers of the front-line outfits felt trapped. It was as if the 'Chinks' could see every move they made and this thought lent fear, even panic, to everything they did when they were ordered to hold until the time to withdraw came. They rarely did. As veteran Col Paul Freeman of the US 23rd Infantry Regiment exclaimed bitterly to his executive officer: 'Look around here. This is a sight that hasn't been seen for hundreds of years . . . The men of a whole United States Army fleeing from a battlefield, abandoning their wounded, running for their lives!'

Freeman's regiment never did. He held it together until the whole miserable débâcle was over. But in the end his regiment was the only one of the elite 2nd 'Indianhead' Infantry Division still regarded as combat worthy.

There was no denying the panic. In ten days the men of the US Eighth Army retreated 120 miles! Even the initial week of the Battle of the Bulge, exactly five years to the month before, couldn't be compared with that terrible 'Big Bug-out'. Men abandoned their weapons, their wounded comrades, their honour. Nothing was sacred. In their unreasoning panic the green young soldiers, who mostly made up the US divisions, constantly feared they would be left behind at the mercy of these 'Chink' supermen.

The North Korean capital of Pyongyang was abandoned. But before they left, the troops torched the huge supply dumps located there and much of the rest of the city. Others simply looted 'booze and butts' and hurried on. Let the Chinks have the rest. It was no use senior officers telling their frightened men that the Chinese were miles behind them. They simply weren't listening.

A tank commander of the 8th Irish Hussars, which had charged at Balaclava, recalled:

> Millions of dollars worth of valuable equipment had been destroyed (at Pyongyang) without a shot being fired or any attempt made to consider its possible evacuation. Seldom has a more demoralising picture been witnessed than the abandonment . . . of the American forward base, before the unknown threat of Chinese soldiers – as it transpired, ill-armed and on their feet or horseback.'

The British, often on foot, had the benefit of the corset of regimental tradition to stiffen their resistance. Even though most of the rank-and-file of the 1st Argylls were short-service conscripts, they carried out what the Jocks called 'The Death March'[1] in an orderly fashion. They marched back in companies, each one led by a regimental piper. Each night the men were briefed as best their officers could on what was happening and what was the plan for the next day. Young Mitchell used a map torn out of the *Daily Telegraph* for his briefings! Then feet would be inspected by the officers to see if they were all right, hot food would be served (even if it was only compo M & V stew) and position would be sited for the night.

Nightly the Argylls worked out an escape route, designated by stakes, with the sergeant-majors who might have to take charge of the men in an emergency walking the route to ensure they knew it in the darkness and under fire. That done, the fire plan for the battalion's mortars and the supporting artillery was worked out. It could be called down in a matter of seconds, if there was any threat of the retreating Jocks being cut off. Then one final order was given out as the men huddled in their blankets and tried to sleep in the bone-chilling cold of the freezing darkness: 'We shave and wash at . . . so-and-so time.' If the Jocks were going to die the next day, they'd do it in the time-honoured British Army fashion – with their boots cleaned!

Not all the British retreated. By 1 December, Gen Laurence Keiser's US 2nd Division found itself in a terrible mess. With Keiser's battered 9th

Infantry Regiment leading the way, the men of the 'Indianhead Division' found themselves trapped in a six-mile-long narrow defile. Bumper to bumper, the vehicles carrying the retreating GIs were easy meat for the Chinese who dominated the heights on both sides, pouring a merciless hail of mortar bombs on to the packed road. Officers were picked off one by one by the enemy snipers and although they tried desperately to keep control it was clear they were going to have to get out of the trap soon – or else.

Air was whistled up to help. Fighter-bombers ranged the length of the convoy, which was already beginning to burn and smoke at front and rear where the Chinese had knocked out vehicles in order to trap the Ninth. Anything catching their attention on the heights was attacked immediately. Zooming in at almost ground level, they loosed volley after volley of deadly rockets which sped to the Chinese like swarms of angry white-and-red hornets. Where the cannonfire didn't seem to do the job, napalm followed. It exploded with deadly intent, splashing the suddenly-screaming panicked 'Chinks' with its all-consuming mixture of oil and chemicals from which there was no escape. Still it was obvious that time was running out for the men of the 'Indianhead'. A desperate Gen Keiser raced up personally to take command. He knew their only salvation was to attack both sides of the pass to their front and clear the roadblock which trapped them.

'*On your feet, men! . . . Let's go! . . . move out!*' he yelled the old cries given in such make-or-break situations. No one moved. The terrified GIs continued to cower in the ditches or hugged the ground beneath their vehicles. Keiser pushed on. It was the Gen Dean situation all over again; his division was falling apart in front of his eyes. He had to do something – anything – before it was too late.

He found a single man firing a mortar. That didn't help much. He rushed on. In his haste he tripped over what he thought was a dead GI sprawled in the track. The 'corpse' sprang to its feet and yelled angrily, 'You damned son-of-a-bitch!'

All that the Major General could think to say in way of reply was: 'My friend . . . I'm sorry.'

Finally the harassed general managed to find some clerks and cooks and ROK soldiers who were prepared to fight. He directed them up the heights to slog it out with the Chinese hidden in the rocks. In the meantime, volunteers in bulldozers took their lives in their hands and, with slugs pattering against their machines like heavy tropical rain on a tin roof, managed to clear away the wreckage. The 2nd Infantry Division was moving again. But they weren't out of danger yet. A desperate Walker asked the Middlesex, who were closest to the 'Indianheads', if they could attempt to break through to the 'Yanks' and relieve the pressure.

The 'Diehards', knowing there was little hope, pushed forward all the same, glad to have the opportunity of showing what British soldiers could do. They entered the hills and started winkling the obstinate 'Chinks' from their positions. At one stage they heard that almost forgotten command

'*Fix bayonets*' . . . *at the double now . . . CHARGE!*' and they did. It would be the first time but not the last (as we shall see) that British infantry dashed forward to give the enemy 'a taste of cold steel'. But in the end all their efforts came to naught.

Still the survivors of the 2nd US Infantry Division managed to make it back, pushing through the 3rd Australian Infantry, one of whom remarked that when they did, 'their cigar butts went by like tracer bullets in the night'. But the cost had been high. Three thousand casualties – as many as George Washington's Continental Army took in the 1777 winter at Valley Forge.

But even the British, held together by excellent leadership, stern discipline line and a centuries-old tradition, were beginning to feel the strain of that constant retreat. As Colin Mitchell of the Argylls recalled: 'Our morale held because we were the Argyll and Sutherland Highlanders – though people did show signs of strain. I remember one of my Company HQ, a quiet reliable chap, who was sitting on the ground next to me about to open a tin of baked beans.' Suddenly he 'stood up and screamed. He ran wild-eyed' into the middle of a field. He ignored the sergeant-major's order to come back so Mitchell went after him, as he stood there defiantly, holding the can like a grenade. 'Don't come any nearer!', he shouted. Mitchell ignored the warning. The man threw the can, missed and then collapsed into the officer's arms. Mitchell told him he, too, felt the same sense of despair, but 'we were all in this together and just had to stick it out or go under. At this he broke down and sobbed.' Still the man allowed himself to be led back to the column to continue the march back. The Jocks were going to have no cases of 'combat exhaustion' in their battalion . . .

'Drummer' Tony Eagles of the 'Gloomies', as the Gloucester Regiment was called then before it became the 'Glorious Gloucesters', was a young soldier who, cut off with a chum, nearly panicked. For all around him there were fleeing Yanks, crying 'Get ya ass outa here – the commies are coming!' But he and the other man driving a three-ton truck didn't. Instead they soldiered on only to find at one re-fuelling stop that the retreating 'Wolfhounds', as the 2nd Infantry Division's best regiment was nicknamed, had 'nicked his rifle', and that of his comrade. They had taken the weapons as 'souvenirs'.

Now with a faulty truck, unarmed, feeling that if they ever reached the regiment they'd be court-martialled for having lost their 'personal weapon', they fled after the vanishing Yanks. Their private odyssey would remain with them for the rest of their lives. In those few crowded days while they were 'lost', they delivered a Korean woman of her baby, washing it in a nearby river; they joined a group of Korean students who showed them a concealed underwater bridge which they crossed 'Christlike, walking on the water'; and heard in the distance the blare of Chinese bugles, the burr of machine pistols and the screams as the Chinese raped the captured local women. Finally, shaken, but in one piece, they were overjoyed to report to their stern, unyielding adjutant Captain Farrar-Hockley, one day to be one of Britain's most senior generals; even though they thought they'd be court-martialled for losing their rifles. They were not. Bodies in the line were more important than one in the 'glasshouse'[2] that week.

Walker had already thrown his strongest British battalion, the 'Geordies' of the Northumberland Fusiliers, into the battle in another attempt to stop the prevailing rot. Fusilier 'Thommo' Thompson had had his first taste of action after four years as a regular soldier and still did not know whether he liked it or not. Long afterwards, he wrote that the 'gooks' had come 'running up the slope, ghostly white in the gloom, overrunning our positions, surging by, scrambling upwards . . . *to me!*'

There had been 'panic and discipline', 'John Wayne would have waited until they were on top of him and mown them down . . . but I decided there and then that no one was going to get close enough to harm the most precious thing worth fighting for – Fusilier Thompson'. Without an order and feeling himself the only British soldier in the whole of Korea, he had let rip with his Sten gun. 'I killed. We all killed. I let rip at shapes that bobbed near . . . until the gunfire and the bugles and the screams died away and we got out of our slits and cheered as the gooks streamed from the hill. Cheers, laughter, hysterical back-slapping laughter. The first taste of victory!'

Afterwards had come the counting of the cost of victory – the missing, the wounded, the dead – 'three canny lads laid out in the happy warrior position, covered in blankets. I turned my head from them, tried to weep for them, found I couldn't.' All he could feel at that moment of first victory was the need 'for revenge. I vowed I'd get ten gooks for everyone of those mothers' sons.'

That had been only days before but, to 'Thommo' the veteran, it seemed years as the Fusiliers retreated with the rest, living for the hour, being carried along all those weary miles by the knowledge that a new defensive position awaited them – or so the young infantrymen hoped – where the Chinese had to be stopped, 'otherwise all the fighting and dying would have been in vain'. But just as for so many other soldiers in this war and all wars, living life as automatons, wondering afterwards how they ever made it through, Fusilier Thompson's thoughts kept straying to the one happy spot in his whole life – 'dear old Blighty'. 'Will I ever see it again,' I thought. 'It seemed a million miles from here. Ah well. Let's get on with the war . . . QUO FATA VOCANT!'[3]

But despite the resilience of those 'canny lads' and the professionalism of their officers, the British top brass in Korea were desperately worried that December. The Koreans seemed to have turned against the Allies: when some Gloucesters asked an English-speaking Korean woman if there were anything they could do to help her and her miserable refugees, she asked in return, 'Haven't you done enough already? Just go away, all of you, and leave us with what's left of our country.' As for the Yanks, the British senior officers thought that they were not prepared to fight to the end of their strength for this 'stinking, miserable country – give it back to the frigging Gooks!'

On 5 December, Brig Coad, the senior brigadier in Korea, signalled a top secret message to the British Commander-in-Chief, Far East, Gen Sir John Harding. The battle-seasoned infantryman painted a gloomy picture – and he was a man who had been through the desperate fighting in Normandy, Arnhem and the Reichswald five years before. He was not given to despair when the going got tough. After all, in the North-west European campaign his old division had had a complete turnaround, 12,000 of them, including every frontline commanding officer. In essence, Coad felt it was now virtually impossible to just keep on working with the Americans.

Harding was 'shocked'. He informed London at once. Still he knew that he couldn't wait for the War Office to reply. He had to stamp out the 'rot' immediately. He replied to Coad's signal in the sharpest terms. He made it absolutely clear that the British must support their American allies by holding firm whatever the difficulties between the Anglo-Americans were. He wrote: 'Everyone . . must do their utmost with what they have . . . If you are given a task which, in your considered opinion, does risk your troops to an extent exceptional in war . . . you should make a formal written protest to your immediate superior commander.'

We do not know Coad's reaction. But the message was unequivocal. He'd have to soldier on with Yanks whether he liked it or not. But unknown to both soldiers, right at the very top in Britain's capital a major difference of opinion between the two chief Allies was about to burst into the open. In London, it was believed that the situation in Korea had got out of hand. MacArthur, the ageing soldier, possibly senile and living off past victories, had run the war too long. In Washington, his nominal military chiefs and even the President had allowed him to do so without criticism. Now it was obvious that MacArthur was thinking the unthinkable, thus raising the question of whether the President would supinely allow him to translate those thoughts into action. Urgent decisions were needed, soon!

There was, however, one unit of the British Armed Forces in Korea which, although under American command and fighting side by side with the Yanks, had no complaints about the 'cousins from across the sea' or the command structure. This was Lt Col Drysdale's 41 Marine Commando. The 'Green Berets', of which they were so proud, were attached to Gen Smith's 1st Marine Division, in particular to Colonel 'Chesty' Puller's 7th Marine Regiment. Here the British 'sea-soldiers', who wore the same globe-and-laurel emblem as their American counterparts, were among friends: men who subscribed to the same 'gung-ho' philosophy that they could overcome all difficulties in battle whatever the cost. As their new commander, the barrel-chested Marine veteran Puller put it: 'They've got us surrounded. The bastards won't get away this time!'

But naturally it wasn't going to be as easy as that. The Marines, part of Almond's X Corps, had been trapped in the far north for days now. Isolated and cut off from Walker's retreating Eighth Army, living on short rations in the freezing Siberian cold, Almond's 25,000 soldiers were in a parlous state. Not that that seemed to worry Almond. Even as the general order from MacArthur came through that the whole of the UN forces were going to have to pull back under Chinese pressure, Almond told his new aide, a certain Lt A. Haig (who himself would eventually achieve the highest rank in the US Army), 'The enemy who is delaying us for the moment is nothing more than the remnants of Chinese divisions fleeing north.' He turned to the shaken soldiers all around him, standing numbly and hollow-eyed in the new snow, and added 'We're still attacking and we're going all the way to Yalu. Don't let a bunch of Chink laundrymen stop you! Retake the high ground lost during the night.' They never did. Now the 1st Marine Division and its comrades of the 41 Commando, those British marines whose predecessors had fought together with the 'Leathernecks' half a century before,[4] had to fight their way out of the Chinese trap or die. Surprisingly enough in a war in which the Americans held all the command jobs, although a dozen non-American countries fought in it, Colonel Drysdale was given an American Marine company, another from the battered and demoralized US 31st Infantry Regiment and some 29 US tanks. It was now his task with this mixed force of Commandos, US Marines and soldiers, plus a handful of ROK troops – a total of 922 men, 29 tanks and 141 other vehicles – to blast his way out of the mountains, to break through the encircling Chinese and free the road ahead.

It was a tough assignment even for the commandos and the US Marines; both forces knew the honour of their countries and their corps were at stake. Almost as soon as they set off, without having had time to eat, they were attacked. Unlike other troops of Almond's X Corps, who had stuck by their vehicles in similar circumstances and let the enemy dominate the fight, the British and US Marines deployed at once. They headed up the hills, looking for the Chinese, winkling them out of their ambush positions at the point of the bayonet.

The Chinese who hitherto had underestimated the Allies' will to resist, were taken by surprise. There were casualties, both British and American. But the surprise attack paid off. Soon they were moving again. But the 'opinionated young man', as an angry Drysdale called the US tank commander, refused to distribute his Shermans down the length of the tightly-packed column. The result was that his tanks at the point burst through the next Chinese roadblock a few miles further on, leaving the soft-skinned remaining vehicles to their fate.

Marine James Stanley, a wartime spy-saboteur in the Far East, later said 'This was the worst experience of all my career. Nothing as bad as this had ever happened to me before. . . . The early North American covered-wagon stories had nothing on this.'

The Chinese blasted away at the trucks, slowing down to a crawl, at six-foot range. Men crouching behind the thin canvas hoods were riddled by machine-gun bullets. The holes jetted bright red blood. 'Even a blind Chink couldn't have missed then.' Drysdale's own jeep was hit, though no one was injured. Still their luck held out and in the end they got through the next section of that 'highway of death'.

But Drysdale, the veteran of jungle warfare, knew they weren't going to get out of this mess so easily. He was fully aware, from the flares sailing into the night sky and the slow chatter of machine-guns ahead that the Chinese were still attacking further up the hill road. He ordered his men to take a brief rest. At dawn they would assault the hills dominating the way ahead: there were supposed to be guerrillas up there.

That dawn, as Marine Stanley remembered, 'we shook the ice from our boots before we put them on and got ready. I've been to Iceland, Norway and Russia, but I've never known cold like that night.' But they attacked successfully and the convoy rolled on, though dwindling in size and number by the hour. As Stanley recalled, 'After the first two miles, it was pretty quiet. Then the Communists gave us all they'd got. They were using burp guns and machine-guns. The jeep in front of us had three drivers killed in one hour.' Then more tragedy struck. 'They hit the ammunition truck with a phosphorous bomb and set it on fire.' Another British Marine, a 22-year-old Scot named Andrew Condron (later to gain some notoriety as we shall see), was appalled to pass one of the casualties of that bomb: an American, his body burning away with the phosphorus, screaming 'for someone to shoot him'. No one did. They were too busy. For the burning truck had effectively blocked the road for the other half of the convoy.

Drysdale had to make an immediate and brutal decision. Should he stand and fight there and try to unite the convoy once again? But he remembered that 'Chesty' Puller had warned him that there was to be no stopping 'at any cost'. Those in the rear – about sixty-one British commandos, most of the Army GIs and some US Marines – would have to fend for themselves in what became known as 'Hell Fire Valley'.

Marine Condron was one of them. He tried to make a break for it on his own. Around him all was confusion. Angry flame stabbed the gloom. There were raging shouts, cries for help, curses. He fell in with two other British privates who were wading a stream. A challenge. A sudden shot. One of the unknown Britons fell face forward into the water, dead before he hit it. An American loomed up. He and his escaping buddies had fired the fatal shot. Condron rounded upon him angrily. 'You've killed my fucking mate!' he yelled. For a few moments it looked as if the two British soliders would start firing themselves at the shocked 'Yanks'. But in the end their tempers cooled and the mixed bunch of fugitives went to ground, listened to the screams, shots, cries of supplication coming from half a mile away.

Then they began to think practically. Condron took off his socks, as he had been trained to do with wet socks. He hung them on the skeletal branch of a tree nearby. They froze immediately. That didn't stop the resourceful

Marine. He put his beret on one bare foot and his camouflaged netting scarf on the other and tried to dress the wound of a US Marine shot in the hip. Suddenly he looked up. A soldier that he took for a ROK was standing there in a snowcape, carrying a tommy-gun. The gook grunted aggressively 'Bugger off!' Condron snarled and was about to bend down to his self-imposed task once more until a scared American called across to him, 'Hey, buddy, you'd better drop that rifle fast . . . We've surrendered.' The 'gook' soldier was a Red Chinese.

They were everywhere in 'Hell Fire Valley'. Their casualties in the trap had been horrific: by now they were down to forty men who could fight, and they had only eight rounds of ammo each. An American Marine Sergeant tried to buy time by bargaining with the Chinese. A wounded US major named Eagan told him sourly, 'You don't have a snowball's chance in hell.'

They didn't. The Marine noncom and the Army major watched glumly as the Chinese raided the surviving trucks, looting Christmas presents from home. Others swarmed over the holed PX truck. They littered the snowfield and road around with wrappers from Toostie Rolls, Hershey bars and Dentyne gum, chewing happily like excited schoolkids. Then they started rounding up their prisoners, including Condron, who one day would be reviled as Britain's leading traitor in Communist hands. They were heading for three years in the 'cage'. There'd be no more Hershey bars or Toostie Rolls for them for a long time – perhaps there would never be again.[5]

Still, with what he had left after the débâcle of 'Hell Fire Valley', Drysdale pushed on through nightmarish conditions. It seemed that everything of Man and Nature was conspiring against him in his desperate attempt to link up with the rest of the US Marines. At one point their luck seemed to be changing. The lead element of the fugitives, for that's really what they were by now, sighed the Seventh Marine positions some two thousand yards away. Salvation was within sight.

The Chinese, however, were not going to allow them to escape that easily, and suddenly launched yet another attack. Bugles blaring, shouting crazily, as if drugged or drunk or perhaps both, they came out of the hills once more. A sharp, bitter fire-fight started at closer range than ever, with no quarter given or expected. Drysdale, exhausted as it was, was hit by a grenade. Gamely the Commando officer tried to fight off the loss of blood and exhaustion. He couldn't. He was almost out on his feet after six days of fighting and running in Arctic weather.

US Marine Capt Carl Sitter took over. Above the confused bedlam of close-quarter fighting he barked: 'Everyone off the trucks! Face out and shoot!' The reluctant GIs obeyed the tough Marine's command. Stopped temporarily, the Chinese rallied and counter-attacked – the best part of a Chinese regiment. Sitter crawled from gun position to position, rallying, exhorting, cajoling, threatening the defenders. The Chinese infiltrated his command post and hand-to-hand fighting ensued. Bitter, cruel and animal. Sitter was wounded in the face, arm and chest.

In the meantime, Drysdale had rallied sufficiently to order his surviving thirty-two commandos to attack a hill on the left flank from which the US Marines had been driven off. Out on their feet, running low on ammo, relying more on their bayonets and entrenching tools, they staggered up the hill and recovered the lost position. Immediately the pressure was off Sitter, brave Leatherneck, tried to relax while a corpsman attempted to staunch his many wounds. (Later he would be awarded the US's highest honour, the Congressional Medal of Honor.)

Up on the recaptured hill Marine Stanley, who would be wounded himself in two days' time, stared around at the stark reality of the battlefield in the dawn light: 'I saw dozens of dead Communists from where we were . . . They must have been thousands round the defence perimeter' (i.e. that of the Drysdale force). Then he turned and looked down below as the survivors pushed forward to meet Puller's waiting US Marines.

In the lead was that cocky young US tank commander whose first thought had been his own safety and that of his seventeen tanks. All of them had survived. Now in his panicked haste, he crashed through the US Marine roadblock and smashed headlong into a jeep. Behind him came the British commandos. To the startled US defenders they looked more like a raiding party. They raised their weapons to shoot. Hastily a Commando shouted, 'Don't shoot, Yank!'

Now the survivors started to pass into the American lines. One in three of the 922 men with whom Drysdale had started out had been lost; half their vehicles, too. The wounded Colonel has fewer than a hundred of his Commandos. But they were in good heart and as Captain Peter Thomas, bringing up the rear with the last two trucks laden with wounded, exclaimed happily, 'I never thought I should be so glad to see an American.' Despite the comment, a friendship between these 'Limeys' and 'Yanks' had been bonded in blood. In due course Drysdale's 41 Commando would be awarded a rare honour for a British unit – the Presidential Unit Citation.[6]

By now, though, Anglo-American solidarity needed all the help it could get, for finally this December there took place within the top levels of the US command and at the highest political levels between the two major allies a series of showdowns which would change the whole course of the war in Korea and, in essence, save the world from potential nuclear disaster.

CHAPTER THIRTEEN

What about the Workers?

He was a bastard, a former heavyweight trade-union bully-boy and now probably the best Foreign Minister Britain would have in the second half of the twentieth century. He was the bespectacled, roly-poly 'Ernie' Bevin, who had been a government minister for nearly a decade now, right through the Second World War in Churchill's cabinet and now, since 1945, in that socialist one which was going to create a new world in 'England's green and pleasant land'.

However, although the dying Foreign Minister owed his native land very little – born out of wedlock, raised in poverty, educated solely by his own efforts – Ernie Bevin was a patriot of the old school. He had little time for his parlour-pink socialist fellow ministers who had 'found their faith' in their public schools and Oxbridge colleges. He had come to Labour as a working man, not out of dogma but out of hunger and despair. Marx's *Das Kapital* meant nothing to him. He'd probably never read a single page of it in his whole life. Besides, he hated communists anyway.

Yet as the man who would have to plead Britain's case in the international forum as far as the war in Korea was concerned, he found himself becoming increasingly isolated in the cabinet. In addition, public support for the Korean War was waning. It was remote and at the most it was affecting not more than 20,000 British servicemen and their families.

At the 1950 Labour Party Conference, Bevin (who still liked to use the working-class term 'mate' when addressing his fellows) laid it on the line: 'Do you think we like it?' he thundered in that South Country accent of his. 'Do you think after all the years of fighting we have done in the Labour movement in the hope of getting a peaceful world, that we like having to do it?' (He was referring to Britain's part in the Korean War.) 'Is there any minister who likes to go down to the House of Commons to ask for £3,600 million for war? . . . We blamed the Conservatives for knowing Hitler was on the move and not making adequate preparations . . . *We* are in office now and shall we refuse to do what we called upon others to do which would have prevented the 1939 war if they had only done it?'

Bevin, sick and worn, was received by luke-warm token applause. He didn't even get a vote of thanks.

Still, Truman's declaration at the Washington press conference on 30 November, that the nuclear option was being considered, forced his chief's hand. It was decided that Prime Minister Attlee and his military advisers would go to Washington to discuss the matter with Truman and his advisers in person. Britain was now only a minor power, yet she was America's most powerful ally against communism. Truman agreed to the meeting and thus they met in the first week of December 1950 while in Korea the war continued to rage and the Allies retreated and then retreated again.

There were points of discussion enough – and many of those points made the American participants realize, perhaps the first time, the implications of having allowed MacArthur his head. For it was becoming ever clearer to both parties before the sessions had hardly got under way that the Americans were heading for disaster if they continued to follow their present course.

That veteran soldier, the one-time commander of Britain's 'Forgotten Army' in Burma, Field Marshal Slim (whose own son was currently serving with the infantry in Korea), for instance, asked whether, if UN declared a limited war against China after that country's aggression in Korea, the Russians might come in. Truman said they might. Slim's reaction was to moan, 'if that's the case, we can say goodbye'.

At a dinner at the British Embassy on 7 December, significantly enough the ninth anniversary of Japan's surprise attack at Pearl Harbor, the two positions were made clear. Acheson stated that it was doubtful if any government 'had any control over General MacArthur'; Marshall, the wartime chief of the US Army, snapped that wars cannot be 'run by committees'. The points seemed disparate, but they weren't: it meant that the Americans knew they'd have to get rid of 'Dug-out Doug', but that *they* were going to fire him, *not* a group of Allies.

Still the British stuck to their viewpoint. They wanted to have a substantial say in the conduct of the war. They didn't want it to involve a 'limited one' with China, which might escalate into a nuclear conflict. Most of all they didn't want the Americans to become bogged down in the Far East; the security and future of Europe were more important to them. All the same they knew they *had* to support the Americans in Korea. If they didn't, the Americans might feel a sense of betrayal and concentrate on the Far East altogether.

Truman and his advisers understood the British motives and felt they were one-sided and shoddy. Still they agreed to consult the British and their other UN allies before they took any more major steps. But at the same time Truman didn't reveal to his British opposite number the extent of the US's nuclear planning. He had told his advisers that he would 'work in step with the British . . . but will agree nothing that will restrict . . . [our] freedom of action'.

Thus it was that Attlee and his advisers returned to London unaware that US army commanders in the field had been warned that 'the general situation in Korea has greatly increased the possibility of general war'; and that the US Army Plans and Operations Division had already recommended that the military should ensure they were ready to make 'prompt use of the atomic bomb . . .'

The writing was on the wall. The United States was coming ever closer to that terrible, overwhelming decision; and a nation which had never suffered mass bombing – as had most of Europe and Asia – was actually *clamouring* for 'Harry' to use the bomb. The situation couldn't be worse.

Bradley and Collins, still in awe of MacArthur, were in the meantime concerned with more immediate decisions. They were essentially about dealing with the US Eighth Army, still retreating, and with its commander 'Bulldog' Walker. In mid-December they knew that the time for a decision on this had come. Should they order Walker to pull out of Korea altogether, to evacuate his hard-pressed men through Pusan in a kind of second Dunkirk?

Both Bradley and Collins came to the conclusion that they couldn't risk such an operation as the British had carried out – successfully – a decade before. As Bradley stated: 'A withdrawal could turn into a frantic desperate affair in which we had to leave masses of equipment behind, all of which would fall into the hands of the Chinese armies . . .' and further that 'if the Chinese decided to commit air power, the evacuation might turn into a disastrous and bloody operation costing tens of thousands of lives'.[1]

So the Eighth Army would stay and slog it out, the top brass decided. Besides, Bradley and Collins felt that retaining a 'foothold' in Korea would mean that Japan would be saved for a future Chinese attack. (Already the US military were secretly considering re-arming their bitterly hated enemy of five years before, the 'Nips'.)

But what about Walker? Ridgway, the airborne commander, who was in the running as the leading contender for the command of the battered Eighth, was more concerned about MacArthur than about his subordinate Walker. For the tough Second World War soldier, who had learned to jump when in his early forties and who was known to his troops as 'Iron Tits' because of his habit of carrying a grenade pinned to chest equipment on one side of his uniform and a field dressing on the other,[2] felt that MacArthur was the real root of the Eighth Army's problems.

Matt Ridgway, craggy-faced, tough and highly experienced, thought that the US Joint Chiefs-of-Staff had been too soft with MacArthur; that they held the old man in 'almost superstitious awe'. In Ridgway's opinion he (MacArthur) was 'a larger-than-life military figure who had so often been right when everyone else had been wrong'. Ridgway maintained that 'Too much blame cannot be attached to his superiors and his colleagues who, after the blazing success at Inchon, hesitated to question MacArthur's military judgment or even the hazardous disposition of his forces.'

As it grew ever closer to a bleak Christmas, with Truman declaring a state of national emergency on 17 December, Ridgway for one thought the time had come to question the judgement of the old man in Tokyo. But how? The answer was clear to an ambitious Ridgway, but for the time being he restrained himself. He would go to Korea once more. As Deputy Chief-of-Staff he could be spared from Washington. He would see how Walker's

Army was making out. (He had been ordered to concentrate his fleeing troops now in the old Pusan beachhead area.) As for Walker, Ridgway already knew officially from Collins *and* MacArthur that he would replace the little pouter pigeon of a man if he became a casualty. When that would be, however, was anybody's guess. In the event, the problem was solved by a *deus ex machina*. Matt Ridgway would become Eighth Army commander sooner than he anticipated, and with MacArthur's support: 'Do what you think is best. Use your own judgment. I will support you. You have my complete confidence.' That 'complete confidence' in the airborne general would vanish rapidly four months later when it was MacArthur's turn to be replaced by the ambitious younger man, as will be seen later. Meanwhile the 'big bug-out' continued.

At the front, if it could still be called a front, conditions were horrific. Even the veterans of Arctic warfare and those who had fought through the Battle of the Bulge in the worst winter in Europe for a quarter of a century had never encountered anything like it. If you were wounded, even slightly, your only chance of survival was a speedy evacuation to one of the seven MASH centres by one of the new-fangled 'choppers' – and helicopters weren't equipped to fly in snowstorms.

The result was that the wounded, if they could be recovered, were stacked up like piles of logs outside the unheated medical tents, where operations were done on tables balanced on saw-horses. At 30 degrees below zero, blood froze on the wounds and stopped the bleeding. That was fortunate, save for one thing; a man out in the open in those temperatures could suffer frostbite after a mere couple of hours. Medics kept plasma under their armpits to keep it fluid. Morphine ampoules were placed in mouths. Under such conditions, care was crude in the extreme. Medics couldn't tie bandages with gloves on so they worked without. But after a few moments their fingers became numb and useless so they dipped them in their patients' blood to keep them warm! There were so many frostbite cases that they weren't considered battlefield injuries; they afflicted both the wounded and the unwounded. As Marine surgeon Captain Hering stated: 'The only way you could tell the dead from the living was whether their eyes moved. They were all frozen stiff as boards.'

The men who were still 'fighting' moved like very old men: not because they were weighted down with all the clothing they could find, but on account of that terrible mind-numbing cold. Colonel Davis of the US Marines recalls just how difficult it was to give orders to his men and remember himself what the orders had been, with them all in such a daze. 'I'd get up [to give orders], say a few words and by the time I'd ended, I'd forgotten what it was I was trying to do. Everybody had to repeat back to you two or three times to be sure of what was supposed to be happening.'

Naturally the US Army had still not provided Arctic greases and oils for the men's weapons, even after its experiences in the Ardennes. The men had to make do the best they could. Marines used a hair oil called 'Wild Root Cream Oil' on the moving parts of their rifles and BARs[3] to keep the action moving. When they didn't possess the highly perfumed 'city slicker' hair pomade, they resorted to the time-honoured method of ripping open their rifles and urinating over the breech of their weapons. When tank fuel froze up, the tankers took the risk of lighting fires beneath their tanks to start them up or ran burning strips of the Army newspaper *Stars and Stripes* along the fuel lines to thin the turgid oil. Every action, even the simplest, seemed to take infinite time-consuming energy. Even to light a cigarette with the soldier's standard Zippo lighter in the Siberian wind became a major operation.

But still they fought – and retreated – 'We're not retreating,' General Smith of Marine Division insisted with typical gung-ho panache, 'We're merely attacking in another direction' – and fought again. A former Marine himself and now a photographer with *Life* magazine, David Douglas came across another Marine picking frozen beans out of a C-ration can. 'If I were God and could give you anything you wanted, what would you ask for?' Douglas asked. Momentarily, the hollow-eyed, unshaven Marine looked at the civilian and said in a husky voice, 'Gimme tomorrow' and then went back to his ration can.

'*Gimme tomorrow*' – that seemed to sum up the attitude of most of the men that December. If they believed in the great cause, the fight against communism, they didn't mention it. They simply wanted to survive to see another day, however grim that morrow might be. But slowly their odyssey was coming to an end. The steam seemed to be running out of the Chinese attack, which up to now had been relentless. Perhaps it was the Allied air forces which slowed the enemy down. For the arctic weather with its clear blue hard winter skies did allow the Allied fighter-bombers to range far and wide to strafe enemy concentrations wherever they were found. Even the Chinese, masters of camouflage as they were, could do little to hide in those barren white-coated hills against which everything stood out in stark contrast.

The Chinese, however, soon learned the danger from the air, just as the Vietcong would fifteen years later. They realized that their trucks couldn't move by day because drivers wouldn't be able to hear the approach noise of attacking enemy aircraft. Somehow or other they never learned the trick of having an 'air sentry' with his head poked out of the roof of the cab as had been done by British and Germans during the Second World War. It was the same with the mass movement of troops, which had to be completed by first light; and wherever possible the tell-tale marks left by the troop movement had at the same time to be cleared away by brooms.

By the time the Chinese advance had passed into the south, the Chinese commanders had instituted a crude but fairly effective system of air-raid precautions. Sentries were posted every two hundred metres or so along the Chinese supply route. As soon as these lookouts saw a dark spot on the horizon which could only be an enemy aircraft, they fired a shot, blew a whistle or whirled a rattle for the men and vehicles on the road to disperse at once. The British had done it all before in their native country and the Western Desert back in the early 1940s.

Still, despite all the precautions, logistics became one of the Chinese High Command's major problems throughout the great bug-out, especially when they started to use the coastal routes as the beaten Eighth US Army retreated toward the port of Pusan. Here the really obsolete planes carried by the four British carriers – the *Triumph*, *Theseus*, *Glory* and *Ocean* – joined in, with the vintage wartime Seafires and Fireflies (which had been used on the wartime Arctic convoys to help the now arch-enemy Russia) winging their way down to attack at a steady 300 mph, till replaced by the new Sea Furies.

They made up to sixty sorties a day to help the 'Yanks'. During those terrible first three weeks of December 1950 they flew 650 attacks, destroying 32 railway bridges, eight tunnels, 30 boxcars, etc. (Later the Sea Furies would successfully tackle the brand new MIG jets used by the Chinese.) The cost in human life was fifty pilots and observers killed. Not many on the surface of it, but in such a small force it was too many 'going for a Burton', as the Fleet Air Arm termed death in action in a typical understated British manner.

Still, despite Allied air supremacy and the fact that they themselves were experiencing severe logistical problems (back in China housewives were being urged to fry flour for the troops' rations!), the Red Chinese kept up their relentless pursuit of Walker's beaten Eighth Army. The British managed to keep their battalions intact and effective, but even that proud soldier Colin Mitchell of the Argylls, whose First Battalion had the lowest frostbite rate of the whole army (three casualties) due to excellent man-management, had to admit they were leading an 'animal existence', with men downing a bottle of whisky sometimes between just two of them 'in less than ten minutes'.

It seems, though, that the Americans were falling apart. This fact was a great help to the Chinese with their tremendous logistics problem: they lived off abandoned US rations and used captured US weapons. As one of their leaders told British writer Max Hastings long after the war: 'We quickly got used to American biscuits and rice . . . We were particularly glad to get carbines because we found rifles so heavy to carry.' The same informant added, 'Without the American sleeping bags and overcoats that we captured, I am not sure we could have gone on. Two thirds of our casualties were from cold . . .'

Most of the British involved in the retreat never saw the Americans. To them, the Yanks were still the boastful, generous, gum-chewing GIs of the Second World War.[4] The only British to have any real contact with their allies were their senior officers and, as Coad had found out, they were ordered to keep their mouths shut about the shortcomings of their allies and 'get on with it'.

All the same, the British top brass were worried about the resolution of the American rank-and-file in battle and their officers' ability to direct them correctly. All the British generals agreed that the Marines couldn't be faulted, nor could the American gunners who fired most of the artillery support missions for the British brigades – they were 'better than the US infantry'.

Trained senior officers sent out from London on Far Eastern Command were dismayed by what they saw of the US Army in Korea. (In a couple of weeks' time, its new commander Ridgway would experience the same kind of shock.) Veteran British Gen Leslie Mansergh, who had seen tough fighting in the Far East as an infantry commander, reported: 'I doubt whether any British really think that the war in Korea will be brought to a successful conclusion. The reason for this is primarily because of the lack of American determination and their inability to stand and fight . . . I would judge that American morale is low and in some units thoroughly bad.' In essence, the British general thought the trouble was caused by three things: the Americans didn't want to be in Korea in the first place; they had lost most of their regular officers; and in an Army which had always emphasized attack *à la* Patton, they had never been taught to defend.[5]

Brig Coad, who was on the spot and had had more experience of American officers than most, in particular of the hated commander of the US 24th Infantry Division, felt that it was the Army's senior field officers who had let it down: 'Since the withdrawals started,' he reported in a secret signal (which, naturally, in due course the Russians – and the Chinese – read) 'the behaviour of some senior staff officers and Formation HQs was, at times, quite hysterical and resulted in impossible orders which, if obeyed without question, would have resulted in unnecessary loss of life . . .' He concluded that the men of the British brigade under his command felt a sense of 'contempt' for their fellow American infantry.

Another observer reported to the British War Office on 27 December 1950 that the average GI wanted to get out of Korea as soon as possible. He felt Truman should stop consulting the other allies and drop the atomic bomb straight off – on Moscow! The unknown observer had little time for the US Army and he maintained that the US Marines experienced the same feeling.

> Offensive thinking among junior officers and men was confined almost entirely to the Marines . . . [It] was accompanied by a distrust and contempt for higher leadership, almost more frightening than the lack of fibre of their army compatriots. There can be few occasions in history when officers and men of a fighting force have expressed themselves so freely and violently in public on the subject of their commanding officers.

No doubt these observations stemmed from a member of the somewhat superior and supercilious British professional-officer caste, the sort who had been fighting what they must have regarded as 'colonial wars' for centuries and with forces used to fighting against mass native armies outnumbering their own by many times. But they had always been better-trained and – naturally – better officered, with rank-and-file being mostly hard-bitten professionals, the traditional 'old sweats' of the British Regular Army who had always felt themselves superior to the 'darkies', 'fuzzy-wuzzies', 'wogs' and all the rest of those inferior beings.

The Americans were different, even the regulars. In the twentieth century they had fought only large-scale wars against 'civilized' nations. They weren't used to assaults by hordes upon hordes of 'natives' in the wilder parts of the globe. As one typical PFC wrote to his folks in the Bronx at the end of that unhappy year:

> The Chinese are kicking the hell out of the US Army . . . It's impossible to stop these Chinese hordes . . . The troops over here are mad, mad at America, Americans and American leadership. If we must fight communism, let's do it in Europe . . . It seems to me that's more worth fighting for than some barren oriental wasteland, with uncountable hordes of savage warriors.

Three years later, by the time the shooting war finally ended, the successors of that unhappy Private First Class would still be fighting those 'hordes of savage warriors' in that 'barren oriental wasteland'. But they would be doing so (perhaps reluctantly, it must be admitted) successfully and professionally. They would have saved Europe as well as Asia, too. But they didn't know that; for in that dark December of 1950, the hard-pressed leaders of the United States were damnably close to dropping that atom bomb which might well have started an all-out nuclear war. In the exact middle of our terrible war-torn century, the fate of the world was to be decided.

CHAPTER FOURTEEN

'Iron Tits'

On the morning of Sunday 9 December 1945, General Patton and his friend and former staff officer Gen Gay set off, with Patton's driver taking them in the direction of Mannheim, Germany to do some pheasant shooting. The morning was crisp and bright and his shoot promised to be good. For nearly six months now the beaten Germans had been forbidden to hold hunting rifles on the pain of death. The result was that there was plenty of game.

Still, 'Ole Blood an' Guts' Patton was in a disgruntled mood. Three months before, Eisenhower had taken his beloved Third Army away from him and he felt himself surrounded by 'a bunch of sons-of-bitches'. At sixty he felt he had no future in the US Army in which he had served since his teenage days at West Point. He was right. There wasn't. But not in the way Patton had visualized. Just outside a barracks on the edge of the shattered city of Mannheim, an Army truck driver turned without a signal. Patton's driver, distracted for a moment by a ruined tank, hit the truck, damaged the car's fender – and broke Patton's spinal cord. For eleven days, Patton lingered at the US hospital in Heidelberg before he passed away in his sleep – 'What a goddam way to die for a soldier!'

On Sunday 23 December, a special train set off from Heidelberg bearing Patton's body to its last resting place in the US Army cemetery at Hamm, Luxembourg. (No American soldier killed in the war was buried in Germany; remains of the 'glorious dead' were to rest in the former Allied countries such as the little Principality.) Neither Eisenhower nor Bradley, his former comrades and superiors who owed Patton so much, attended the funeral. They were back in the States, and that was a convenient excuse. One who did attend was his former Corps Commander 'Bulldog' Walker who, at his own expense, had flown to Europe for the solemn ceremony. Now, due to the foggy winter weather over the countries where he and Patton had once fought, he was forced to follow in a light plane the slow train carrying Patton's body. It was a final act of devotion to the man he had tried so often to ape – or so Walker had thought.

But he had been wrong. By an amazing act of coincidence five years later, Walton Walker, who like his former master felt himself in the 'doghouse' in December 1950, would now suffer an almost identical fate. A broken man, knowing that he had lost the confidence of his superiors on account of the way he had handled his Eighth Army and that he was scheduled to be relieved soon, just as Patton had been, Walker set out to do two things on the morning of 23 December. He would award the Silver Star to his son for bravery in action; then he would drive to the HQ of 27th Commonwealth Brigade to pass on a Korean Presidential Unit Citation Award.

He never got there. Unexpectedly a ROK truck turned across the road in front of his jeep. Just as Patton's driver had done, Walker's tried to save the strutting little general. To no avail. He was thrown out of the little vehicle and suffered head injuries from which he would later die in hospital. (Syngman Rhee, the Korean President, wanted to have the unfortunate ROK driver who had caused the accident to be executed there and then, but the worried Americans hastily stayed his hand.) Just as in the case of Patton's death, which had come at an opportune time for the top brass (for Patton had been threatening that December in 1945 'to spill the beans'), rumour and counter-rumour about Walker's death flew thick and fast. The American authorities wanted no more problems than there already were. There were no recriminations. Official comment about his past performance as the commander of the ill-fated Eighth US Army were hushed up. The fact that that December his staff officers had openly talked of evacuating their army to Japan was forgotten. The brave but not too bright little General was buried with due military honours – and promptly forgotten. In his place at the head of the Eighth Army, there would be another equally tough and brave general, who would – unlike Bulldog Walker – carve a sizeable niche in military history.

Gen Ridgway was sipping a highball at a dinner party given by Army Chief-of-Staff Joseph Collins, a fellow former corps commander in the 'old war', when the news came. It struck him 'with the suddenness of a rifle shot'. Walker was dead and he was to fly to Korea immediately and take over the battered and demoralized Eighth Army. He stayed on a few minutes more and then he was off, hoping that no one had noticed his sudden departure and concluded that something important was happening in Korea. For Ridgway, although capable, was a suspicious man. In addition he had acquired that airborne habit of never quite trusting the 'straight-legs' as they called non-airborne soldiers somewhat contemptuously.

Christmas was looming up fast, but there was no time for the festival of 'sweetness and light and goodwill to all men'. A brother officer was delegated to select and deliver a Christmas present for his long-suffering wife. Twenty-four hours later, on Christmas Day 1950, he was facing the august presence of General MacArthur, a man that Ridgway thought should have been relieved weeks before, in the former's Tokyo HQ.

MacArthur, whom Ridgway had known since his days with him at West Point, was his usual dramatic self with the 'great actor's instinct' for gesture and physical presence. Still, Ridgway thought his briefing was down-to-earth, fluent and lucid. All the same, MacArthur wanted a victory in Korea, not on account of his own prestige apparently, but because it 'will strength our diplomacy.' Ridgway didn't quibble, though he knew the state of the US Army in Korea and that MacArthur didn't want to retire on a defeat but a victory.

But as vain and as self-centred as the old man was – he had been like that ever since Ridgway had first met him as a young instructor at the Academy – he did seem to be giving him carte blanche in Korea. When Ridgway asked: 'If I find the situation to my liking would you object to my attacking?' MacArthur replied: 'The Eighth Army is yours, Matt. Do what you think best?'

With that, Ridgway set off on a freezing winter's day, minus his red flannel longjohns (he'd forgotten to pack them in Washington), to meet his new command. It was not a very encouraging encounter. 'Every command post I visited,' he wrote later, 'gave me the same sense of lost confidence and lack of spirit. The leaders, from sergeant on up, seemed unresponsive, reluctant to answer my questions. Even their gripes had to be dragged out of them and information was provided glumly, without the alertness of men whose spirits were high.'

Ridgway held no brief for the British. He had had several run-ins with the British brass during the Second World War, in particular with Montgomery in the Ardennes, yet he had to admit 'I could not help contrasting their attitudes to that of a young British subaltern who had trotted down off a knoll to greet me and identified himself as to name, rank and unit.'

Ridgway knew that the British were holding a large sector of the front line with a Chinese attack on their positions expected almost hourly. So he asked how the young officer found the touchy, even dangerous situation in his sector. 'Quite all right, sir,' he swiftly answered the three-star general with the craggy, hook-nosed face. Then he added with a warm smile, 'But it *is* a bit draughty up here.'

'Draughty' it was. Now Ridgway realized that there would be no immediate attack with his new command. The Eighth Army was thoroughly demoralized save for certain units and there were 'gaps in the line wide enough to march an army through', even in small-size company fronts. His first priorities, he realized as he toured his new command extensively in that supposed 'festive' season (the men at least got a chunk of tinned turkey, often cold, as a treat) were to stabilize the line; inspire the Army's leaders to do battle with the enemy; and not let themselves be roadbound as they had been so far, with disastrous results for American arms in particular.

Ridgway, a leader and a driver, kept reminding his hidebound commanders, who at West Point had never been taught defence or the real task of footsoldiers, that their men had go to into the hills if necessary and engage the enemy up there. Then they'd beat them at their own game. Time and time again at one command post after another, he would snap at his subordinate generals and colonels that ancient Army adage: 'FIND 'EM! . . . FIX 'EM! . . . FIGHT 'EM! . . .FINISH 'EM!'

Twenty to five on the morning of 31 December 1950. At the other side of the world in London, they would already be celebrating New Year's Eve. In the pubs and clubs, they'd be drunk, festooned with streamers, wearing funny paper hats, waiting for the first boom of Big Ben heralding the start of 1951. In New York, those who were prepared to stand the bone-chilling cold were thronging Times Square, trying to avoid the pick-pockets and the perverts, hoping for better times ahead. In Germany, where the 'Economic Miracle' was already under way – thanks to the surge of business due to the Korean War – they were already drunk, letting off the traditional fireworks and preparing for the equally traditional *Bleigiessen*.[1] It was no different in Japan. That one-time enemy country also knew the bad times were over. The war had turned the hated 'Nips' into our 'Japanese friends'. Everywhere the Western World seemed to be celebrating the approach of the second half of the twentieth century, but not in Korea.

There the soldiers of the Eighth Army waited and waited in tense and miserable expectation, for Intelligence had already warned their commanders that the Chinese were massing. Normally a warning of that kind would have pleased a commander in a well-prepared defensive position: conventional military wisdom taught that attackers usually lost three men for every defender who became a casualty. But that didn't apply on the Allied front for, as Ridgway had noted, there were too many gaps between individual units and even within those units themselves. In essence, the Eighth Army was defending a too-long front with troops who had been beaten time and again since the previous October and now expected to be defeated once more.

Opposite them the Chinese gathered silently. Their leaders had already stated that 'the Imperialists will run like sheep. Our problem is not Seoul. It is Pusan. Not *taking* it – just *walking* there.' Their enemy had taken enormous casualties, but the Chinese knew that they themselves had too. However, they felt they had the measure of the 'Imperialists': both sides were weak, but the Red Chinese Army had the supreme advantage of morale. The 'Imperialists' *expected* to lose and so they would, mainly because of that.

It was now almost time. The Chinese assault infantry which had slopped warmed-up lard on their feet and legs to keep out the biting cold, started to wade the frozen or icy Imjin River. Now the only sound was the harsh gasp of their breath, as they felt that awesome cold. Wave after wave of them. Here and there their fixed bayonets gleamed silver in the light. But as yet the enemy sentries huddled in their greatcoats and parkas hadn't heard whatever noise they made.

Behind them their gunners tensed behind the long lines of artillery. For the first time, the Chinese were going to use a mass bombardment, Soviet-style, for the attack, once the first assault waves were in position. All along a forty-mile front the brown-clad wave rolled closer and closer to the enemy line, held by three American divisions, the British 29th Brigade, two ROK divisions and a brigade-strength group of Greeks and Filippinos. On and on. Behind the advancing infantry, the artillery commanders kept throwing anxious glances at the green-glowing dials of their looted watches. The minutes were ticking away rapidly. Behind them the gun-layers fidgeted behind their pieces. On the other side of the artillery pieces, the loaders prepared to spring into action once the breech ejected the first smoking empty shell case. It wouldn't be long now.

Zero Hour!

Flares sailed into the night sky everywhere. The bugles sounded the call to attack. Whistles shrilled. NCOs gave hoarse angry cries. Officers raised their Soviet automatics above their heads. 'ATTACK!' they bellowed as, to the rear, the massed guns opened up with a massive ear-splitting roar. In an instant, as if the door of a gigantic blast furnace were being flung open, the whole horizon was aflame. The great final Chinese offensive had begun.

Back of the Allied line, as the very earth trembled and shivered like a suddenly live thing, the first reports started to flood in. Each was more alarming than the one before. Telephones jingled. Teleprinters clacked out their messages of defeat and doom. Harassed sweating staff officers strode back and forth, trying to make some sense of it all, restore some order. But they were out of luck. The ROK soldiers, the first to be hit, were already scrambling out of their 'hooches', as the Americans called them, running to their rear, throwing away their rifles and helmets in their unreasoning panic. Angry shouting officers tried to stop them, arms outstretched like kids in a playground trying to catch their fellows in some kind of lethal game of tag. But there was no stopping the fugitives. They brushed the importuning hands to one side. Even threats of immediate execution couldn't stop them, as they brushed by their officers, their slant dark eyes wide and wild with fright. The Chinese were coming. It was every man for himself!

Ridgway reacted at once. He ordered a cohesive orderly withdrawal. To no avail. The ROKs and their comrades of the Allied armies were beyond reason. As Ridgway himself described what happened that last day of the old year:

> I'd never had such an experience before and I pray God I never witness such a spectacle again. They were coming down the road in trucks, the men standing, packed so close together in those big carriers that another small boy could not have found space among them. They had abandoned their heavy artillery – all their crew-served weapons. Only a few had kept their rifles. Their only thought was to get away, to put miles between them and the fearful enemy that was at their heels.

Ridgway, who had stopped a riot like this once before, albeit on a much lesser scale, hastily posted MPs who were to set up roadblocks and stop the ROKs' mindless, panic-stricken flight. But it was no use. Even firing above their heads and threatening to shoot their officers if they didn't turn and fight didn't work. As Ridgway noted ruefully: 'I might as well have tried to stop the flow of the Han [River] . . . We were obviously a long way from building the will to fight that we needed.'

The 'Geordies' of the Northumberland Fusiliers of Brodie's Brigade did at least try. 'Thommo', now acting corporal (unpaid) and section leader, was trying to warm himself and ward off what his mates called the 'Korean lazy wind' (instead of going round you, it was so lazy that it went right through you) when the call came.

It was dawn and further up their valley, known ironically as 'Happy Valley', he could hear the rattle of musketry – obviously their forward companies were engaged in a major fire-fight. Indeed they were, and they were also cut off. Now, Thommo's company commander told them urgently, as the noise of battle grew ever louder, they of 'W' Company were to fight their way forward to the rescue. In fact, he said, not pulling his punches, they were going to make a counter-attack against the 'Chink' hordes, supported by exactly *two* tanks of the 8th Irish Hussars.

Thommo couldn't remember later what the men's reaction was to that 'massive' support of two tanks, but he could guess. Still, their mates of the 'Fighting Fifth' were cut off and they had to do something. So they set off at the double until they came to a burning hamlet of miserable straw-roofed huts. The tanks halted, and the gunners of the Irish Hussars pumped a couple of rounds at the place – just in case. The tank commanders had guessed right: as the 20-pounder high explosive shells exploded, sending gleaming shrapnel scything through the air, scores of enemy soldiers broke cover. They scurried away like ants whose nest had been disturbed. But the Geordies' company commander wasn't taking any chances. He shrilled a blast on his whistle. '*Fix bayonets!*' he yelled above the racket.

Thommo gulped. 'There's nothing like a bayonet to galvanize the mind! Bayonets meant hand-to-hand fighting!'

'*CHARGE!*' the company commander bellowed.

Like automatons the young soldiers, most of them teenage conscripts, moved forward, firing single shots from the hip as they did so. All of them remembered their training. They had to save a last round to blast away the flesh of some unfortunate if their bayonet stuck in his guts.

Thommo saw his first prisoner advancing towards him – 'a little bloke with his hands aloft'. He jerked his rifle to the rear and hoped 'the bloody remainder was to do the same'.

That wasn't to be, for as the long ragged line of men in khaki continued to advance up the hill, the Chinese defence began to harden and their snipers took up the challenge. Thommo knew that Chinese snipers were hand-picked and masters of camouflage. He began to pray. They started to take casualties; his officer was hit – a piece of shrapnel from a mortar bomb had struck him in the foot. The officer went down on one knee, blood spurting in a bright red arc from his boot laces. As the stretcher-bearers doubled up, red-faced and panting, he gave a last wave to his platoon and shouted a little weakly now to Thommo: 'Take command!' With alacrity he did so. He felt 'awfully proud' of his little command. 'They were putting up a tremendous fight and were now definitely in control of the situation.'

Suddenly he received 'an awful blow' to the back of his head and he blacked out immediately; how long he was 'out', he never knew. When he came to, he felt something warm trickling down his neck. 'Christ Almighty,' he told himself, '*blood*!' Already he could visualize the telegram from the War Office being delivered to 'my poor old mum'. Next moment he felt a great sense of elation and relief as he discovered that the 'blood' was melting ice and mud from the back of his helmet. The mortar bomb which had exploded close by had merely knocked him out.

Now men in khaki started to filter back through their position. The relief was only too obvious on their tired worn faces. Suddenly three figures burst from one of the burning village huts and started running to the Geordies' positions in 'a strange, stooped way'. The young soldiers squinted down their sights. 'More of the buggers!' they yelled and prepared to fire. Abruptly the leading man began to shout – in English! Thommo, as dizzy and as exhausted as he was, caught on immediately; 'Don't shoot!' he warned urgently, 'They're prisoners.'

And so they were: men of the 170th Battery, 45th Field Artillery who had been captured earlier on. The Chinese had tied their hands behind them as they usually did with Allied prisoners they would soon shoot, but these three gunners had struck lucky when the Geordies had arrived on the scene before they could do so; the gunners lived to fight another day.

Thommo nearly didn't – for a second time. He was sorting things out before his section moved back, stepping over 'dead' Chinese sprawled out in the grotesque unreal postures of those violently done to death, when his mate, ex-wartime paratrooper Ted Shorthouse, shouted, '*Look out!*' The acting section-leader reacted instinctively. He swung round and pressed the trigger of his cheap unreliable Sten gun in one and the same movement. This time there was no stoppage.[2] He could see the burst 'rip through' the supposed dead soldier's thick uniform. The 'dead man' went limp, this time for good.

'Once again "the Fighting Fifth" had done their bit,' Thompson wrote long afterwards. 'For a little while at least, they could rest on their laurels, bury their dead, tend their wounded.' But it wasn't over yet, by a long chalk. It wouldn't be the last time in Korea that the Geordies would hear that alarming if exhilarating command: '*Fusiliers bayonet – Charge!*'

Seoul was again threatened. Ridgway would have liked to save it as a prestige object, but that wasn't to be. As always with the Allies, little thought was given to the Korean whose country this was and who would be left behind to the mercy of the Chinese, who despised Koreans as much as the Japanese had done.[3] Ridgway decided the place didn't have much military value, and that it would be better to defend the high ground to the south of the capital. Hastily he and the rest of the Americans in the capital's one surviving hotel packed and prepared to 'but out', just as the Eighth Army was doing.

Veteran war correspondent Hal Boyle of AP, who had been instrumental in reporting from Belgium the 'Malmédy Massacre' of December 1944 and who was a hardened old hand, found an abandoned baby on the steps of the capital's city hall. He told his fellow correspondents, the child's plight wringing his heartstrings, 'We can't just leave him here.' So he bundled him up in a heavy quilt and took him to the Chosun Hotel for a night of warmth and food. But that was it.

Ridgway, for his part, left behind a pair of ripped pyjamas with a message that read: 'To the Commanding General, Chinese Communist Forces, with the compliments of the Commanding General, Eighth Army.' It was a nice professional humorous gesture, typical of military men who fight each other, using the same basic knowledge, founded on the same histories and textbooks: one with no hostility or rancour. But at that moment it was out of place. The professional soldiers of both sides were making the innocent civilians, whose country they fought over, pay a terrible price for that 'honour' in blood and sorrow.

On 5 January 1951 Seoul fell. The capital had changed hands for the third time in less than six months. Again the retreating troops torched the place. Bewildered citizens and the peasants from the outlying countryside whom they had sheltered fled yet again. In their hundreds, thousands, perhaps even hundreds of thousands, they trudged south once more, carrying their pathetic bits and pieces in bundles on their heads or in rickety two-wheeled carts. Men, women, children, sick and well, pregnant mothers due soon to give birth, old women about to die – the whole pathetic horror of a totally bewildered civilian population fleeing to God knew where.

Later Ridgway wrote:

[What was] being enacted was one of the greatest tragedies of our time. In a zero wind that seared the face like a blowtorch, hundreds of thousands of Koreans were running, stumbling, falling, as they fled across the ice . . . [they] prodded oxen, piled high with goods and little children . . . Now and then an ox would go down, all four legs asprawl, and the river of humanity would break through and flow around him, for in this flight no man stopped and helped his neighbor . . . Without a sound, except the dry whisper of their slippers on the snow and the deep pant of their hard-drawn breath, they moved in utter silence . . .

Now the Eighth Army was retreating southwards at twenty miles a day. Town after town, for which much Allied blood had been spent in MacArthur's triumph march northwards when he was about to 'put an end to the war', was lost. Ridgway desperately tried to kindle the fighting spirit of his disheartened troops. As he cabled Washington: 'My one overriding problem, dominating all others, is to achieve the spiritual awakening of the latent capabilities of this command.' It was official gobbledegook and Ridgway knew it. What he really meant was: '*I want the bastards to fight!*'[4]

MacArthur, becoming increasingly isolated in his Tokyo ivory tower, suggested to Washington in his turn that the war should be extended to China to save Korea. What *he* meant was: 'use the bomb!'

At the end of those terrible first six weeks of the new year the Eighth Army had retreated 275 miles, panicked more by the thought of a Chinese attack than by the reality of one. As one US noncom, who had joined the 25th Infantry Division in December, complained bitterly: 'I had seen no enemy, fired no round and the company had sustained no casualty. I felt disgusted, ashamed and frustrated. Talk that the Eighth Army was about to evacuate Korea was common. . . . My morale was at bottom.'

But Ridgway tried his best. Here and there he attempted local counter-attacks, often using new foreign troops which had just arrived on the battlefield. In late January he employed a mixed force of GIs and French volunteers. The French lost 125 men, a sixth of their battalion, but together with the Americans, they killed 1,300 Chinese and captured or wounded another 3,600. It was the first time the Army's PR men made a great fuss of that 'body count' which became so notorious in Vietnam. They called it the 'Wonju Turkey Shoot'. It made a great headline.

All the same the combination of Ridgway's resolution and drive and the growing number of Chinese casualties, aided by the fact that the Chinese supply lines were ever longer so that replacements for frontline units were not coming up fast enough, started to bring the big bug-out to an end. The Chinese *knew* they were exhausted; the Allies *thought* they were. But these factors didn't matter. It was as if some deity on high had, for the time being at least, had enough of the horrors of war being carried out here below and wished to draw a curtain over them, banishing them from his or her shocked and disapproving gaze. One day the battle raged in full fury; the next it had begun to subside dramatically. In that early spring of 1951, a stalemate descended on the killing fields.

But it was a stalemate that even the dumbest private knew instinctively wouldn't and couldn't last for long. A final decision had to be made. One side or the other had to win before those currently thinking the unthinkable finally employed that most terrible weapon of all. As the GIs wise-cracked in the rough but totally apt language of the man at the 'sharp end', it was time 'to piss or get off the pot'.

CHAPTER FIFTEEN

Ass and Alcohol

Dig or die was now the motto of the British Tommy.

As the retreat slowed down and stopped virtually altogether, the battered British regiments, which had brought up the rearguard for the most part[1] started to dig in. In the past, the British had been almost as lazy as the Americans were still at digging themselves in as soon as they came to a halt, but the last year of the war against the Germans had taught them that 'digging saves lives'; the Americans never learned. Now the British dug as if their very lives depended upon it, which indeed they did. Elaborate defensive positions were burrowed into the hard unyielding Korean earth. Great screens of barbed wire followed. Weary as the men were, they constructed, as one observer reported, 'the most sophisticated defences under the most impossible conditions – lugging great pillars of concrete and huge baulks of timber up to the forward posts.'

Here their newly-acquired Korean 'coolies' came into their own. These hardy peasants, often forced into the front line by press-gangs or sheer hunger (the only food in Korea that winter seemed to be that of the Allied troops), carried huge loads on their 'A-frames', working from dawn to dusk for a handful of cigarettes and three meals a day. Not that the meals were very exciting. They were basically warmed-up tins of US C rations with additional items such as fresh bread and tea, which the British soldier demanded as his right. No Tommy would fight well without his mug of 'char' and his 'wood' (i.e. Woodbines), though if needs be he could make do with US Lucky Strikes and Camels.

These Koreans, soon to appear as ROK 'auxiliaries' to fight in the line alongside the British troops, as they were supposed to have done with the Americans (without much success, it had to be admitted), were already used in a military role as well. At the headquarters of the British Brigade, busily taking in scores of reinforcements before the nasty business of war started once more, an officer known as 'Beetle' had recruited a small force of young Korean men. It was their duty to penetrate the enemy's lines and bring back information about his strength (still unknown after two months of fighting) and his dispositions.

Soldier and war correspondent Col Eric Linklater was taken by 'Beetle' to see them that spring. They lived in a brown shattered hamlet under the command of a lance-corporal of the Royal Northumberland Fusiliers. There, after passing a warning signpost intended to put off unwelcome visitors: 'DANGER . . . SMALLPOX!', the two officers met the 21-year-old corporal.

He was surrounded by eight or nine devoutly attentive Koreans . . . changing his trousers . . . He received us with dignity, and laced his boots, put on his beret with its red-and-white plume and conducted us around his 'estate'.

In a country notorious for its dirt and unwashed masses, 'it was remarkably clean. He had been giving his cut-throats lessons in sanitation and hygiene, he had had them vaccinated, he insisted that they wash themselves.' An astonished Linklater, veteran of two wars, asked 'How do you make them do what they're told?'

'I keep them in,' the Corporal said severely. 'They get leave to go out in the evening, but if they haven't done their work, I keep them in. And as an extra punishment,' he added, 'and they get a bit excited sometimes – I make them stand on their hands.'

Linklater didn't ask how. But as he walked away, he said to 'Beetle', 'if empire-building wasn't so unfashionable, he ought to be given a bag of sovereigns and told to go out and found a colony . . .'

But if temporarily the British were building a little empire (including in one case, the Colonel of the 8th Irish Hussars growing flowers: 'My Provost-Sergeant does the flowers!') here in the Korean wilderness, the men were more concerned with 'getting their legs over', as they phrased it. For by now Ridgway had come up with a brilliant idea to raise the morale of his troops. Every fighting man, from private to general, would get five whole days in Japan. 'R and R' – Rest and Recreation was now part of their activities.

The programme began slowly. Perhaps two hundred per division per week were allowed to fly to Tokyo or one of the other big Japanese cities. But the knowledge that one day, perhaps soon, they would be leaving behind the dirty hell of Korea, with its all-pervading stink of *kimche*, was a significant factor in keeping the men going.

The GIs soon dubbed their R&R breaks 'I&I' for 'Intercourse and Intoxication'. Cruder types even entitled them aptly and more succinctly 'A&A', standing for 'Ass and Alcohol'. But all of them were entranced by the rapid transition – a mere airplane flight away – from the foxhole to the 'fur-lined' ones among the dazzling lights of the Japanese capital.

They got drunk first, as all young men on leave in war always do. They came from a 'dry' army (at least officially)[2] and now they could sink as much good Japanese 'suds' as they could afford. Thereafter it was the 'joints' with the girl vocalists singing last year's US pop tunes. Finally would come the 'broads'. But these 'broads' were unlike the brassy, loud-mouthed predatory 'B-girls' and 'hookers' they had known from around Army camps back home.

Even the prostitutes in the official Japanese red-light districts were different. Perhaps it had something to do with the language difficulty and the traditional submissive role of the Japanese woman. But these demure women, small and lacking the long legs of the US women they were used to, seemed to aim to please a man. It wasn't just 'a short time' for dollars. It appeared to be a genuine need to help young men who could be dead the following week enjoy what might well be their last five days on earth. Their conversation in English was limited. 'You go Korea . . . You been Korea . . . How long you stay . . . when you go?' seemed to be the extent of their interest and knowledge of the war raging on the other side of the Strait. But actions spoke louder than words, and when the action was over the GI could 'shoot the breeze', drink his 'suds', and enjoy unlimited undisturbed 'sack time'.

There was a question of cleanliness, too. After Korea, Japan seemed a paradise as far as personal hygiene was concerned and even the business of keeping clean was associated in a delightful way with sex. The Japanese inns, with their traditional hot baths, to which the more enterprising GIs took their 'shack-up jobs', came as a wonderful surprise. The washing and rinsing with the tiny cloths not only took away the grime and weariness of the front, but in the cunning little hands of these professional – or amateur – Japanese misses did a lot for the GI's libido as well.

But it wasn't always sex. It was the warm cleanliness and the feeling of being wanted; the proximity of a soft shapely body; the birdlike chirping quality of the speech and movement of these little slant-eyed girls. As Bevin Alexander, the combat historian of the 5th Historical Detachment in Korea, wrote later, probably very truthfully:

> Despite all the talk (and some action) regarding wine, women and song, the most lasting and happy memories that most men carried back from the R&Rs were remembrances of being clean and being able to lie down in peaceful sleep untroubled by mortars or wet or cold. Few veterans of Korea would ever admit it among their associates, but a great many of them *slept* great portions of their R&Rs . . .

For some of the British squaddies who enjoyed the same five days of freedom, they might well have slept the whole 119 hours allotted them away. For apart from the free bed, the cheap beer, constant hot-water showers, they simply didn't have the cash to compete with the Yanks for the favours of the 'good-time girls', however much they might have liked to do so.

Yorkshire volunteer Pte Denton, who had transferred from the West Yorkshire Regiment to go on a draft to Korea, although he was six months under-age and barely trained, remembers he had just enough

> money to buy myself sixteen pints of Jap beer. As good as it was, it wasn't what I thought the front-line squaddie was supposed to do when he went on leave. You know – the *second* thing that a soldier does when he goes home to his missus is to take his small pack off and 'Take a look at the floor, dear, cos all you'll be seeing for the next forty-eight hours is the ceiling.' Still I went back without a little souvenir of Japan as a lot of the Yanks did – some of 'em, so they say, with a full house.[3]

Another British soldier in the same position remembers that apart from 'the ale' and the usual physical comforts, his main amusement was watching some Koreans who had somehow got to Japan because they had been wounded in Allied service, 'playing a kind of marbles for fags – with their glass eyes! When they were finished with the game, they spat on their eyes, polished the glass optic and popped it back in the socket as if it was the most natural thing in the world.' His comment fifty years later: 'Funny lot, the Gooks . . .'

But now all the humble, underpaid British soldiers were content to watch the goings-on of the Gooks, as strange as they may have seemed. Thommo, that irrepressible Geordie of the Northumberland Fusiliers, had been sent to Japan after the bayonet charge and what followed, to the British rest camp at Kure, 25 miles from Hiroshima, to recover from exposure and sundry other illnesses.

At 22, he soon recovered and started to explore the backwaters of the port. He discovered an 'inn' with a good selection of 'bottled ales' and more importantly a very beautiful 'mine host', called Mitchiko, nicknamed 'Mitsi'. Naturally he was smitten at once. But first before he 'got my feet under the table', he had to deal with her father, a former major in the Imperial Army and 'a tough cookie to say the least'. Oaki, as he was called, was proud of his arm-to-arm wrestling and even more of his leg-to-leg variation in the middle of the bar room floor. Finally Thommo convinced the older man of his worth as a Japanese-style wrestler and was tacitly allowed to go to bed with his daughter in which he engaged in a more 'pleasurable tussle' with the ex-major's offspring.

As always, love was accompanied by 'sweet sorrow' and Thommo found it difficult to dodge out of the supposed 'rest camp' to continue the struggle with Mitsi. Once he sneaked out under the wire, just as an MP patrol hove into sight. Thommo reacted quicker than the MPs. He dived into what he thought was a monsoon ditch. It wasn't. Later he arrived at Mitsi's place for another 'tussle', 'stinking and dripping with mud and slime'. Mitsi took it in good part. Next morning just before he sneaked away to be back in camp before roll-call, he found his filthy clothes washed and dry and 'smelling of sweet violets'. It was another plus point for the Japs, he told himself.

After another episode, though, when high on sake he took on a whole Jap hotel staff, charging them with a drunken '*banzai*' when he thought they were overbilling him and scattering the 'terrified Japs in all directions', it was time for him to return to Korea. Here, he told himself, he'd find some peace at last after his hectic time in Japan. But that wasn't to be.

For Ridgway was trying to give backbone to his demoralized Eighth Army not only by means of those delightful R and R's in Japan, but also by means of limited localized attacks. He hoped that if they were successful, these minor victories would convince his soldiers that the Chinese were not the super-soldiers they believed them to be; they, too, could be defeated in battle. In most cases these attacks had been a success. The Chinese, for the most part, had hardly reacted.

As far as the British were concerned, they, the Australians and the Canadians had actually beaten off a major Chinese attack, with the Canadian Princess Patricia's Light Infantry being cut off and dependent on air-supply for twenty-four hours and still emerging victorious from the fray. Now the British 29th Brigade was dug in on the hill range south of the Imjin River, right across the historic route southwards to the Korean capital. To Ridgway, it must have seemed an impregnable position. Almost every metre of the river bank below was visible from the heights, and flanking the British were two good infantry divisions, the 1st ROK to the west and to the east the US 3rd 'Rock of the Marne'[4] Division, which had gained more Congressional Medals of Honor than any other US division in the Second World War at a cost of 35,000 casualties.

However, the Imjin position looked better than it really was, as events would show tragically. The river below was shallow. It could be forded at most points. Any attacker wouldn't need to alert the British troops on the heights to their presence by bringing up bridging equipment, etc. Besides, the defenders really didn't know where exactly the Chinese might attack and although Brodie's Brigade was supported by the excellent gunners with their Second World War 25-pounders of that old standby, the 45th Regiment Royal Artillery, their range was limited. Unfortunately, as it would turn out, Brodie couldn't call upon heavy artillery from Corps to 'see off' Chinese troops massing further back.

In essence, Brig Brodie had a front far too long to defend against first-class troops: a brigade of perhaps two and a half thousand riflemen to cover seven and a half miles. (Textbooks taught that a *division* couldn't defend more than a five-mile front against first-class troops.) Still he did his best, according to his own lights, though he was criticized later on the way he deployed his meagre forces. He decided to position his individual battalions on key heights. The Belgian Battalion, all volunteers and including two platoons from Luxembourg (the smallest contribution of all the Allied nations)[5] was positioned to the far right, north of the Imjin River. The Geordies of the Royal Northumberland Fusiliers, veterans now, though they had taken up lots of green replacements, were on the right flank on the south bank of the river. On the left were the 'Gloomies', the Gloucester Regiment, with the 'iron men' of the Royal Ulster Rifles – 'a tough mob', as they were known throughout the British Army[6] – in reserve.

Some of Brodie's officers were highly critical of his dispositions. They felt he had scattered his troops too much. They knew that the Brigadier had been a staff officer before he had been sent to Korea with his 29th Brigade, but staff officer solutions, all neat and tidy and according to the book, didn't always work in the hot fury of battle. They felt he should have concentrated his men more, basing them on the dominant heights of Kamak-san, where the height's natural defences were virtually impregnable – and there was water: that vital element for man and machine in battle, more important even than food.

One British Major, who read in the US Army Paper *Stars and Stripes* that the Chinese[7] might attack on the Imjin and flew back to the Brigade from Japan, was dismayed at what he found there. As he stated later: 'We were not really in a defensive frame of mind. We had been crawling forward, probing forward for months. We didn't even really know where on our front the Imjin was fordable.'

Thommo of the Royal Northumberland Fusiliers, back with his regiment, thought that debacle to come was not the fault of the Brigadier. He put the blame squarely in the court of the 'Yanks'. As he said fifty years later: 'I think the mess was caused by the Yank command. They gave us too much of a front to cover – they always did all the time I was in Korea. The result was we had to take the can. But I'll say this for the Yanks. When the balloon went up, they did try to get us out of the mess with all they had. Too bad for the Gloucesters that the rescue attempt ended in a ballsup.'

But that was later.

Now in the first week of April, Brig Brodie did his best to find out what was going on. On the fourth he sent out some of his Belgians and a patrol of the 8th Hussars' Centurion tanks to search the no-man's land in front of their sector.

The Belgians were all volunteers, led at first by a man renowned after the fact for his activities as a secret agent in the Second World War, code-named 'Pat O'Leary'. The Irish-sounding name concealed that of a Belgian aristocrat who had suffered mightily in the Allied cause when he was captured by the Gestapo and thrust into one of their more notorious concentration camps. As always 'Pat O'Leary' survived, for the Baron was always a survivor.[8] Expert in Intelligence matters as he was, he was determined that his battalion, whose proud banner inscribed '*Vive La Belgique*' flew over their hill positions, should know all they could about any possible attack.

The mixed Hussars-Belgian infantry struck lucky. For days now it had seemed that the Chinese had vanished from the face of the earth. Now, suddenly, they bumped into an enemy fighting patrol four miles north of the river. An immediate fire fight broke out. Slugs zipped back and forth while the Centurion turret gunners sprayed the area with their Besa machine-guns. In the end the Chinese broke off the unequal fight, leaving one of their men behind as a prisoner.

He was the usual tough Chinese peasant, his broad face revealing nothing, neither fear nor defiance. Hastily with the help of a ROK interpreter they questioned him. They knew the value of getting information out of a prisoner just after he had been captured, was in shock and hadn't had time to recover his nerve, but he could tell his interrogators little. Nevertheless, the sheer fact that he and the rest of his patrol were four miles into no-man's land was indication enough that something was going on.

Now it was the turn of the Gloucesters to send out a listening patrol. It consisted of Cpl Cook, Drummer Anthony Eagles (who had already had a bellyful of the Chinese during the big bug-out) and Pte Hunter. At ten o'clock that same night, Drummer Eagles nudged Hunter. He'd heard the sound of troops on the opposite bank searching for a ford and they could only be 'Chinks'. He had been considering where he was going to spend his five days' R&R in Japan. The 'what' needed no thought; he knew that already. In the event, there'd be neither.

Now the thoughts, delightful as they were, vanished hastily. Cpl Cook counted the shadowy figures on the other side of Imjin and reported over the 'blower' to the Gloucesters' tough adjutant Capt Anthony Farrar-Hockley what he had seen.

Farrar-Hockley, a tough former parachutist during the Second World War who had twice joined the Army under-age in that war and would rise from private to full general, contacted the artillery immediately. Moments later, star shells burst over the river, illuminating its surface in their harsh and unreal silver light. The listening patrol didn't move. They continued to observe the enemy as they stopped, tense and rigid, hoping they might be mistaken for trees if they didn't move.

Cpl Cook and the other two weren't fooled. In a whisper Farrar-Hockley told the three to open fire, now that they had started to move again. They were to wait till the Chinese were halfway across the ford; then they'd be easy meat. Hastily the three soldiers prepared for action. They agreed to lob their grenades and then use their rifles. They felt that the grenades exploding would so disconcert the enemy that they'd panic. At that point they'd open fire, using the rapid fire that had always been the strong point of British infantry since the days of the nineteenth-century colonial wars.

Then it happened. The grenades hissed into the darkness, spluttering as they flew through the air. They exploded in great spouts of water. Screams, yells of rage – agony. The three grabbed their rifles. Working the bolts of the Second World War Mark IV rifles, they poured a hail of fire at the disorganized Chinese caught by the ambush.

Over the field telephone the Adjutant demanded angrily who had told Cook to take a precious Bren gun on a standing patrol. An excited Cook retorted it wasn't a Bren gun firing, but Drummer Eagles and Pte Hunter pouring on rapid fire for all they were worth. As one of them described the effect later: 'Some disappeared altogether. Others screamed like tormented men. Bullets tore into their bodies. Walking wounded tottered back to the bank.'

In the end, panting like men who had just run a great race, they ceased firing and waited for the Chinese reaction. There was none. Apart from two dead Chinese sprawled out in their sodden uniforms on the opposite bank, they might well have never been there . . .

On 16 April, Col Kenneth Foster, a big bluff man who had also been a staff for several years after the Second World War, took out his entire battalion of the Royal Northumberland Fusiliers on a reconnaissance. Perhaps the 'recce' was intended as a provocation to lure the Chinese into a large-scale confrontation. But we don't know now. At all events, nothing of significance happened, although the Geordies, accompanied by tanks of the Hussars, advanced *nine miles* into no-man's land. They were met merely by token fire and succeeded in taking a few Chinese prisoners, from whom little was forthcoming: the process of interpreting from Chinese into Korean and then into English was too laborious. As one participant noted in exasperation: 'Battleground interviews of this nature were often more exacting than instructive.' So the Geordies returned to their fortress height no wiser than before. Unknown to them, their beloved CO had less than a week to live now.

In the end, Brodie and his staff concluded that despite their extended front, they had little to fear from the 'Chinks'. Perhaps, they told themselves, they had heard of the reputation of the men of the 'frozen rectum' and were keeping well clear of them. They were merely keeping a cautious eye on the 29th Brigade. If the Chinese did attack, it would probably be on the poor hopeless ROKs on their flank, and the South Koreans would run at the drop of the hat. But the men of the 'frozen rectum' brigade were wrong. Before this week was out, a third of them would be dead, wounded or destined for that terrible living death of a Chinese POW camp.

CHAPTER SIXTEEN

Old Soldiers Never Die

The downfall of Gen Douglas MacArthur began at the start of the uneasy stalemate in Korea. At that time it was generally thought that the ancient autocrat had brought it on himself: he had defied his political and military masters in Washington and was threatening to endanger the whole world by his advocacy of the atomic bomb, so he had to go – and it was his own fault.

But in American politics – and in the final analysis, the dismissal of Gen MacArthur did have a strong political rationale – things are never that simple. It was clear to Truman that MacArthur had an immense following in the States. Ordinary men and women, who knew little or nothing of the horrors of total war as did the Europeans, *were* prepared to think of the unthinkable – the use of the nuclear deterrent – if its use would bring the Korean War to a speedy and successful conclusion. If he, Truman, and his top generals (who detested MacArthur on account of the old man's treatment of them) weren't prepared to use that terrible weapon, then MacArthur might well go public. He could resign and, with the backing of the Republican Party (MacArthur was a Republican), successfully run for President in 1952.

After all, right throughout the history of the United States, successful generals from Washington, through Grant and soon on to Eisenhower had always been regarded as ideal candidates by the political machine for the greatest office in the land. Truman, the Democrat, couldn't allow that. Carefully he, Secretary of State Dean Acheson and Gen Bradley prepared the ground for the confrontation they knew had to come soon. In retrospect now, it is obvious that, thanks to the death of poor old bumbling 'Bulldog' Walker, Ridgway was in an ideal place to take over as soon as MacArthur had been dismissed. Ridgway, in his turn, would be speedily replaced by another very capable Second World War Corps, Gen van Fleet, known and trusted by Ridgway, now waiting in the wings. In other words, the military under the command of Gen Bradley was already prepared in March 1950 for what was to come.

At the same time Truman and Acheson were busy taking care of the diplomatic and political side of the intended dismissal. In terms of fighting men sent to Korea, the British were of little importance (both Turkey and Canada had dispatched twice the number of Britain's initial contribution in the form of the 'Woolworth's Brigade'); but of all the twelve UN nations involved in the conflict, that country was the most important *politically*. In upper-class British terms, that poor old broke country, already beginning its long period of inversion in the form of the 'Welfare State', still 'sat at the top table'.

Thus it was that the two 'plotters', Truman and Acheson, made much of Britain's alarm at the prospect of MacArthur convincing them to allow the military to intervene in China; of introducing Nationalist Chinese troops in Formosa into the conflict as UN troops; and, most importantly, of employing the atom bomb. Truman and Acheson ensured that America's thinking classes and the media became well aware of Britain's feelings as expressed in London's broadsheets. The emphasis the two Americans wanted was on MacArthur's alleged role as a 'warmonger' and the British papers did them proud. MacArthur was the 'tail wagging the dog'. He was 'overruling' his own 'political bosses'. As the French paper *Le Franc Tireur* summed it up, while European ambassador after ambassador protested to the State Department about MacArthur's conduct, 'An Asiatic war is too serious to be left in the hands of a military man.'

The time was ripe. All that the plotters needed was for MacArthur to make one of his more lunatic public statements. As Dean Acheson put it, quoting Euripides, 'Whom the gods destroy they first make mad.'

In the last week of March, MacArthur seemed to do exactly what his 'enemies'[1] in Washington wanted him to do. By now the State Department and the Pentagon had decided that the time had come to offer Red China a truce. The proposal was put to all of the USA's allies *purposefully* with a copy to MacArthur himself. Four days later MacArthur reacted.

It was exactly what the plotters were waiting for. In essence it was an ultimatum to the Chinese, its tone taunting and naturally calculated to anger the latter. MacArthur opined, '(China) lacks the industrial capacity' for the 'conduct of modern war.' Its troops had displayed an 'inferiority of ground firepower', and all these 'military weaknesses . . . have been clearly and definitely revealed since Red China entered upon its undeclared war in Korea'. The real sting came in the tail of MacArthur's extraordinary statement. He wrote that China had 'shown its complete inability to accomplish by force of arms the conquest of Korea. The enemy, therefore, must by now be painfully aware that a decision by the United Nations to depart from its tolerant effort to contain the war would doom Red China to the risk of imminent collapse.'

The Chinese reacted as expected. The communist leaders' sense of outrage and anger were all too clear. Radio Peking expressed their mood. It stated that MacArthur had 'made a fanatical but shameless statement with the intention of engineering the Anglo-American aggressors to extend the war of aggression into China.'

MacArthur's message reached Washington on the evening of Friday 23 March. Acheson arranged a meeting with his advisors at once. Some were for informing the President immediately but Acheson thought they should sleep on it before they did. Perhaps the slick, immaculately dressed

Anglophile did so in order to refine his arguments and convince the President that at last something had to be done about the opinionated maverick in Tokyo. He need not have bothered: Truman flew off the handle. Later he recorded he was 'deeply shocked'. MacArthur's statement was 'a challenge to the authority of the President under the Constitution . . . By this act MacArthur left me no choice – I could no longer tolerate his insubordination.'

On 24 March Truman ordered Bradley to send MacArthur an order telling the latter that if the Chinese military leaders requested 'an armistice in the field' he was to 'inform the Joint Chiefs of Staff at once'. That did it. MacArthur later stated that he thought what was now happening was one of the 'most disgraceful plots' in US history. He threatened to go public, knowing that he had the support of the US public who wanted a victory in Korea and that many of the Republican Party would follow suit.

On Thursday 5 April MacArthur really went to town. He stated that Korean soldiers were begging to fight the invaders but the lacked weapons to do so because of 'basic political decisions beyond my authority'. He fed the *Daily Telegraph* a heartfelt complaint that 'the UN forces were circumscribed by a web of artificial conditions' and then capped it all by a statement obviously leaked[2] to Joe Martin of the US House of Representatives. That noon the latter got up and complained that the President was preventing a force of '800,000 trained men' in Formosa, i.e. Nationalist Chinese, from fighting on America's side. As Martin cried: 'if we are not in Korea to win, then this Truman administration should be indicted for the murder of thousands of American boys.'

That was the clincher: now Truman was determined to get rid of MacArthur, and he would not allow the General to resign, as was now being predicted – Truman was not going to give him that satisfaction. As he exploded to an aide: 'That son of a bitch isn't going to resign on me . . . *I want him fired!*'

On 12 April (despite Truman's anger it had taken so long for him and his advisers to figure out how to get rid of a man who was a national hero, a general who had won the Congressional Medal of Honor, beaten the Japs and had 52 years of military service behind him), the President cabled MacArthur that his time had come. He was dismissed.

In his autobiography MacArthur noted that 'No office boy, no charwoman, no servant of any sort would have been dismissed with such callous disregard for the ordinary decencies.' Still, outwardly, the 71-year-old General accepted his fate with dignity and calm. When he departed from Tokyo for the last time, two million ordinary Japanese men and woman lined the route to the airport. One of Japan's leading newspapers said of the warrior who had conquered them but not humbled them as a lesser man might have done: 'We feel as if we had lost a kind and loving father.'

At San Francisco Airport, MacArthur and his family were received by half a million cheering supporters and it was clear from the Press and public statements that the average American man-on-the-street thought that the old soldier had been dismissed unfairly. Truman received a torrent of angry mail, including death threats. He was forced to go on national radio and tell his listeners: 'In the simplest terms, what we are doing in Korea is this: we are trying to prevent a third world war.'

That couldn't have been clearer. But for the time being the nation wasn't listening to President Truman. They wanted to hear what MacArthur, the hero, had to say. Being MacArthur, the General gave them their money's worth in a 37-minute televised address. He said he wasn't 'a warmonger', as some people had suggested:

> Nothing could be further from the truth. I know war as few men now living know it and nothing to me is more revolting . . . But once war is forced upon us, there is no other alternative than to apply every available means to bring it to a swift end . . . There can be no substitute for victory . . . There are some, who, for varying reasons, would appease Red China. They are blind to history's clear lessons, for history teaches, with unmistakable emphasis, that appeasement but begets new and bloodier war.

His audience undoubtedly knew at whom these barbed references were aimed. But MacArthur knew, as a master of sentimental rhetoric, that they alone wouldn't suffice. He was well aware of what a sentimental, emotional nation the American people had become in the twentieth century, totally different from the hard-bitten no-nonsense American men of his youth. Thus he laid on the schmaltz to emphasize his point – a simple old soldier, who had served his country long and well and had been kicked out by devious office-seeking politicians. He said:

> The world has turned over many times since I took the oath on the Plains at West Point and the hopes and dreams have long since vanished, but I still remember the refrain of one of the most popular barrack ballads of that day which proclaimed most proudly that '*Old soldiers never die, they just fade away.*' And like the old soldier of that ballad I now close my military career and just fade away – an old soldier who tried to do his duty as God gave him the light to see that duty. Good bye.

Despite the sentimentality of that talk, which was received by wild enthusiasm, there was a certain nobility about it, for MacArthur carried it off with dignity and aplomb – no one else could have done it quite like that. Undoubtedly there was many a tear in the eyes of his listeners that day – and not just in women's eyes either. But Douglas MacArthur had had his moment of history. He would live on for another fourteen years before taps finally sounded for him. But a third call[3] never came.

He must have died a bitter man, though he continued to joke and maintain: 'Years may wrinkle the skin . . . but you are as young as your faith . . . as young as your hope, as old as your despair . . . When . . . your heart is covered with the snows of pessimism and the ice of cynicism, then and only then you are grown old – and then indeed, as the ballad says, you just fade away.'

In 1964 just before he faded away and one of his doctors quipped he'd better buy that ticket to his beloved Scotland but that he should not expect to get there, an old, frail and weary MacArthur rallied with the remark that he was going and that just in case he didn't make it, he as a canny Scot would be 'buying my ticket from station to station'. He never got there.

In Korea in that spring of 1950 MacArthur was already forgotten. A Chinese attack was imminent – where the top brass didn't know, but they were certain it was coming: the Chicoms would undoubtedly make one last attempt to finish off the Allies in Korea.

With expedition, Ridgway took over MacArthur's post. In the meantime, the Allied army waited for their new commander-in-chief, their senior officers knowing that he would have to be someone special, not only because of the precarious situation. For by now in Korea there were approximately 40,000 non-US troops – in addition to the ROK formations – in the field.

About half of them were British or from the British dominions. The rest were from all over the free world. They spoke thirteen different languages plus dialects. They ate food totally unknown to the average American. The Greeks wanted olive oil; the French baguettes and wine, the strong red pinot; the Greeks and Turks ate lamb, but the former wanted their lambs to be virgin and ritually slaughtered; the Turks wouldn't eat pork; the Indians no beef. Naturally the British wanted their 'char', hard booze and 'wallop'.

Even clothing and footwear differed according to nationality. The Turks wanted wide shoes; the Thais small ones; the Brits hobnailed boots and not the American rubber-soled ones. The crazy logistics even went as far as contraceptives – 'rubbers' and 'French letters' – as the Americans and British called them. The Mohammedans among the Allied troops looked at them with suspicion; the French-Canadian battalion commander wouldn't have them in his outfit – his men had 'to save themselves' for the 'girls back home'; and the Americans used them primarily to cover the muzzles of their rifles. They quipped routinely, 'What we supposed to do – fight 'em or fuck 'em to death?'

The general whom the Joint Chiefs-of-Staff had already selected to take over the Eighth Army from Ridgway was James van Fleet. He was naturally a West Pointer, who in the First World War had served as an infantry officer. Thereafter he had gone through the usual 'schools', as most officers between the wars seem to have done. Some US officers seem to have spent most of their careers before the Second World War either being taught or teaching; perhaps the US Army was unable to find any other employment for them.

Van Fleet's career had progressed nicely during the Second World War, where he had risen rapidly from major to one-star general and had been an able front-line commander in Germany, ending as a corps commander. Now, Korea was his big chance: finally he was going to command an army. But van Fleet fully understood the difficulties: the unreliability of the ROKs, the strange assortment of allies and the wishy-washy policy of his predecessors who had had to fight with an unreliable demoralized US Army.

Now, as the General faced the Press and was asked by a correspondent what the official policy in Korea was, he answered: 'I don't know. . . . Somebody higher up will have to tell us.'

It was an answer typical of the new commander, whose own son would be killed in action in Korea, because he really *didn't* know what Washington planned for his Army. Nor did he know much more of the Communists' intentions, despite a new intelligence campaign conducted by the CIA behind enemy lines; the Chinese didn't signal their punches either, neither to the enemy nor to their own people.

But from what van Fleet *did* know, he guessed that trouble was brewing. The Chinese were not probing for weak spots in the Eighth Army's lines and were not carrying out any large-scale patrolling and, as well, had imposed radio silence. These were all give-aways to an experienced officer like van Fleet: the enemy were trying to avoid losing prisoners who might be captured on a patrol and who might give away secret information to the 'round-eyes' under duress. On 19 April the Chinese started setting fire to the forests along the front held by units of the US I and IX Corps. The smoke was being used as a kind of primitive smoke screen to shield their movements from the Allies. It was yet another indication to the trained soldier that something was in the offing.

Something else as well alerted van Fleet: the 'feel' of coming major attack. All soldiers know it – a kind of dread excitement: the sound of vehicles moving in the middle of the night, strange lights flashing to no apparent purpose, the appearance of bushes that surely weren't there the day before, faint angry faraway voices carried to the tensed listeners unwittingly by some freak of the wind . . . a hundred and one things that later would be rationally explained but which now meant in the vaguest of ways that something untoward was afoot.

And it was: almost under the very noses of the puzzled and anxious defenders were 350,000 Chinese soldiers waiting for the order to attack. This time, their officers and *politruks*[4] told them confidently, they'd chase the 'round-eyes' out of Korea for good!

CHAPTER SEVENTEEN

The Battle of the Imjin River

Thursday 22 April 1950 was a fine mild day in Korea. Spring was in the air. Both the wind and the earth smelled of new life. The dwarf oak and the scrub, so recently covered with heavy snow, were beginning to shoot with new green life. There was a feeling of hope in the air.

Even the war seeming to have vanished. On the British front there had been some sporadic rifle-firing and the occasional mortar stonk, but that was about it. The Chinese who had seemed to be so threatening a month before appeared to have vanished from the face of the earth. The soldiers reasoned they had taken so many casualties in their recent attacks that they were considering whether there was any future in attacking any more. The word was that there might be a little more fighting just to prove to the 'commies' that the Eighth Army was ready for any major offensive, but in reality their missions was 'to die for a tie'. A truce was on its way soon.

So the three battalions of Brodie's Brigade went about their routine duties this warmish Thursday, enjoying the balmy air and the freedom from their heavy winter clothing, keeping up the 'bullshit' as all good British soldiers should.

The Northumberland Fusiliers were preparing a little feast. The next day would be 'St George's Day' and the men who wore his insignia on their cap badge always celebrated the birthday of the Patron Saint of England. The cooks were already racking their brains for some way to turn the standard C ration into the annual celebratory meal – at least something better than what the GI called contemptuously 'shit on shingle', i.e. hash on toasted bread.

The Ulsters in reserve weren't the best-disciplined of troops, but they were perhaps the wildest in the whole brigade, including those of the all-volunteer Belgian Battalion, which was now under Brodie's command. Now they were busy strengthening their positions, knowing that they'd take some 'stick' from their English comrades later for doing so. For everyone knew that the 'Micks' were all 'brickies' by trade and took a delight in digging. 'Give 'em a bag o' cement and they'd turn the bleeding Sahara into a housing estate before yer can say bleeding Jack Robinson!'

'The Gloomies', as the other two battalions of Brodie's Brigade called the Gloucesters, were a little worried, it had to be admitted. There seemed to be some sort of mild flap going on. Indeed the CO Col Carne, old-looking for an infantry colonel, appeared to have vanished.

That afternoon, the broad, tough-looking young adjutant of the 'Gloomies', Capt Anthony Farrar-Hockley, was a bit worried by his absence.

He asked a fellow officer at Battalion HQ where Carne was and was told: 'They're all down at the river. There's some sort of flap on.' The adjutant decided to have 'a look-see' himself and on the way to Imjin in his scout car he was told by the driver, Yates, that a couple of hours before their OPs and those of the Northumberlands had spotted Chinese patrols heading for a ford called the 'Gloster Crossing'. According to Yates, it was no big thing; just 'very small parties'. All the same the pipe-smoking adjutant was puzzled. He told himself 'How very odd that, after concealing their hand for so long, they [the Chinese] should alert us by sending down *daylight* patrols.' He frowned and dismissed the thought. He'd wait and see what the CO had to say.

Some time later Farrar-Hockley reached the river and was met by Henry, the Battalion Intelligence Officer. Together they wriggled their way to the edge of the Bund and peered across.

'Over there,' Henry whispered, as if the Chinese might well hear him. 'That's the fourth group we've seen. The Colonel's got the mortars on them.'

He had. Carne barked an order. Almost immediately the men manning the Battalion's 3-inch mortars opened up. A line of flashes. Black smoke balled up and started to drift in the wind across the hills.

'That ought to tickle 'em a bit,' the Intelligence Officer commented with a grin.

But Col Carne wasn't so sanguine when the two officers crossed to where he sat on a rock staring at the map through his issue glasses, looking for all the world like some retired officer reading his morning *Daily Telegraph* somewhere in Gloucester. 'This looks like the real thing,' he announced shortly in that unemotional manner of his. 'We'll have a fifty per cent stand-to tonight, I think.' Suddenly the man who had commanded an infantry battalion in Burma and knew just how tough combat could be looked worried . . .

Unknown yet to Carne, he had good reason to do so, for by the light of the full moon in the early hours of that Thursday, the Chinese had launched their last great offensive of the war. Some 350,000 Chinese, outnumbering the Allies by about three to one, had attacked, while Communist 'Radio Pyongyang' boasted that this new 'rapid' offensive would throw the enemy back into the sea from which it had come.

Already the signs were bad for the Allies. The US 24th Division, mainly black, and its sister division the 25th had been badly hit. The US 3rd, that veteran formation, which had produced the most decorated soldier in American history – movie star Audie Murphy – had also been attacked in force, while its neighbour the ROK 1st Division was on the point of collapse.

The 6th ROK Division was already retreating. By the end of that Thursday, it would have fallen back ten miles, with Corps Commander Gen Almond ranting to one of his regimental commanders, Colonel McCaffrey: 'Make them return to their positions. Shoot them if you have to!' In the event, the harassed regimental commander couldn't bring himself to shoot the troops of his allies, but there was no denying the fact that, by retreating, the South Koreans had allowed a ten-mile hole to be opened by the attackers in the central front.

Van Fleet, directing his first battle in Korea, reacted at once. He hadn't yet had time to assess the fighting qualities of the various Army units under his command. But he *did* know that the US Marines wouldn't let him down. Like most Army commanders he frowned upon the Marines' tactic of always attacking frontally. It was old-fashioned and it wasted far too many good troops. But the 'Leathernecks' would try and try again to take an enemy position – and *they* didn't run away!

He ordered Gen Smith of the 1st Marine Division to rush to the front and bolster it up the best they could. Smith snapped into action at once. Huge convoys of Marines in open trucks left their reserve areas in a matter of hours and rolled forward the best they could struggling against a crazy tide of thousands of retreating panic-stricken ROK soldiers. The whole of the 6th ROK Division had now collapsed totally.

The Leathernecks tried to stop the rot at a spot called Horseshoe Ridge, the hill formation giving it its name. Almost immediately, hardly before they had had time to occupy the abandoned ROK trenches and site their weapons, to their front the Chinese were clearly preparing to attack. There was the incessant shrilling of whistles, the bellowed commands and, most unsettling of all, the blare of Chinese bugles.

As one Marine, PFC Floyd Baxter recalled: 'The hair of my neck stood up. Trying some humor, I told my foxhole buddy, "They sure could use some music lessons".' His buddy wasn't amused. 'All of a sudden, it got quiet. You could hear the guys bracing themselves, you know, getting ready. I thought who's gonna live and who's gonna die?'

So far the British had not begun to die. But it was obvious to the forward companies and observers of the Royal Northumberland Fusiliers, the Gloucesters and the Belgian Battalion that soon there would be killing. Everywhere they started to signal the rear that large parties of Chinese were massing for the attack. The British, too, could hear that terrible overture to sudden death, typical preliminary accompanying music to the offensive.[1]

Farrar-Hockley listening to the ominous rumble of the guns in the distance, as the light started to give wondering what was going to happen, and observing the CO, Col Carne, who sat smoking, one hand on his knee, lost in thought. He could guess that the CO was reviewing his dispositions. What fears, what doubts were going through his mind, he wondered. For the young adjutant, who had seen much of battle himself, knew that success or failure in the fight to come depended upon so many imponderables, mechanical, military and human. But of all the latter, the 'moral strength imparted by the troops' stout hearts' was the most important. But could the old colonel have guessed at that moment of silent reverie before they joined in the sound and fury of desperate battle, that within the next forty-eight hours his obscure English county battalion would become known throughout the whole free world, praised by monarchs and presidents as the 'Glorious Glosters'? But the cost of such glory would be high. Before that time limit expired, that same famous battalion would be 'liquidated' . . . would no longer exist . . .

In the Northumberland lines, their Colonel – Kenneth Foster – might have felt a little more at ease, less introspective. Broad, bluff and hearty, well-liked by his men, he wasn't given to emotionalism. After all, as an infantry officer, in charge of those 'at the sharp end' who would do most of the fighting and suffer seventy per cent of an army's casualties, it wasn't advisable for him to give way to emotions. *He* concerned himself with the problems of the following day, in particular with upholding the age-old regimental tradition of celebrating the birth of St George. How, for instance, was he to get the special meal to the men already in the Battalion's forward positions, observing the 'Chinks'? Men in the line, whose lives consisted of dull and sometimes dangerous routine, mostly with no kind of entertainment whatsoever, needed the stimulus of something extra tasty to relieve the tedium. But everyone had to have his share of it. He didn't want any 'bitching' afterwards about 'one law for the rich and one for the poor . . .'

Thus he too sat and thought. Like Carne, Foster couldn't possibly have conceived what the next day would bring. His battalion also would be badly hit. But whereas Col Carne would survive and live to die in bed, Col Foster wouldn't. On this Thursday evening, the last twenty-four hours of a life mostly devoted to the service of his country were upon him.

To the flank of Foster's Battalion, the Belgians also waited. The Belgian volunteer battalion, who wore the Belgian lion in dull gold on their sleeve, were the 'new boy's in Brodie's Brigade – they had arrived in Korea on 31 January 1950; they were also the strangest unit of his varied formation. Indeed, one might say they were the strangest formation of all the Allied forces in Korea.

Not that a casual observer would have known it. They wore British battledress with beret, though their beret was a distinctive dark brown, and they spoke French which everyone else expected Belgians would speak. In reality, they were an unusual disparate formation, sometimes at each other's throats on account of their regional backgrounds, and speaking three languages, two of which for the most part weren't understood by their commanding and company commanders. Their heavy weapons and headquarters companies were mixed: Walloon soldiers who spoke their own peculiar French, and Flemish ones who spoke their form of Dutch. Rifle Companies A and B were exclusively French-speaking Walloons, while C was Flemish. In addition there was a 48-man contingent from the Grand Duchy of Luxembourg with A Company, who with their Belgian comrades spoke French, but among themselves spoke their own little-known *Luxembourgeois* German dialect, unintelligible to the Walloons. And to cap it all off, among the three companies there were German-speaking soldiers from Belgium's three *Ostkantonen* who had actually been serving in the *Wehrmacht* only five years before!

Disparate as the *Bataillon Belge* was, it did contain a large number of experienced fighting men who had served in half a dozen armies in the Second World War, sometimes on opposite sides, as well as others of the Armée Blanche, the 'White Army' (on account of the fact they wore a white overall) of the Resistance, who were not inclined to be namby-pamby in their methods. After all the Gestapo had not exactly been the Salvation Army! This battalion, which would have 103 men killed in action (including two Luxembourgers) before they were finished, would now – as one chronicler put it – 'fight magnificently at the Imjin River'.

But just like the rest of the 29th Brigade, as that Thursday started to come to a tense and uneasy end, they were still unaware of what awaited them. It wouldn't be pleasant.

Young Lt P. Kavanagh, son of the 'ITMA' scriptwriter, had volunteered for Korea. Now he and his patrol commander, Lt Hedley Craig of the Royal Ulster Rifles, peered through the darkness north of the Imjin. The two young officers thought it 'looked fishy'. All the same they started to push on under the cold silver light of the stars. Both were aware that something was going on this night – they could hear the grind of motors and the rusty rattle of tracks in the far distance – but they couldn't make out what.

Then it happened. As Kavanagh wrote later, displaying some of his father's talent: 'Flames, rockets, yells, a thousand Cup Final rattles. Guy Fawkes, one of the carriers in front of us goes up. Fifty of us have run into a bloody army!' His men reacted at once. They fled for the cover of the darkness pursued by a swarm of angry hornets which were enemy red tracer slugs.

Kavanagh who had been slow off the mark – or brave – yelled at the retreating figures of his men, 'Come back!' A few did. Others vanished, never to be seen again.

'Lie down. Face your front,' the greenhorn commanded, 'and return the fire!' A wild volley of rifle fire erupted from their scattered ranks, but Kavanagh, now the man of the moment but sounding more confident than he really was, couldn't hear the reassuring steady rattle of their Bren gun. 'Get that Bren going,' he hissed.

An Irish voice answered out of the glowing darkness, 'There's something wrong with it, Sorr.'

'Mend it,' he snapped. How the unknown soldier would do so under fire, he didn't know. Still he consoled himself with the thought that this was 'Splendid stuff. And will the First Cavalry, just in the nick of time, pennants a-flutter come riding, riding.' Next instant he told himself that they wouldn't. Suddenly he wished he wasn't there. Out of the dark came that splendid bog-Irish voice once more, 'I can find nothing wrong with the Bren, sorr, known to God or to man.'

That 'God or man' pleased the young officer no end. Suddenly he felt reassured that everything would go right in the end. He told himself, 'Oh, the Irish, the irresistable cadence, unresisted.' He opened fire . . .

Now everywhere, the forward posts of the Belgians, 'Geordies', Ulstermen and 'Gloomies' were under fire. The four infantry battalions of Brodie's Brigade were dug in on the invasion route to Seoul, the South Korean capital, and it was a matter of prestige and 'face' for the Red Chinese to capture the capital yet again. It would be a prime propaganda coup and might well swing things in their favour, when the American people had lost it. Everyone in the States knew where Seoul was.

So by dawn three Chinese divisions were attacking the 6,000-odd British force along a seven-mile-wide front. Their plan was to cut off the individual battalions and then destroy them piecemeal. It was not a difficult task due to the way that Brig Brodie had deployed his four units. Even within units, such as the Geordies of the Northumberland Fusiliers, there were gaps of up to two miles.

In itself such gaps would have not been a very great problem. The Russians and Germans had used positions of that kind, called 'hedgehogs' widely in the Second World War to protect the huge Russian front. But with typical Russian and German persistence, hard work and thoroughness they had made each 'hedgehog' into a mini-fortress. But Brodie's troops had not done so. They had believed they would hold these positions only for a short while so that they had not bothered to lay minefields, put out wire and prepare mutual-support fire-positions. Instead they had cleared the scrub to their front, repaired whatever foxholes (some left by the Japanese five years before) they could find and waited for the order to advance once more. After all they were tired after a two-month retreat and were busily engaged in absorbing replacements from 'Blighty'. As one gunner major commented on the Glosters just before the Chinese attack, they were 'relaxed, perhaps *too* relaxed.' Now they were going to pay the price for letting down their guard for even a few days. As always the Chinese were quick to take advantage of any laxity on the part of their enemies.

'Thommo' Thompson was one of those still relaxing as Friday 23 April dawned. After the customary 'shit, shower and shampoo' (though these last two pleasures were noticeably absent in the line) he had a good strong mug of 'sar'nt-major's char,[2] and took stock of the day the battalion would celebrate St George's Day.

It looked as if it was going to be a fine day and there was an appetizing smell coming from the cookhouse where the cooks were already busy with their dixies, portable stoves and all the other trappings of their trade. All in all, the young Fusilier told himself, it looked as if it was going to be a 'canny' St George's Day. Little did he realize as he took in the snap-and-crackle of an angry fire fight to his front somewhere that this St George's Day of 1950 would be one he'd never forget for the rest of his life.

At the Ulsters' forward positions, the Chinese attack had slackened somewhat. Surprisingly, although the attackers outnumbered the Irish by at least ten to one, they were now allowing the survivors of that first brush to withdraw. As Lt Craig, wounded in the shoulder and inclined to drift into unconsciousness, covered him, Kavanagh pulled back with five riflemen. In the morning gloom, there were Chinese everywhere, thrusting forward, occasionally firing short sharp bursts with their 'burp guns' – at whom a confused Kavanagh couldn't guess. But luck was on their side – they managed to escape the mêlée. He didn't know it but this short engagement, a matter of minutes in total, was his first and last battle. Soon thereafter he was evacuated to hospital in Japan.

He was transported there with hundreds of other wounded of half a dozen nationalities to be treated by the overworked staff of the Britcom General Hospital at Kure. By that time the nurses would discover to their horror that most of the men's wounds were crawling with 'the nightmare of maggots' . . . 'inside plasters and under scalps and even the first colostomy dressings produced thousands of these horrors.' But that was later.

Now as it grew ever lighter, the fighting was hotting up on the fronts of all four battalions. The Chinese poured in wave after wave of yelling cheering troops. Bugles sounding, whistling shrilling, they challenged, '*Come out . . . English – COME!*' and fell dead the next instant. But there was always another apparent fanatic ready to challenge the defenders, braving that merciless hail of fire which at times must have appeared to the Chinese like a solid wall of whirling sudden death.

Nevertheless the pressure was beginning to tell. As 'Thommo' of the Northumberlands' W Company was alerted for action, all thoughts of a festive meal vanishing in a flash, the leading companies of his own and the other battalions were being forced back. The intensive pressure was just too much.

So far the Glosters had fought off the repeated attacks on their forward positions, though they had been forced to give ground. Now on the morning of 23 April they waited for the new attacks that even the dullest of the infantrymen realized had to come; the Chinks wouldn't let them get away that easily.

They were right. A tin can full of stones rattled. Straining their ears, the listeners waited for the next indication that the enemy was close to their front. A scrape of metal against the barbed wire. Another tin can rattled. An order was whispered down the trench line. The men took out their grenades and twisted the cotter pins free. Suddenly something came whizzing through the air. A Chinese stick grenade, like the wartime German 'potato masher'. It exploded. A flash of violet light. A muffled crump. The ping of shrapnel. The battle was on again.

As Farrar-Hockley recalled:

Echoing now, the hill is lit with flame . . . Mortars begin to sound down near the Imjin . . . Slowly like a fire, the flames spread east and west around Castle Hill [one of the Glosters' strongpoints]. Now, almost hand to hand, the Chinese and British soldiers meet. Figures leap up from the attacking force, run forward to new cover and resume their fire upon the men of the defence.

The Vickers guns cut across the cliffs and slopes by which the Chinese forces climb to the attack . . . The mortars and the gunners drop their high explosive in among the crowded ranks . . . Fresh hundreds are committed to the attack and the tired defenders, much depleted, face yet another assault . . .

But as the Chinese prepared for that next attack, the officers of the Glosters' company knew they weren't going to be able to hold the position. The heights above the Castle site had fallen into Chinese hands and as the officer in question informed his subordinate by field phone, 'At the present rate of casualties we can't hold until we get the Castle back. Their machine-guns up there completely dominate your platoon . . . We shall never stop their advance until we hold that ground.'

With a growing feeling of apprehension, but knowing it had to be done, the assault group which would attempt to recapture the Castle site moved. Like grey ghosts they passed to the wire. But despite their silence, the Chinese had spotted them and were waiting. A machine-gun ripped the air apart. Tracer sped towards the attackers in a lethal Morse. Two men were down, moaning. Somehow or other the rest, cursing and sweating, the rusty barbs ripping cruelly at their uniforms, got through the wire. Over at the bunker, which they thought was abandoned, a machine-gun suddenly spat fire. It was one of the old Russian 05 models; as it tatted away, though, it was effective, since at that range the hidden Chinese gunners couldn't miss. Men went down everywhere: some for good, others just hugging the ground for cover, pressing their bodies close to the damp earth like lovers in the throes of physical passion.

The machine-gun ceased firing as abruptly as it had started: it had done its job for the time being, and the attack had stopped. On the ground, the wounded commander of the attack, a young officer barely into his twenties, moaned, and with a supreme effort of sheer willpower raised himself on one knee. The dark smudge on his uniform spread. He was undeterred. Someone held on to his swaying body as he gasped with agony and said through gritted teeth, 'We *must* take the Castle site!'

His men protested. But already the young officer was gone, staggering through the wire, heading for the damned bunker. As Farrar-Hockley wrote afterwards, 'the others come out behind him, their eyes all on him. And suddenly it seems as if, for a few breathless moments, the whole of the remainder of that field of battle is still and silent, watching, amazed, the lone figure that runs so painfully forward to the bunker holding the approach to the Castle site: one tiny figure throwing grenades, firing a pistol, set to take Castle Hill.'

It wasn't to be. The machine-gun in the bunker raked the brave young officer's body with bullets. He stumbled as if he had run into a brick wall and had been stopped in his tracks. But even with the blood jetting in a bright red arc from his wounds, he was still on his feet, fighting to the last. With his dying strength he threw a grenade. It exploded in the mouth of the bunker. Hurriedly three of the dead officer's platoon rushed forward to pick him from the ground, braving sudden death themselves. But the enemy gun remained silent, its muzzle blown off, its crew sprawled in a confused dead tangle around the shattered weapon. Dead before he had really begun to live, the officer had done his duty to the bitter end.

Many did, that terrible Friday. Some died in lonely obscurity, no one present to record their bravery. Others were observed by officers and comrades and would be remembered – at least for a while – because their bravery would be recognized. In the cold unfeeling prose of the official Gazette, it would begin with 'Citation in respect of —— to support the award of the ——' And that day many such citations would be earned, too many of them awarded posthumously.

One was for the brave young officer who died trying to stop the Chinese attack on his company. His name was Lt Philip Kenneth Edward Curtis, whose parent regiment had been The Duke of Cornwall's Light Infantry. But he fought and died a Gloster and that regiment and its successors will always claim him as one of their own. For he won his country's highest award that Friday – the Victoria Cross. The *London Gazette* called his conduct 'magnificent throughout this bitter battle'.

Many men that day seemed to have been carried away by the wild, unreasoning atavistic fury of battle, carrying out reckless acts of bravery that under normal circumstances they wouldn't even have dared to contemplate. But then the Battle of Imjin, in which Brodie's Brigade faced up to the tremendous manpower of three whole Chinese divisions, could not have been regarded as 'normal' whichever way one looks at it. And some continued the fight against overwhelming odds in the hard, bitter years to come.

Fusilier Derek Kinne of the 'Geordies' was one. He was captured in the confused mêlée that followed the withdrawal of the Fusiliers' survivors. Even as the Chinese captors roughed him up, the infantryman told himself that he would escape as soon as he could and until then he would treat with contempt the Chinks and the Northern Korean Gooks who would hold him prisoner under appalling conditions until he was released from their captivity in August 1953. He first escaped within twenty-four hours of being captured, which earned him a black mark and special surveillance for the rest of his imprisonment. It didn't help much that he punched a Chinese officer who had assaulted him, for which he was tied up repeatedly for as much as 24 hours with a running noose around his neck which would have throttled him if he had attempted to relax in any way.

That terrible torture didn't break the young soldier's spirit. While too many of his fellow POWs from many countries compromised and tried to live with their captors, his resistance grew apace. He escaped again and was recaptured. Terrible beatings followed. He was thrown into a dank rat-infested hole for days on end. On 16 October 1952, eighteen months after being captured, a shadow of his former self, crippled by a double hernia incurred while trying to escape, he was court-martialled. Again he fought back at the tribunal but was sentenced to a special penal company. Weak and emaciated he continued his lone fight, being sentenced to solitary confinement for wearing a home-made rosette in celebration of Coronation Day 1953. As the *London Gazette* commented when he was awarded the George Cross for gallantry one year later, after he had come out of a British hospital, 'His powers of resistance and his determination to oppose and fight the enemy to the maximum were beyond praise. His example was an inspiration to all ranks who came in contact with him.'

Fusilier Derek Kinne was typical of all these Geordies, who had started that Friday 23 April 1950 by placing the proud new red-and-white plume of their regiment in their bonnets in honour of their patron saint, St George of England, and had gone to do battle whatever the outcome.[3] Most of them weren't professional soldiers; they were young conscripts still in their teens, dragged out of their cosy little world of pub, pictures and palais de danse to fight in this remote country, which meant nothing to them. But those same poorly educated, poorly paid, poorly trained youngsters, armed with the weapons of the First World War, absorbed the century-old traditions of their proud regiment and fought as if they were old bearded veterans of the Fifth of Foot . . .

But even a bitter determination not to let their 'mates' or the regiment down was little avail against the overwhelming might of the Chinese divisions. By now the Northumberland Fusiliers' main defences had been shattered, as had those of the Ulsters and the Belgians. Maj Winn of the Geordies' Z Company conducted a fighting retreat, knowing that he was cut off on both flanks and virtually surrounded. Still, he wasn't going to surrender if he could help it, and his men supported him to the hilt. One by one his senior men were hit. Finally he was reduced to one officer, the company sergeant-major and one seriously wounded sergeant who, however, still carried on, trying to lead a depleted company burdened by a score of lightly wounded and 27 stretcher cases (who Winn was determined were not going to fall into the hands of the gooks). By now all of them knew what the Chinese did to POWs who couldn't be moved. They were quickly shot in the back of the head and slung into the nearest drainage ditch like pieces of tainted meat.

In the end when Winn's company was at the end of its tether almost, another was rushed up to break through to it. Suffering casualties itself, the relief force managed to reach the heights on which Winn was holding out, doing as one of his men quipped 'His Custer's Last Stand' thing. They got the survivors out, including the stretcher-cases, evacuating them under fire from nearby Chinese snipers. It was only then that Winn hobbled down the hill unaided except by his own officers' ashplant.

Ammunition was running out rapidly. Col Foster, the Fusiliers' CO, knew the moment of crisis was almost there. He pushed on up to his men's scattered positions. He didn't get far in his attempt to reach the heights from which Maj Winn was attempting to withdraw. His jeep was hit and overturned and in the mêlée which followed, he was mortally wounded.

The death of their well-liked commanding officer was a bad blow for the Northumberland Fusiliers. The heart seemed to go out of the men for a while. 'This was an enormous setback for our regiment,' Thommo Thompson wrote afterwards. Now 'in a sorry state and with the casualty rate rising dramatically', the remnants started 'fighting our way out with whatever ammunition we could muster'.

By now the situation was becoming critical. Already the Belgians were being forced to withdraw, according to a hastily worked out plan at Brigade HQ. Still, they too were taking casualties, although they were protected to a certain extent by US tanks. The Ulsters and the Royal Northumberland Fusiliers, who didn't realize till later that their desperate counter-attack had served merely to cover the Belgians' withdrawals, were suffering badly and, as has been seen, were running out of ammunition. Here and there, where officers and senior NCOs had been knocked out, there was a feeling of *sauve qui peut* among the rank and file. Understandably so: the Chinese seemed to be everywhere and, in some cases, retreating British soldiers were mingled with excited Chinese soldiers advancing confidently on enemy positions which had long been breached or abandoned.

Brig Brodie, whose Brigade was in the direct path of the enemy advance on Seoul, was terribly worried as the first of the survivors began to trickle into the Brigade area. Casualties were flooding the HQ, originally eight miles behind the 29th's front: scores of them and then hundreds. When the first of his artillery positions were overrun, he signalled the US I Corps that his situation was 'a bit sticky'.

General 'Shrimp' Milburn, the I Corps commander, had never served with British troops and didn't know the average British officer's dislike of emotionalism, especially in a crisis: that, in British Army circles, was 'not the done thing'. So when Brodie told the American that things with his brigade were 'a bit sticky', the latter did not take into account British understatement. As one of Brodie's staff officers related afterwards: 'they (the Americans) simply did not grasp that in British Army parlance, that meant "critical".' As one American commented: 'If he (Brodie) had been an American officer, he would have screamed, "We're being overrun by Chinamen. Pour everything you got into here".' But Brodie didn't. The result was that Milburn ordered him to hold his positions; there would be no withdrawal. Naturally 'Shrimp' Milburn knew that both Ridgway and the new Eighth Army Commander, van Fleet, wouldn't take kindly to a US

Corps Commander who sanctioned yet another withdrawal that might well turn into a retreat, which they so often did in Korea; there had been too many bug-outs as it was.

By now Brodie was under tremendous strain. His battalions were melting away under his very eyes. The 'Rock of the Marne', 3rd Infantry Division promised assistance. But so far nothing of importance was forthcoming. In his bunker HQ, controlled chaos reigned now. The field phones jingled non-stop. Anxious staff officers paced back and forth, scribbling their approval to new 'last ditch' orders. Quartermasters and supply officers sought fresh ammunition, radio batteries, even food – fruitlessly. The whole British front was up in the air.

Again Brodie appealed for permission to withdraw. Again he was turned down. His staff officers knew that the 'Brig' was working under intolerable pressure. The strain on his face revealed that all too clearly. His brigade had been almost shattered and there seemed little he could do to save the survivors. He had no clout at US I Corps HQ. He was just a 'Limey one-star general' and Corps HQs in the American Army crawled with such creatures. Finally he realized that all hope had vanished. He could expect no further assistance from 'Shrimp' Milburn. The final act of the tragedy could now begin . . .

A harassed Brig Brodie had just returned from visiting what he could still find of the Fusiliers, the Ulster Rifles and the Belgians when the radio link with Colonel Carne of the Glosters came alive. Brodie's mood was low. The Belgians had withdrawn successfully, but their casualties had been heavy. They too, like the Fusiliers, had lost their CO, who had been standing next to a tank's smoke discharger on the side of the vehicle's turret when it had been hit by a Chinese bullet. Phosphorus in the smoke bombs had been discharged in a deadly unstoppable spray which had burned the Belgian colonel so terribly that it was feared he might not live.

The Fusiliers had virtually run out of ammo. The men had been reduced to throwing their C-ration cans of cheese at the advancing Chinese in the hope that the latter would think they were grenades and go to ground! The Ulsters had got out too, but again with heavy casualties. It had been gloom, gloom, gloom, gloom everywhere. There had been only one moment of light relief when a company commander in the Northumberlands related how one of his reluctant heroes had stopped dead in the middle of a charge, let his rifle slip and had proclaimed solemnly that he couldn't carry on with the nasty business of battle because 'the Lord Jesus had instructed him to take no further part in the attack'. The Fusilier so suddenly converted to Christian good-will and charity to all men, even the Chinese, was now on a 'fizzer', waiting for a court-martial in due course.

Now a deeply despondent Brodie laid it on the line to Col Carne of the Glosters. The Brigadier said that an attempt was being made to break through to his encircled battalion by a Filippino outfit, supported by US tanks. Till then, however, the Glosters would have to stand and fight it out until they were rescued – *if* they were rescued, an unhappy Carne must have told himself. For he had already told one of Brodie's staff officers that he had only four hundred effectives left. If they were to reach safety, he would have to order the withdrawal *now*.

So in his gentle somewhat oblique manner, Col Carne, who had been a Gloster for twenty-seven years, attempted once again to obtain permission to break out now before it was too late.

Brodie wouldn't have it. Farrar-Hockley listening in closely could tell by 'his (the Brigadier's) voice that he didn't like committing us to such a desperate task'. But he did. The Glosters would have to stay where they were, fight and then probably die. 'He said, he realised how things stood with us, but the job had to be done . . . we were the only ones who could do it.' With that the radio went dead. The Glosters' fate was sealed.

Carne's face revealed very little. He wasn't a very vocal officer. He had reached the peak of his career back where he had been five years before in Burma, commanding an infantry battalion. Under normal circumstances, back in the UK, it would have been about time for him to ask for his 'bowler hat', i.e. put in for his retirement pension – 'ask for his papers', as the military jargon of his caste had it.

Apparently now, as he puffed at his old pipe, he told himself he wasn't fated to die in bed of old age, remembered only in a passing notice in the regimental journal. No, he was going to die in battle. For a professional soldier of so many years that realization wasn't so shocking as it might have been for a 'civvie'. It was the price you always had to be prepared to pay, once you had accepted the 'King's shilling'. Still the thought of losing all those young men, some of them barely out of their teens, must have appalled him. But as always he couldn't articulate his emotions. He was too much of an old-school, somewhat tongue-tied type for that.

Instead he said to Farrar-Hockley, as he walked away from the radio link: 'You know that armour-infantry column that's coming up from three div to relieve us?' He meant the Filippinos attached to the 'Rock of the Marne'.

'Yes sir,' Farrar-Hockley said dutifully.

'Well, it isn't coming.' Carne had already made up his mind that Brodie was in no position to help. The Americans were under heavy attack themselves.

'Right, sir,' the adjutant answered promptly, just as unemotional as his CO.

On the morning of 25 April 1950 began the final breakdown of the 1st Battalion the Gloucester Regiment.

The weary defenders of the shell-pocked perimeter littered with the ugly debris of war – empty ammo packets, unfurled yellow shell dressings, gleaming pieces of shrapnel, brown still-steaming holes caused by the mortar bombs looking like the work of giant moles and the dead – were awakened reluctantly from a drugged sleep by the sound of bugles.

The regulars had lived much of their lives in garrison timed to the bugle – reveille, cook-house call, officers call, lights out and all the rest – but this bugle, now being joined by another and yet another all along the Glosters' sector, was different. The call was unfamiliar. Yet Farrar-Hockley, waking at his position on the parapet of his defensive position, recognized it for what it was, all the same. It was the signal to attack. *The Chinese were attacking again!*

The drowsiness vanished immediately. His nerves jingled electrically. He got to his feet. There was a job to be done. The first angry snap-and-crack of a small-arms fight was coming from the south-east. A Company was under attack.

'The noise of battle grew around us. Soon the coloured lights of tracer rounds were flying over us from somewhere to the west. From the knoll and saddle, held by the Battalion the previous day there came the shrill blare of Chinese bugles too. The enemy was preparing yet another assault from that direction as well. Farrar-Hockley knew one didn't need a crystal ball to see that this was an all-out Chinese attack. This day they wanted to eradicate the last of the 'round-eyes' who stood in their way.

Now the reports came in thick and fast. The Chinese were making probing attacks all around Hill 235 (or as it would become known, 'Gloster Hill'), everywhere. With their usual tactics they were looking for the weak point. Here they'd make their all-out assault.

Farrar-Hockley contacted the Colonel, who during the night had insisted that he take his place on the perimeter like an ordinary rifleman. He was irate. It was obvious that the blare of Chinese bugles was getting on his nerves. He said, 'It'll be a long time before I want to hear a cavalry trumpet playing after this.'

The young tough Adjutant nodded his understanding. Then he had a brainwave. 'It would serve them right, sir,' he said, 'if we confused them by playing our own bugle. I wonder which direction they'd go if they heard "Defaulters"?' Farrar-Hockley was really attempting to cheer up the CO; his suggestion was 'half joking'. But Carne took him seriously. He went along with it. The drum major, who could play the bugle and had one with him, was whistled up. Farrar-Hockley gave him his orders hastily.

The NCO did not hesitate. A few 'peeps' on his gleaming brass bugle with the regimental crest adorning its polished side and the 'tall lean figure, topped by a cap comforter' started to go through his whole repertoire. He played 'reveille', 'Orderly NCO', even 'Officers Dress for Dinner'. Later, as old men, some of those who heard that lone bugler play that terrible day remembered their sense of wonder and pride, 'though God only knows what the Gooks made of it'. But for a while it silenced 'the opposition' and Farrar-Hockley records 'For a moment (after the Glosters' bugler ended) there was silence – the last note coincided with a lull in the action. Then the noise of battle began again – but with a difference; there was no sound of a Chinese bugle.

It was the last happy moment. Half an hour or so later, Col Carne was informed by the Brigade Colonel that in an hour's time he would lose all artillery support. The Royal Artillery's 45th Field Regiment, which had served the British Army so well in Korea, would cease firing then: they were in danger if they remained in their present positions and the Brigadier had ordered them to pull back. The Glosters were on their own . . .

Now Carne was free to make his own decisions, and he did so. But it was a decision that every large unit trapped in an impossible situation hated, especially its officers and their commander. For it was one that seemed always to bring ruin and disgrace. Throughout history there were only a very few examples of the tactic Carne was now going to order ever succeeding.

However, as the wounded started to flow back to the dressing station in ever-increasing numbers, and with the air on the height black with enemy mortar smoke, he gave that order: his company commanders, all veterans of the Second World War, were to make their way back to Brigade as best they could. Gathering them a little way off from their men, Carne then told his officers the real facts of the situation. They were to move towards the right flank of the 1st ROK Division that still seemed to be fighting. There, he hoped, US tanks would come forward to assist the fugitives.

His officers said little, made no objections or suggestions. They knew, however, that the old Colonel was grasping at straws. Both the ROKs and the US tankers were noticeably reticent when the chips were down. Indeed, from past experience of their South Korean allies, they could expect the latter to 'go on the trot' if the Chinese pressure got very much harder. As for the tankers, they were notorious for declining to advance along the narrow valley roads if they didn't have infantry to protect them from the enemy on the heights.

Finally Carne turned to the battalion medical officer, Capt Bob Hickey. He hesitated and then said a little sadly, 'I'm afraid we shall have to leave the wounded behind.' If the doctor was shocked, he didn't show it, but the company commanders didn't like it. They understood the Colonel's reasoning. All the same, though, to leave men – helpless men for the most part – behind at the mercy of Chinese cruelty and lack of medical supplies appalled them. They knew well why the US Marines always took their wounded with them in Korea. Wounded men didn't survive too frequently in enemy captivity; it was a simple fact of life.

Still no one protested and Capt Hickey accepted his own fate without emotion. For already he and the chaplain, Padre Davies, had decided to stay behind with the eighty wounded in that particular section of the Glosters' front. Indeed the Padre had even joked about it, with a kind of gallows humour, to the RAMC NCO, remarking, 'This looks like a holiday in Peking for some of us.' It would be the last joke that the Padre would crack for many weary bitter months, and then years, to come . . . and he never *would* see Peking!

CHAPTER EIGHTEEN

Finis

That day one of the first US veterans of the conflict on the other side of the globe, Cpl William Jensen, shot through the leg in the first Chinese attack, limped through the downtown area of his home town, Hastings, Nebraska. Jensen, accompanied by a reporter trying to get his 'story', paused at the entrance to Second Street. He leaned on his cane and stared at the new glittering stores along the street, all full of goods the like of which he had never seen before. Outside rows of new cars were parked and well-dressed folk – at least for Nebraska – were happily engaged in spending a lot of greenbacks on these same TVs, pop-up toasters and the like. Finally the wide-eyed corporal gasped: 'Man, I never saw anything like it. This town is just one big boom!'

The astonished veteran was correct. Everywhere America was booming after the post-war slump induced by the rundown of the wartime economy. Now there was another war, not as big perhaps but still a war, and the new surge in heavy industry manufacturing tanks, cannon, trucks and the like was reflected in the money in their pockets which people had to spend.

The war itself had been relegated to the middle pages of the newspapers. It was no longer the first item on the news bulletins and in the infant TV programmes. Indeed one cynical Oregon newspaper editor ran the same Korean war story two days in a row. The editor placed the item in the same place under the same headline and with the same by-line in his paper – and not a single reader noticed!

It was typical. Even the surge of interest occasioned by the sacking of MacArthur had vanished as abruptly as it had been awakened. People were getting on with their own lives, engaged primarily in the race for money. It didn't help that the new master in Tokyo, Gen Matt Ridgway, had introduced strict censorship, instead of the voluntary kind that had existed under MacArthur. By the time the Chinese had attacked Brodie's ill-fated 29th Brigade, correspondents were not even allowed to mention the 38th Parallel! The result was that Eighth Army communiqués were dull, full of officialese and invariably upbeat and optimistic, even when the Allied armies were fighting with their backs to the wall. Besides, who really was interested in what was going on 'over there'? Korea wasn't Europe with its familiar place names and characters. Most Americans – and natives of other Allied countries for that matter – barely knew who Syngman Rhee was.

Former enemy countries such as Japan and Germany, as we have seen, were beginning to prosper too, under the business impetus of the Korean

War: German and Japanese goods were needed to make up the shortfall in American-produced consumer items, while US industry was geared to war production. Unburdened by the economic demands of paying for a war or even for a military to protect itself, West Germany in particular was beginning to boom. The 'economic miracle' which would amaze the free world, coming as it did a mere five years after Nazi Germany's catastrophic total defeat, was well under way.

Only Britain did not seem to notice the boom. Rationing was still in force. The nation was in debt and the great hopes raised by the ending of the Second World War seemed to have vanished. Britain seemed to be wallowing in self-pity. The country had begun to lose an empire but hadn't found a new role for itself. (Some cynics would maintain fifty years on that it still hasn't.)

Thus it was that on 22 April, the day the great Chinese offensive began in Korea, Aneurin Bevan resigned from the post of Minister of Labour. On the surface of it the cause was the Welsh demagogue's opposition to the new prescription charges imposed that month. By 1950, ministers and governments in Britain were agitated by such trivia, making major issues of them.

In this case the Bevan resignation did address a major issue as far as the left wing of the Labour Party was concerned: Bevan felt that the right wing of the party under Hugh Gaitskell was too subservient to capitalist America, which country's blind anti-communist hysteria would, in Bevan's opinion, drag the world into a nuclear war. Gaitskell, though, was 'wildly pro-American and anti-Russian'.

The blatant anti-Americanism of the Labour left infuriated Dean Acheson, the American Secretary of State. He asked the British ambassador in Washington if his government back in London wasn't being 'blackmailed' by the 'Bevanites'. The British, he felt, would have to learn to 'toe the line'. If they wanted a truce in Korea, they would have to work for it. As Acheson saw it, the British war aim was to allow the Chinese a means of ending the war without losing face, that critical factor of their culture. All right, then, they should put their backs behind the current bitter battle in Korea. Stop the Chinese first – then talk.

So, unknown to Brodie's soldiers fighting for their very lives in Korea,[1] they had become pawns in an even greater struggle: that between the two radically opposed factions in the Anglo-American camp wanting to win the power to make the geo-political decisions. Before the relatively pro-American Gaitskell faction could gain the upper hand and try to swing America into talking peace with the Chinese, those hard-pressed young men at the front would have to help to win their desperate battle on the Imjin . . .

The Glosters, the last of Brodie's Brigade engaged as a coherent unit, weren't doing well. By now the men had absorbed the Colonel's order that they were to break out in companies, and prepared to do so. The Glosters'

A Company took stock of their ammunition supply: for those who hadn't been wounded and could bear arms, there were exactly three rounds per rifleman. Each Bren-gunner still possessed a magazine and a half and there were seven grenades left for the whole company! Not exactly a plentiful supply of ammo to fight through the enemy and four miles on after that to safety.

Trying to ignore the fact that he, like the rest of the men, was suffering from a raging thirst, Farrar-Hockley walked back to Battalion HQ through the lunar landscape where they had held out for over three days now and reported to HQ. There, the destruction of equipment and secret documents, codes and the like was in full swing. Farrar-Hockley nodded his approval and crossed to where the MO stood, as the HQ group prepared to move out after what was left of 'A' Company.

'Come on, Bob,' he said to the doctor, 'We're about the last to go. You ought to have gone before this. The Colonel will be off in a minute and that will be the lot.'

The MO stared at him for a few moments, as if seeing him for the very first time, before saying, 'I can't go. I must stay with the wounded.'

For what seemed an age, the adjutant couldn't seem to comprehend. Then he got it. It was something that he had read in history books, but he'd never been witness to such an action. Then 'I realized that he had weighed all this – weighed it all and made a deliberate choice: he would place his own life in jeopardy in order to remain with the wounded at the time when they needed him most.' His heart went out to the brave medic. Too moved to speak, he clapped Bob's shoulder and went about his duties.

By now the greater part of the defeated battalion had vanished. Behind them they left the badly wounded; those of the Glosters who wouldn't 'soldier' any longer and had thrown themselves to the ground, weary and too heart-broken to care; and the Padre, who on the day before had enjoyed a few moments of respite, longing to say 'Stop to the rushing minutes: to prolong this quiet sunny afternoon indefinitely.' But that wasn't to be. Already the first of the Chinese scouts were beginning to sneak into the abandoned positions like grey predatory wolves intent on their prey . . .

At higher headquarters, after most of the survivors of the shattered Brodie Brigade had reported in, they were preparing a news release – with a certain amount of trepidation. Ridgway in Tokyo was particularly worried. The British had led the US Corps advance to the Yalu. Together with the Turks of the Turkish Brigade they had covered the December retreat. That had occasioned him to issue an order against 'sacrifice missions'. Shortly thereafter he had discovered that a British group had been left behind as a rearguard at Seoul and he had lost an equal number of GIs trying to rescue them.

Now he was informed that a British battalion – the Glosters – had been apparently wiped out in their defensive position on the Imjin. He flew into a rage, blaming the corps and divisional commanders, i.e. those of the US I Corps and 3rd Infantry, for not having pulled the Limeys out more quickly. As he was to write,

> I cannot but feel a certain disquiet that down through the channel of command the full responsibility for realising the danger to which this unit was exposed, then for extricating it when that danger became grave, was not recognised nor implemented . . . There are times when it is not sufficient to accept the judgement of a subordinate commander that a threatened unit can care for itself. Colonel Carne of the Glosters – 'a most gallant officer' – should have been ordered to withdraw.

It was now that the Glosters unwittingly stepped on to the wings of the free world's political stage – much to the chagrin of other survivors of that shattered 29th Brigade. In that last week of April, as has been shown, Anglo-American relations were fraught at the best. There had already been criticism in the British press of the manner in which British troops had been used to 'carry the can back' for the Yanks. Ridgway knew that well enough. Now nearly 1,000 British soliders seemed to have disappeared in the jaws of the war in Korea. What would the anti-American faction in Britain make of that? As Ridgway reiterated: 'We must not lose any battalion, certainly *not* another British one.'

But the Glosters *had* been lost. So what was he going to do?

It was here that the PR machine stepped in. Korea was no Vietnam, where the blood-letting of the morning could be seen in the parlour TV of the evening in full colour. Still, the US Army was very conscious of media scrutiny. To ensure they didn't make publicity mistakes, they had developed their own publicity organization headed by one-star generals and staffed with senior officers and noncoms. They set about ensuring that this defeat of British arms would be turned into a victory of a kind.

Certainly the British had lost a thousand men, they said, but they had made the price of victory tenfold by inflicting 10,000 Chinese casualties. How the PR 'feather merchants' (as the GIs called them contemptuously) came up with that figure, no one questioned at the time. Later it was suggested that this was an arbitrary number based on what the battalion and the supporting artillery *might* have killed.

Van Fleet was quoted as saying: 'The most outstanding example of unit bravery in modern warfare'. Brodie's log was publicized and he was found to have declared proudly on behalf of his lost battalion, 'Only the Gloucesters could have done it!' In due course Col Carne was awarded his country's highest medal for gallantry in action – the Victoria Cross. Afterwards, long after the machinations of the US PR feather merchants were forgotten, the other survivors of the 29th Brigade still disagreed with the massive publicity given the unfortunate Glosters – 'the Glorious Glosters', as they were known ever afterwards. In essence, the Northumberlands and the Ulstermen suffered far higher casualties in battle than did the Glosters who received all the eulogies – and the gongs! The latter had marched through the major city of their home county with bayonets fixed and drums beating, not only to a mere civic welcome, as had had the Royal Northumberland Fusiliers and Royal Ulster Rifles; but to a momentary national upsurge in military pride. The 'Glorious Glosters' were featured in the newsreels and TV news. There was even some talk of making a movie of their famous 'last stand'.

But what, the Geordies and the Ulstermen asked, had the 1st Battalion, the Gloucester Regiment really done to deserve all this praise and admiration? The former thought they knew the answer: not much, in reality. After all – *they had surrendered*!

What was left of 'D' Company wandered through the hills for two days under the command of Captain Harvey. They met only one group of Chinese. They killed the lot of them. Unsuspectingly they bumped into some American tanks. Without hesitation they exposed themselves to their 'big friends'. It was the wrong thing to do without warning in those circumstances. The Yanks opened fire at once. When the desperate Glosters finally managed to identify themselves there were thirty-nine of them left. Back at base they and the other survivors were mustered and the NCOs commenced that terrible roll-call of death. Out of 850 Glosters on the Battalion's strength, there were 169 left. Over two-thirds of the 1st Glosters had vanished in sixty hours. Where had they gone?

Captain Farrar-Hockley, who would escape from the Chinese time and time again over the next three years, came upon the survivors of the other three companies in a 'dark and cheerless' ravine dominated by the fire of three Chinese machine-guns. Instinctively he knew that they wouldn't live another five minutes if he didn't do something at once.

'Feeling as if I was betraying everything that I loved and believed in, I raised my voice and called: "Stop!"'

They stopped and 'looked towards me, their faces expectant. I shall never know what order they anticipated'.

Now Farrar-Hockley would give that dreadful order he wouldn't forget to his dying day, long after the Gloucester Regiment no longer existed.[2] He raised his voice and called the best he could: 'Put down your arms.' The Glosters surrendered. The Battle of the Imjin River was over. The long road to peace in Korea was open at last . . .

Envoi

'You eat the Queen's salt and you obey the Queen's regulations. It's no good suddenly saying: "Oh my conscience tells me something else." To hell with your bloody conscience. Get out of the Army.'

Gen Sir Anthony Farrar-Hockley, 1998

On 25 May 1953, the Chinese struck for the last time.

For years now there had been periods of alternative stalemate, interspersed by those of brief, bitter and very bloody fighting. Still the Chinese came in 'waves' or 'human waves', as the Tokyo feather merchants called what seemed the enemy's inexhaustible supply of manpower. Indeed the outposts on the heights of Southern Korea from which the Allies fought stank, as one GI put it, of 'flies, rats, garbage, fecal waste' . . . with the 'worst job covering the Chinese bodies that lay everywhere on the side of the hills'.

The British of what was now the 'Commonwealth Division' played their role in those bloody skirmishes, which sometimes developed into outright battles. One after another the first battalions of these infantry regiments, which have now long disappeared, took their place in the line In Korea. They fought their private battle, tended their wounded, buried their death and vanished thereupon into the obscurity of that 'forgotten war'. The Royal Warwicks, the Royal Irish Fusiliers, the Royal Sussex, the Cameron Highlanders, the Essex Regiment . . . they were all there, fighting to gain 'honours' the glory of which has faded over the years. In that last spring of the Korean War it was the turn of that regiment bearing the name of the most famous soldier the British Army has ever produced – the 1st Duke of Wellington's Regiment.

The position they would defend was the notorious 'Hook', part of that range 'Old Baldy', 'Pork Chop Hill' which would go down in the folklore of the US Army afterwards.

The battle for the 'Hook' had commenced back in October 1952 when the 7th US Marines had fought a successful defensive action on those grim, barren, shell-pitted heights. Thereafter, the position had fallen into the care of the British Commonwealth Division. Again it tempted the communists into attacking it, for as one of the officers of the Duke of Wellingtons said later: 'It was a sore thumb, bang in the middle of Genghis Khan's old route into Korea . . . it commanded an enormous amount of ground.'

On 18 November 1952, it was the turn of the 1st Black Watch. Again the Chinese attacked in their usual wasteful manner; but then, they had the men. Human life didn't count for much in that huge country with its tremendous population. Nor were the Jocks inclined to take the Chinkies prisoner. Twice the Chinese attempted to swamp the Black Watch positions and twice they were forced back. At tremendous cost they failed to shift the men of Scotland's elite regiment.

However, the British casualties as well were mounting in the defence of the 'Hook' – indeed the Army lost more on the height's steep flanks than in any other battlefield in the three-year struggle for Korea. Now they were going to lose some more – but they would never lose the 'Hook'.

On the night of 28 May, 1953, the 'Dukes' were warned by the urgent brassy blare of bugles that a Chinese attack on the 'Hook' was imminent. As the sound died away, there was the first obscene thump and whack of mortars being fired. To the defenders' front, cherry-red flames erupted everywhere as the Chinese artillery joined in. The Chinese were coming!

'Stand to,' the NCOs and officers yelled urgently. Men grabbed their equipment and sprang to the fire-steps of their deep weapon pits. They slammed the brass-clad butts of their rifles and Brens into their shoulders. Others placed their grenades, already primed, in handy little holes in the sides of the slit trenches. The fire swept over them in fiery fury. Now they could hear the commands, the shouts, the angry orders coming from below. The Chinese were attacking in strength. As all around them their trenches started to crumple under a series of direct hits, the defenders began to fire furiously into the darkness.

Both dug-in Centurion tanks being used to support the Dukes with their 20-pounder cannon were hit. A half-blinded young officer just out of Sandhurst staggered bleeding into his company commander's dug-out. He reported that his position was 'untenable'. 'Balls,' his company commander snapped curtly, 'get back!' A Browning machine-gun was knocked out, with five killed and three wounded. Another machine-gun took up the challenge. The Chinese fell everywhere. The night was hideous with their screams and yells of pain. Still they kept on coming – and the Dukes kept on mercilessly mowing them down.

Now the Chinese had in places reached the summit. The Dukes went underground in their tunnels. By this time their wireless sets were smashed, so they were cut off from Brigade and had to rely on themselves. They did, fighting back with the desperate courage of men who knew instinctively that they either fought and won – or died. Underground the Chinks would show no mercy. It had become a close-combat battle in which no such mercy was shown or expected.

Commanding the Dukes' Support Company, Maj Kershaw (who had missed out on most of the Second World War because he had been stationed in Iceland and other out-of-the-way places) was now getting his 'bellyful' of hand-to-hand combat. He had already fought his way into a tunnel until it too had been swamped by the enemy. A Chinese only feet away thew a stun grenade. He yelped with pain, as his legs and buttocks were peppered with fragments, the blast knocking his helmet off and his Sten gun out of his hands.

He staggered somehow into another trench. Four wounded Korean 'Dukes' lay in it. Half blinded and threatening to drift into unconsciousness at any moment, he tied a tourniquet with his bootlace. Still he fought back, until the Chinese blew in the entrance to the tunnel.

A Corporal Walker ran with his hard-pressed section into another tunnel. Again the enemy were everywhere. While his men frantically barricaded themselves in, the young corporal fired rapid bursts to keep the enemy at bay. The Chinese retaliated by tossing in satchel charges whose blast slapped the defenders around the faces, buffeting them time after time and almost deafening them. More critically, it blocked the entrance and thus it was that, when they had recovered from the explosion, they found themselves gasping for air like ancient asthmatics in the throes of an attack.

They lay 'doggo' and, as Walker related later, they heard the Chinese demand in English, 'Where your friends?' Private Smith, helpless after having been wounded in both legs, lied weakly, 'They're not in this tunnel,' he gasped.

Walker pulled himself together. He advanced through the darkness further up the tunnel, heart beating furiously, weapon at the ready. He saw torches approaching. He knew instinctively they could belong only to the Chinks. He didn't wait to find out whether his guess was right, but loosed off a burst. In the confines of the tunnel, the racket was ear-splitting, giving way to screams and yelps of pain. Then a loud echoing silence. Not for long. A rumble, a trembling, and the Chinese detonated a charge at the entrance. They were sealed in the tunnel, as if in their own tomb. 'We were in darkness,' as Walker afterwards remembered that terribly long night, 'and choking through dust and lack of air. One chap alone had half a bottle of water and he shared it all round, all getting a lick every hour.'

Maj Lewis Kershaw – trapped, bleeding badly and half-conscious in *his* tunnel – held the survivors entombed there together with his undaunted spirit. 'The Dukes don't die,' he shouted defiantly; '*Stick it!*' And stick it the survivors of the 1st Battalion the Duke of Wellington's Regiment did. When on the next day the rescue parties broke through to the trapped men, Lewis Kershaw was still in command! Blinking in the grey light of the new day, he ordered them, 'See that I am the last out!' It was only then that he allowed himself to finally pass into the boon of unconsciousness.

All that long night and the following day, the Chinese attacked and attacked with savage fury. The British brought down artillery on their positions. Later it was discovered that a whole battalion of Chinese infantry had been wiped out in the course of that suicidal barrage. Their shattered bodies hung from the wire everywhere like bundles of blood-red rags.

But the Dukes didn't only defend, they counter-attacked. Over the previous years the Dukes had always prided themselves on having the best rugby team in the whole of the British Army. Some of the players were indeed international stars. Now one of them, six foot four Campbell-Lamerton, led his company into the attack to regain ground lost by the

Dukes. It was a matter of honour. It was tough going. The day-long artillery bombardments, British and Chinese, had 'literally changed the shape' of the top of the Hook. Rubble and tangled smashed wire – and the enemy – made progress damnably slow, but somehow they did it. At 3.30 on the morning of 29 May, the attackers reported that the Hook was again in the hands of the Dukes. *Virtutis fortuna comes* (motto of the Duke of Wellingtons) – Fortune had indeed favoured the Brave . . . .

As the dawn light came slowly that morning over the shattered lunar landscape, as if some deity were reluctant to illuminate the ugliness below, the search parties started to stumble through the smoking wreckage of the Dukes' positions to recover the casualties. They found 250 dead and 800 wounded Chinese. Of the Dukes some 149 had been killed, wounded and captured (many of the sixteen POWs wounded, too). In a matter of a day, the Duke of Wellingtons had lost one-fifth of its strength.

Brig Kendrew of the brigade to which the Dukes belonged came up to the Hook to see what had happened. Kendrew had seen much of war and had won three DSOs in the Second World War, but even so he was shocked. Grave-faced and shaken, he said, 'My God, those Dukes! They were marvellous. In the whole of the last war I never knew anything like that bombardment. But they held the Hook . . . I knew they would . . .'

Despite the praise, the Brigadier could see they'd had enough. Besides, most of their positions and many of their weapons had been shattered. He ordered the Battalion relieved at once. If the Chinese attacked again, they would be in a damned difficult position, so he commanded the 1st Royal Fusiliers to take over. At noon, long lines of Fusiliers started to wind their way up the heights, including an obscure cockney one day to be known to the world as Michael Caine, actor. 'What's been going on?' one of the Fusiliers asked as he came level with the Dukes and saw the carnage and wreckage. The unknown Duke had his answer ready. Calmly but proudly, he answered: 'Just seeing off a few Chinks . . .'

And so they had. The Dukes, three-quarters of them national servicemen paid £1.62 a week by a grateful country for risking their lives, had fought the British Army's last real battle of the Korean War. It went on for several more weeks, but in the end the Chinese knew they'd never defeat the Allies now. They asked for a truce.

In July 1953 they waited as the final hours ticked away, as had happened in Europe when the armies there had waited for the 11th hour of the 11th day of the 11th month of 1918 till that year's Armistice was to come into force. Right up to the last moment on that Monday 27 July, the guns thundered. Half an hour after the last bomb had been dropped by the US Air Force, Gen Trudeau of the US 7th Infantry Division pulled the lanyard of one of the divisional artillery pieces and fired the last round. He kept the shell case and was quoted as saying later: 'I was happy it was over.

It was apparent that all we were going to do was to sit there and hold positions. There wasn't going to be any victory.'

The General was right: there wasn't! What he apparently didn't realize at the time was that it was not a question of a US victory, but rather of defeat or at the best stalemate. In essence the United States of America, one day to be seen as the world's superpower, had lost its first war . . .

Not that the GIs cared. They 'partied'. If they were lucky they got high on hooch and local rice wine. If they weren't they let off rockets and signal flares. The US Marines who had suffered so much in Korea sang dirty songs and told tall tales. One GI seemed to sum up the prevailing mood among the men. Pte Bill Shirk maintained it had all been a 'hell of a waste'. 'Who gives a shit if they're North Korean or South Korean? You can't take a person living like an animal and expect him to act like a human being.'

Perhaps his view was typical. They were all gooks anyway. But whatever the men 'at the sharp end' thought, it really didn't matter on that wonderful July day. The war was over, so they celebrated.

As for the British, nothing much is recorded (as was customary in Korea) of their reaction. More than likely, being the British Army, they were given a couple of bottles of cheap Jap beer and then told to 'bull up'. As they always maintained in the 'Kate Karney' – *'war is hell, but peacetime will kill you . . .'*

Notes

Chapter One

1. General MacArthur was called 'Dug-out Doug' by his wartime GIs because they felt that he was sitting out the war in a safe bolthole, such as Australia, while they were fighting to the death against the Japanese.
2. Due to the time-zone changes, nearly a day earlier than in the States.
3. For a time, the US Army was reduced to 36th in world ranking, lower than that of Chile.
4. Hence the name adopted by the Japanese suicide pilots at the end of the Second World War.
5. The major port of the UN forces in Korea, Pusan was 140 miles from Dean's HQ at Kokura.
6. Nickname given to *Reichmarschall* Hermann Goering on account of his great bulk.
7. The reference is, of course, to the Soviet dictator Josef Stalin. The Supreme Commander Gen Eisenhower often used this term to designate one of the most feared men in history and his troops.
8. When Schoerner returned to West Germany nine years later, he was tried and convicted by his own people. He died in disgrace.
9. As there were naturally time differences between the various localities involved in the Korean War, I have decided to use the time of the area under discussion.
10. The peace negotiations under the control of the UN have never been concluded. The two sides are still 'talking' on the 38th Parallel.

Chapter Two

1. Republic of Korea Army, known to the GIs later as 'Roks' – and other less polite names. Their opponents in the North were known predictably as 'gooks', as were the 'Japs' in the Second World War and the Vietcong in the war to come fifteen years later. The US 'Gook' mentality has a lot to answer for.
2. Afterwards revisionist historians, latching onto this statement, started to point out that Dulles and his awkward aggressive protégé Dr Rhee, President of South Korea, might well not have been so innocent as they had originally seemed. In other words, had they helped in various clandestine ways to provoke a war with North Korea that would bring in a Russia not yet – supposedly – equipped with the atomic bomb, as America was?
3. Eventually, after his failure as a chief-of-staff, Almond became a corps commander in Korea.
4. He had been given this rank by the then island President before the war when he had taken over the Philippine Army.
5. He had caught the flu; just as he crossed the Channel at D-Day, sitting on a rubber cushion and in agony because he was suffering from piles!
6. It is presumed that Blake was recruited by the Soviets during his captivity in Korean hands.
7. Even today, half a century onwards, the Queen's honours awards are based on the 'British Empire' which, as everyone knows, has long since vanished.

Chapter Three

1. Just as President 'FDR' Roosevelt had done with his cigarette holder; perhaps the General had copied it from the dead President, the former having always had an eye for the telling publicity gimmick, even before such things were invented for soldiers. In the Second World War it had been the battered cap he had worn in the Philippines; in the First, it had been an unlikely racoon coat, soon to be in fashion with the post-war 'flapper' generation.
2. According to the US Constitution the Congress had to be consulted first. Although the President was the Commander-in-Chief of the American Armed Forces, he really didn't have the right to declare war.
3. A Civil War between government forces and the communists had been raging in Greece since 1944; Britain had been first to help out, something for which they had been criticized by the Americans. Two years later the Americans had been forced to take over their role.
4. As far as the author can ascertain, that naval action meant that Britain fired the first shots of the 3-year-long Korean War.
5. Contemptuous name given to the Americans by the Germans.

Chapter Four

1. On 13 February 1951.
2. After his court martial, the warrant officer in question remained in the US Army.
3. There had been black rifle platoons within white infantry divisions from 1 March 1945.
4. Paraphrased from notes taken at the time.
5. See the author's *Last Assault* and *Death of a Division* for further details.

Chapter Five

1. They dress as Americans; they talk the same jargon and slang as the Americans; they are just as greedy for status and wealth as Americans are supposed to be, yet the 'chattering classes' – the men and women who pass as intellectuals in the UK – detest their models. Strange!
2. The author, who had volunteered at 16 for the Army in the Second World War was a member of that Reserve. He too was recalled, but his recall notice reached him while he was studying at a foreign university. Two of his fellow undergraduates, still in the UK, both in their mid-twenties, went. They didn't come back . . .
3. The later British formation, which fought as a self-contained division for the most part.
4. As the discredited Chinese leader was known to old China hands.
5. Secretary of State for Defense Louis Johnson.
6. See the author's *Bloody Bremen* for further details.

Chapter Six

1. But they were much older than colonels of 25 and 27 who had commanded wartime infantry battalions in action.
2. The three parts of the bunk mattress.

3. In the author's case, he was ordered to bring with him various articles of clothing, including 'PT shoes'. But rationing of clothing had just ended and he didn't possess such items. Perhaps the Army itself was running short of such equipment, to have to make such a request.
4. Mr Hastings in his book *The Korean War* obviously mistook the 'Fifth of Foot', the Northumberlands' original designation, with a then non-existent 5th Battalion of the regiment.
5. Other other ranks who were present in the Bury St Edmunds training area of that time remember nothing at all of the 'mutiny'.
6. One of the most secret and least-known of Britain's wartime formations, these Marine frogmen swam from submarines to enemy beaches to measure them up and bring back geological samples needed by the commanders of the landing force, often with enemy sentries only a matter of yards away. After the Hitler 'Commando Order', these brave young frogmen knew they would be shot out of hand if captured.
7. Most US accounts of Korea hardly mention the part the British Army played in the war. But they *do* give glowing accounts of Drysdale's force, including the fact that several times the British commanded US 'Leathernecks' in tricky situations.
8. It appears that 41 Commando was too exhausted and depleted to fight seriously after that time.
9. A specialized armoured division, commanded by a former lance-corporal in the Home Guard, Maj Gen P. Hobart, comprised of all sorts of weird and wonderful fighting vehicles, many suggested by Churchill; hence the name.
10. i.e. Guards, 11th Hussars and Iniskilling Dragoon Guards.
11. A.J. Barker: *Fortune Favours the Brave*, Leo Cooper Ltd, 1972.

Chapter Seven

1. Hostilities Only, i.e. men who had signed up just for the duration of the Second World War.
2. Massed half-inch machine-guns in banks.

Chapter Eight

1. If the Scottish reader takes this to be cynicism on the part of the author, let me correct him. As a wartime member of the 52nd Lowland Division I have always had the greatest admiration for the Scottish spirit, though in the years of the author's dotage, they have gone over the top a 'wee' bit.
2. Some of them were paid as little as two shillings (ten pence) a day!

Chapter Nine

1. As the *London Evening News* recorded at the time, under the headline 'GALLANT TRADITION'.
2. It was rumoured that Willoughby paid scores of agents at all levels in North and South Korea, some of whom were really genuine patriots, but most of whom fed the one-time German the information he liked and expected – for money.
3. The Koreans used human ordure from the 'honeydew buckets' to manure their fields.

Chapter Ten

1. The Rt Hon. Hector McNeil, Secretary of State for Scotland. The black singer and screen star Paul Robeson was suspected at the time of being a communist by the FBI and other US authorities. It ruined his life and career.
2. He eventually had it, while on a visit to the Middle East. Perhaps he knew by then that time was running out for him: he should have, for the British counter-Intelligence agent in Washington primarily concerned with discovering the alleged security leak in the British Embassy there was Philby.
3. We shall hear more of this later.
4. Save for one famous French-Canadian regiment, whose CO seemed successfully to have appealed to his soldiers to 'save themselves' for the 'little woman' back home. Well, the CO in question believed he did, at least.
5. Famous at the time, now long-forgotten.
6. Gen Dean had lost over forty pounds in weight now, kept as he was in solitary captivity. His steadfastness over the next three years of imprisonment would earn him the Congressional Medal of Honor.
7. Almond's X Corps was getting most of the publicity at that time.

Chapter Eleven

1. Among other things, in his retirement he would write a fine short history of Korea.
2. In the British Army, front-line troops were allowed an issue of rum daily, measured out under the eagle eye of what the troops called the 'quarter bloke'.

Chapter Twelve

1. Later no one knew whether the name reflected a truth or was meant as a macabre bit of gallows humour. Perhaps it was something of both.
2. Soldiers' slang for the British military prisons.
3. The regimental motto of the Royal Northumberland Fusiliers, with its sombre message – 'Whither Fate Calls'.
4. During the 1900–1 Boxer Rebellion.
5. Marine Condron was the only Briton among a score or so Americans who refused to be repatriated from a communist POW camp in 1953 at the end of the Korean War. He stayed on as a civilian, but in the end the Chinese became embarrassed about him and the 22 Americans who stayed with him. Quietly he returned to Scotland, where the one-time rabid communist sent his son to a public school on the lines that 'If you can't beat 'em, join 'em!'
6. What was left to Drysdale's force would become the 1st Marine Division's garrison reserve, but four months later, in April 1951, the reformed Commando would be storming ashore under US command in another daring operation.

Chapter Thirteen

1. In 1950 the top brass constantly worried about 'Chinese air power'. In the event, when the Chinese *did* commit their air force, including MIG jets, they were no match for the Allies, who dominated the air throughout the war – fortunately for many.
2. It might well be that 'Monty', with his funny hats, old green gamp and civilian trousers had started the military cult of personality back in the Western Desert

in 1942. But the US generals soon got into the act. Not only did they acquire their bold nicknames such as 'Iron Mike', 'Wild Bill', etc. overnight, but the appropriate fighting man's equipment to go with them – Patton's celebrated pistols for example. In truth most of them never went near the real fighting front.

3. Browning Automatic Rifles.
4. Most of the men who replied to the author's questionnaire stated the only Yanks they saw were at the Port of Pusan and on their 'R and Rs' in Japan, where (as one put it grumpily) 'they had more bleeding money than we saw in a month of Sundays.'
5. The US Army had finally learned the defensive lesson in the Ardennes, but soon forgot it again. That was not surprising, given that senior positions in the Eighth Army in Korea were packed with Patton's former officers.

Chapter Fourteen

1. An ancient custom of melting lead, pouring the liquid metal into cold water and trying to read the shapes it formed as an augur for the future.
2. The Sten, which came in three parts and was notoriously unreliable, cost all of seven shillings and sixpence to make: in late twentieth-century money about 40p or well under a dollar.
3. All the author's correspondents hardly mention the Koreans. Afterwards as old men, visiting that still unfortunate country, they had nothing but praise for the descendants of those who were, in reality, their victims.
4. In 1941, after defeat upon defeat, Churchill had experienced the same desperate feeling at the lack of fighting courage of his troops, exclaiming, 'Oh God, when *will* they fight?'

Chapter Fifteen

1. Ridgway ordered later that British troops wouldn't be used as either advance or rearguards in the future; presumably they bore the brunt of the action. Or perhaps a publicity-conscious Ridgway, who naturally wanted his US troops to get the headlines, thought it better to let his GIs have the honour of the task.
2. In the British Army, the men in the line got their daily rum ration. If they were lucky they received a couple of bottles of good Japanese sake beer as well. Officers and senior NCOs received a monthly ration of much prized spirits.
3. British Army slang from the card game, indicating that the unfortunate soldier in question had been infected with both 'gon' and 'siff'!
4. For its stand on the River Marne in France during the First World War.
5. I am grateful to Dr Maquet, Aywaille, Belgium and Jean Milmeister, Luxembourg City, for the obscure details of the Belgian–Luxembourg contribution to the Korean War.
6. In the light of recent events in the sectarian battles of Northern Ireland, it is interesting to note that the Ulsters, predominantly protestant, took catholics into their ranks in the Second World War, when over 100,000 Southern Irishmen volunteered for the British Army, and later in Korea.
7. The then Major MacArthur had been the US Army's first-ever censor. It was something he didn't believe in. More importantly he personally always seemed to give away the US plans by appearing on the battlefield before any new attack was to take place. The Chinese learned a lot of their intelligence from the US media due to the lack of censorship. Ridgway changed all that.
8. He ended his career as a lieutenant-general on the Belgian Army staff.

Chapter Sixteen

1. The word 'enemies' is used here purposely. For, from the records of that time, it seems almost as if Washington was far busier fighting MacArthur than fighting the Chinese.
2. There had been secret links between the two men in early March.
3. Political commissars.

Chapter Seventeen

1. The music of the bugles was copied from the wartime Red Army, which sometimes *marched* into battle in solid parade-ground ranks of infantry, accompanied by brass bands playing martial airs.
2. Special tea, made by brewing an extra long time, and then adding a whole tin of Carnation Milk – and naturally a pound of sugar – to the bucket containing the 'brew-up'.
3. A recent survey of English schoolchildren showed that most of them didn't know who St George was, or even which part of the Union Flag belonged to the colours of the country's patron saint.

Chapter Eighteen

1. Most of the rank and file in that brigade would probably have voted Labour, if they had had the chance. But they hadn't. Most of the national servicemen were just too young – ironically enough – to have the right to vote.
2. It was disbanded and amalgamated after its 300th anniversary parade when the then CO asked Farrar-Hockley's permission in that traditional but heartrending manner: 'May I have your permission, sir, to march off for the last time?' They did and the now General Farrar-Hockley felt a lump in his throat as he spotted the colour-sergeant in a file of his own with 'the tears rolling down his cheeks'.

Index

Subheadings are in chronological order, apart from British Army, where they are in order of seniority in the Army List.